# IN SEARCH
# OF SACRED TIME

Jacques Le Goff

# IN SEARCH
# OF SACRED TIME

Jacobus de Voragine
and
the *Golden Legend*

TRANSLATED BY
Lydia G. Cochrane

Avec le soutien du

PRINCETON UNIVERSITY PRESS

Princeton and Oxford

Published by Princeton University Press, 41 William Street, Princeton, New Jersey 08540

In the United Kingdom: Princeton University Press, 6 Oxford Street, Woodstock, Oxfordshire OX20 1TW

press.princeton.edu

Jacket art: Lorenzo di Credi. Detail of *The Annuciation* (ca. 1480–85). Courtesy of Dover Pictura

Library of Congress Cataloging-in-Publication Data
Le Goff, Jacques, 1924–
    [À la recherche du temps sacré. English]
    In search of sacred time : Jacobus de Voragine and the Golden legend / Jacques Le Goff ; translated by Lydia G. Cochrane.
        pages cm
    Includes bibliographical references and index.
    ISBN 978-0-691-15645-3 (hardcover : alk. paper)    1. Jacobus, de Voragine, approximately 1229–1298. Legenda aurea.    2. Christian saints—Biography—History and criticism.    3. Christian hagiography—History—To 1500.    4. Rhetoric, Medieval.    I. Title.
        BX4654.J4L4213 2014  270.092'2—dc23                                    2013026333

British Library Cataloging-in-Publication Data is available

A LA RECHERCHE DU TEMPS SACRE

Jacques de Voragine et la Légende Dorée

©PERRIN, 2011

Ouvrage publié avec le soutien du Centre national du livre – ministère français chargé de la culture.

This work is published with support from the French Ministry of Culture/Centre national du livre.

This book has been composed in Minion Pro and Bernhard Std

Printed on acid-free paper. ∞

Printed in the United States of America

1  3  5  7  9  10  8  6  4  2

# Contents

*Preface  ix*

*Acknowledgments  xv*

1. Jacobus de Voragine in His Time ........................................... 1

2. The Major Inspirations for Jacobus de Voragine ................. 9

3. The Prologue and the Temporale ........................................ 14

    The Prologue  14
    The Temporale  19

4. The Sanctorale ................................................................... 22

    Saintliness and Christianity  22
    Saints in the *Golden Legend*  24
    All Saints Day  26

5. The Time of Renewal .......................................................... 33

    Advent  33
    The Saints of Advent  35
    Saint Andrew, Apostle  36
    Saint Nicholas  39
    Saint Lucy, Virgin  45
    Saint Thomas, Apostle  47

## 6. The Time of Reconciliation and Pilgrimage ...... 51

The Birth of Our Lord: Jesus According to the Flesh  52
Saint Anastasia  55
Saint Stephen  56
Saint John, Apostle and Evangelist  59
The Holy Innocents  62
Saint Thomas of Canterbury  63
Saint Sylvester  65
The Circumcision of the Lord and the Epiphany of the Lord  68
Saint Paul, Hermit, and Saint Anthony  73
Saint Paul  76
Saint John the Almsgiver  81

## 7. The Time of Deviation ....................................... 84

From Septuagesima to Quadragesima  86
The Ember Day Fasts  89
The Passion of the Lord  90
The Purification of the Blessed Virgin Mary  92
The Annunciation of the Lord  95
Saint Gregory, Saint Benedict, and Saint Patrick  96

## 8. The Time of Reconciliation ............................... 100

The Ascension of the Lord  103
The Holy Spirit  106
The Finding of the Holy Cross  108
The Greater and Lesser Litanies  111
Saint Ambrose  113
Saint George  115
Saint Mark, Evangelist  117
Saint Peter Martyr  118

## 9. The Time of Pilgrimage ................................... 121

The Birth of the Blessed Virgin Mary  122
The Assumption of the Blessed Virgin Mary  126
The Exaltation of the Holy Cross  128
The Finding of Saint Stephen, the First Martyr, and the Beheading
    of Saint John the Baptist  130
Multiple Saints  132
Saint Maurice and His Companions  133
Saints Dionysius, Rusticus, and Eleutherius  135
The Eleven Thousand Virgins  137

The Four Crowned Martyrs 138
Saint John the Baptist 139
Saint Peter, Apostle 141
Saint Paul, Apostle 142
Saint Christopher 143
Saint Dominic 144
Saint Bernard 145
Saint Augustine 148
Saint Michael, Archangel 152
Saint Jerome 154
Saint Francis 156
Saint Martin, Bishop 157
Saint Elizabeth of Hungary 161
Saint Catherine 164
All Saints and the Commemoration of All Souls 165
Saint Pelagius, Pope: The History of the Lombards 170
The Dedication of a Church 176

Conclusion............................................................................181


*Afterword 183*

*Notes 185*

*Bibliography 197*

   1. Jacobus de Voragine and the *Golden Legend* 197
   2. Genoa in the Time of Jacobus de Voragine 199
   3. The "Beautiful" Thirteenth Century 200
   4. The Latin Legendaries 200
   5. The Dominicans in the Thirteenth Century 201
   6. Liturgy and Christian Time in the Middle Ages 201
   7. Christian Time in the Middle Ages 202
   8. Saints and Sanctity under Christianity 202
   9. Various Studies on Time 203
  10. Time and History 205


*Index 207*

# Preface

The *Golden Legend* is an extraordinary work, both in itself and on account of its fortunate history. Written during the last third of the thirteenth century, this text, the 178 chapters of which take up over a thousand pages in the edition of the Bibliothèque de la Pléiade, has come down to us in over a thousand medieval manuscripts, a figure that places it second only to the Bible in its circulation in the Middle Ages.

With the development of printing the *Golden Legend* long held a prominent place among printed books. Unlike most works of the Middle Ages, which were written in Latin because they were destined for a public of clerics and a limited number of educated laymen, the *Golden Legend* was soon translated into the vernacular. We possess, from the Middle Ages, ten manuscript editions in Italian, seventeen in French, ten in Dutch, eighteen in High German and seven in Low German, three in Czech, and four in English, for a total of sixty-nine copies. Printed versions were almost as many: forty-nine between 1470 and 1500, twenty-eight between 1500 and 1530, only thirteen between 1531 and 1560, with the last translation into the vernacular, in Italian, in 1613. The fame of this work was partly due to the fact that it was produced and put into circulation at that essential moment in the history of the written word when vernacular languages began to rival Latin, when a growing number of laymen became capable of reading, and when, during the latter half of the twelfth century, the spread of the practice of silent reading permitted individual reading and put an end to total reliance on reading aloud, the only form of reading practiced in the Middle Ages. Thus the *Golden Legend* benefitted from exceptional historical circumstances. It had, as we shall see, outstanding qualities that enabled it to take advantage of those circumstances. Before we leave the topic of medieval translations of the *Golden Legend*, let me note that one of the most famous of them was made during the second half of the fourteenth century by Jean du Vignay, who held the title of translator to the king of France, having as his royal sponsor Charles V.

Between 1260, the probable date at which he began writing the work, and 1297, the year of his death, Jacobus de Voragine, the Dominican author of this work, enriched or modified his work on a number of occasions. Similarly, the copyists of the Latin text and those who translated the *Golden Legend* into vernacular languages often made modifications in the text. Thus, despite excellent recent editions and translations that make use of manuscripts chosen and established according to the best scientific methods (and on which I shall rely), the text of all the remaining manuscripts of the *Golden Legend* have not been explored completely, hence they remain living and evolving works.

After the great success that it enjoyed for over three centuries, the *Golden Legend* underwent something like an eclipse from the mid-seventeenth century until the beginning of the twentieth. For one thing, whatever the interpretation given to the *Legend*, it is essentially a series of saints' lives, and for that reason it was long (and still is) classified by specialists as hagiographic literature. Chief among those who relegated the *Golden Legend* to the purgatory of oblivion were the Bollandists, the leading specialists in the saints in the modern period. That Jesuit institution, which set itself the mission of presenting the saints in a scientific manner, stripped of the phantasms of medieval credulity, came close to wiping out all knowledge of a work that, as we are now aware, was one of the great masterpieces of the Middle Ages. It was Father Baudouin de Gaiffier who, relying on a study by Monsignor J. Lestocquoy, identified the true source of the unfavorable opinion of the work that was later picked up by the Bollandists. That source was Juan-Luis Virès (1492–1540), a famous Spanish scholar who developed the critical spirit of the Renaissance and who wrote that the *Golden Legend* was in fact a "leaden legend."[1]

In order to measure the meaning and the impact of Jacobus de Voragine's work, we need, first of all, to do away with a notion that does an injustice not only to the *Golden Legend*, but to a large portion of the works of medieval culture. Even as fine a connoisseur of the *Golden Legend* as my student, colleague, and friend Alain Boureau treats the work as a "compilation."[2] Since the eighteenth century, that term communicates a sense only slightly less pejorative than "plagiarism." Compilation was widely practiced in the Middle Ages (Jacobus de Voragine makes use of it in the *Golden Legend*), and its connotations during this period were entirely positive. The person who probably explained this best was the master compiler in the field of etymology, the learned Isidore of Seville, in the seventh century: "The compiler is he who mixes things said by others with his own, in the manner of color merchants whose wont it is to mix different substances in a mortar. A certain soothsayer from Mantua was accused one day of having mixed some verses of Homer with his own, and authors eager to emulate the Ancients denounced him as a compiler. He responded: 'It is to possess great strength to tear Hercules's club from his hand.'"[3] Moreover, Alain Boureau, thanks to his excellent comprehension of the *Golden Legend*, ends up admitting, "The compiler was also an author."

Second, the *Golden Legend* of Jacobus de Voragine is usually placed within the category of Latin legendaries.[4] But although the *Golden Legend* does indeed contain a collection of saints' lives (arranged within a work that treats the liturgy), it reaches far beyond the quite limited character of a simple collection of saints' lives implied by the term "legendary." It is true that the *Golden Legend* is an expression of the Dominican Order, new in the thirteenth century, and of its will to frame in its own way the choice, the presentation, and the use of saints' lives. Jacobus de Voragine did not hide what he owed to two of his Dominican predecessors, Jean de Mailly and Bartholomew of Trent, who authored a true legendary in the first half of the thirteenth century.

Other scholars who have specialized in Jacobus de Voragine have seen in the *Golden Legend* something like a condensation of the Dominicans' intellectual contribution to the Christian apostolate. This view is unacceptable, however, because Jacobus de Voragine, although he did not turn his back on the theological and scholastic activities of the Dominicans, as has been falsely alleged, preferred to leave that side of their intellectual activity to certain of his brothers in order to devote himself to a more active apostolate. For still other scholars, the *Golden Legend* is a veritable encyclopedia. As I myself have attempted to show, the thirteenth century was indeed an "encyclopedic century," for in its course encyclopedias were composed by Dominicans such as Thomas of Cantimpré and Vincent of Beauvais, and by the Franciscan Bartolomaeus Anglicus (Bartholomew the Englishman). Jacobus de Voragine, however, despite the interest he showed in animals (to pick but one subject example), does not include in the *Golden Legend* any entries on God's other great creation, nature, such as were of course included in genuine encyclopedias.[5] Jacobus does link time to the rhythm of the seasons though, something that was rarely done in the Middle Ages.

In my opinion, Jacobus de Voragine's work is indeed a *summa*, as was his intention, but it is a *summa* on time. He says as much in the very first line of his text: "Universum tempus presentis uite in quatuor distinguitur." (The whole time-span of this present life comprises four distinct periods.[6]) The great originality of Jacobus de Voragine is not only that he considers and embraces time, a great question critical to all civilizations and all religions, in its totality;

he also arrives at that total time through a combination of three varieties of time, which I shall examine in succession in this essay: the *temporale*, or the time of Christian liturgy, which is cyclical; the *sanctorale*, or the time marked by the succession of the lives of the saints, which is linear; and, finally, *eschatological* time, which Christianity sees as the temporal road on which humanity travels toward Judgment Day. The combination of these three times is also original to Jacobus de Voragine, as is the essential role that he attributes to the saints as markers of time.

Our Dominican's overriding interest, then, is in demonstrating how it is that only Christianity has the means to structure and sacralize the time of human life in such as way as will lead humanity to salvation. The subject of the *Golden Legend* is not abstract time, but a human time, willed by God and rendered sacred, or sanctified, by Christianity. Marcel Gauchet, returning to an expression of Max Weber's, titled his great book, *Le Désenchantement du monde*. Jacobus de Voragine was attempting just the opposite. He used time to enchant and sacralize the world and humanity—without, however, ignoring the devil's efforts to obstruct that endeavor.

# Acknowledgments

First, my thanks go to the historian Laurent Theis, who brought this essay to the attention of its French publishers, Éditions Perrin—to whom I am grateful for welcoming it—and who gave so generously of his time and energies throughout the writing process, offering suggestions and corrections that proved invaluable in arriving at the final text presented here. His knowledge, intelligence, historical sensitivity, and editorial skills added to the value of his generosity.

My gratitude also goes to Marie-José Bedez, who saw through the material realization of this text with her excellent technical competence and her exemplary devotion to this task in a climate of highly valued friendship.

# IN SEARCH
# OF SACRED TIME

# 1

# Jacobus de Voragine
# in His Time

Jacobus, known in English and in French as "de Voragine," was an Italian whose name in its traditional Italian form is Iacopo da Varazze. Varazze is a small town on the Ligurian coast not far from Genoa. It is thought today, however, that although Iacopo's family came from Varazze, he himself was born in Genoa.[1]

"That year, on Friday 3 June, soon after twelve o'clock, the weather being serene and clear, the sun was obscured and for some time it was night and no one remembered having seen anything similar in other times nor such a great obscurity taking place during the daytime and that lasted so long. As a result, very many were struck by it and much frightened." This eclipse of the sun described by an anonymous layperson in Genoa chronicling the year 1239 is the oldest authentic event to which Jacobus de Voragine alludes in his writings. It is amusing to note that our Dominican's oldest chronological reference concerns a marvel of nature. It is as if he were predestined to be receptive to the marvelous and not over-concerned to separate the natural from the supernatural .[2]

The life of Jacobus de Voragine is fairly well known because, for one thing, he became prominent within a religious order that made liberal use of both the written and the spoken word and, for another, because he himself, despite his humility, was quite sensitive to chronology, which is one expression of time. As a result, the autobiographical information present in his own works, in documents relating to the history of the Dominican Order, and in a series of essential notarial acts (for the most part relating to the last period of his life, 1292–1298, when he was archbishop of Genoa) have been preserved. This great specialist on the saints was himself not canonized, but only beatified, and that beatification came late. It was pronounced by Pope Pius VII in 1816 at the request of the Genoese, who had always been devoted to his memory.

As is usually the case in the Middle Ages, we do not know Jacobus de Voragine's birth date (the keeping of parish registers did not become general practice until the sixteenth century), but it is likely that his family belonged to the minor nobility in Liguria and that he was born in 1228 or 1229. The summary of his life that follows contains only authentic dates founded on indisputable documents. In 1244 Iacopo, who was at the time almost certainly an adolescent, entered as a novice into the Dominican monastery founded in Genoa in 1222. In 1267 the chapter general of Bologna raised him to the post of provincial of Lombardy. This was a highly important post, given the wealth and the prestige of that province and the fact that it was extremely large, including all of Northern Italy, Emilia, and Picenum on the Adriatic coast south of Ancona. He occupied that position for ten years, until 1277. We do not know in which Dominican monastery of the region—whether in Bologna or, more probably, in Milan—he established his seat. He was reappointed by the provincial chapter of Bologna in 1281 and remained provincial of Lombardy until 1286. From 1283 to 1285 he served as a temporary replacement for the master general of the Dominican Order, a charge to which the pope had been unable to name a friar with a wider acceptance in the Order. In 1288 he was a candidate for the archiepiscopal seat of Genoa, which was vacant at the time. He found himself enmeshed in a lively polemic within the Order, however, in which he is thought to have supported the new master general, Muño de Zamora, and in the course of the violent (and at times armed) conflicts that followed, even within the Order, he was threatened with assassination on two occasions and with being thrown into the well of the Dominican monastery in Ferrara. In 1292, when the political winds had shifted, he was named archbishop of Genoa by Pope Nicholas IV. The pope died soon after, however, so it was a cardinal charged with papal functions who consecrated Jacobus as archbishop, in Rome on April 13, 1292. Jacobus de Voragine took an extremely active part in the intense political struggles that shook Genoa at the end of the thirteenth century. Unrest existed in ecclesiastical milieus as well, and here Jacobus launched a legislative reorganization of both the clergy and the laity and attempted to mediate between the enemy Guelph and Ghibelline factions. He managed to reestablish civil peace in 1295 and led an imposing procession through the city, parading on horseback at the head of the population and then presenting a belt of knighthood to the Milanese Iacopo da Carcano, the *potestate* of Genoa (as in most of the larger cities of Italy in the thirteenth century, foreign potestates had replaced the consuls in the city's government). In the same year, Jacobus went to Rome, at the bidding of the new pope, Boniface VIII, to make use of his talent for mediation by reestablishing peace between Genoa and Venice. He failed to achieve this goal, however. On his return to Genoa he was equally unsuccessful at preventing either the breakdown of the peace between factions or the resumption of violent confrontations. In his sorrow, his poetic tastes inspired him to write, "Our zither has been transformed into mourning, and our organ has changed into a human voice of men and women weeping." The violence in Genoa was so intense that the Cathedral of San Lorenzo was burned to the ground; in June 1296 Jacobus obtained an indemnity from the pope for its reconstruction. Having fulfilled his functions as conscientiously as he could and having settled a number of archdiocesan economic problems, he died during the night of July 13 to 14, 1298, aged about seventy, quite advanced in years for a man of his time.

Three elements of his biography throw light both on Jacobus de Voragine as a person and on his oeuvre. First, he was fundamentally—one might say viscerally—a Genoese, totally devoted to the city where he was probably born and certainly died at the head of its clergy, and the history of which he wrote (*Chronica civitatis Ianuensis*) at the very end of his life. From adolescence he had been a member of the recently created Dominican Order, founded by Saint Dominic in 1216 (and as we have seen, his own monastery was founded six years after that). He remained a prominent member of the Order, especially in Genoa and in Northern Italy. We should not forget, however, that although this friar, unlike many Franciscans, was not primarily an itinerant preacher, he did make many voyages, all of them within the Mediterranean basin or the central areas of Christendom (for example, to Pecs in 1273 and to Bordeaux in 1277). Unlike some historians, however, I do not view him as a friar with a special attraction for Mediterranean space, the arena of Genoese commerce. He was essentially a man of the Church, as were all Dominicans, in particular those of the more populated and active cities.[3] Thus the great theologian Albert the Great, a member of the Dominican Order, pronounced an astonishing series of sermons in Latin and German in the mid-thirteenth century, proposing a sort of theology and spirituality of the city according to which narrow, somber urban streets were equated with Hell and large open squares with Paradise. Jacobus de Voragine, who wanted to make pious use of the saints to sacralize or sanctify times and places, believed that just as he did this in writing in the *Golden Legend*, he could also do it in acts, in particular by the transfer of relics. In 1293, during his tenure as archbishop, he organized a provincial council in the cathedral of San Lorenzo to give solemn recognition to the authenticity of the relics of Saint Siro, the patron saint of Genoa. Ecclesiastical authorities, members of the government, the notables of the city, and (in successive groups) the entire population of the city participated. In 1283 Jacobus de Voragine wrote a life of Saint Siro (one of his lesser works) in which he speaks of the relics. Between 1296 and 1298 he wrote, in Latin, a history of the translation of relics of Saint John the Baptist to Genoa in 1099, and he had already written (in 1286 and 1292), histories of relics kept in the monastery of Saints Philip and James in Rome, a convent for Dominican nuns. Jacobus de Voragine himself was first buried in San Domenico, the church of the Dominicans in Genoa, and then in the late eighteenth century his remains were transferred to another Dominican church in Genoa, Santa Maria di Castello, where they remain today.

The second biographical element to be noted is Jacobus's profound attachment to his Order, to its founder, and to his fellow Dominicans. This is apparent in his treatment of the life of Saint Dominic and of the saint chronologically closest to him, Saint Peter of Verona. A fellow Dominican, preacher, and inquisitor, Peter of Verona was massacred on the road from Milan to Como by assassins in the employ of powerful heretics on April 12, 1252, and canonized as a martyr in 1263. During the latter half of the thirteenth century, the Dominicans were a young order, as the official thirteenth-century life of Saint Dominic stresses, and the order almost immediately occupied an eminent place in the urban, social, cultural, and of course in the religious life of Christian Europe. Preaching, as their official name "the Order of Preachers" indicates, was the Dominicans' primary instrument of edification, but they made use not only of the spoken word to sanctify Christian society, but also—as Jacobus de Voragine himself illustrates—employed the written word, in a century when the ability to read was increasing in society. It seems to me that Jacobus de Voragine fully shared in that fondness for novelty and was in no way nostalgic for the past, as some have suggested. The past moved him only when it was the Christian past—the past in which Christianity was born and spread throughout ancient society—a past that was a novelty and, for Jacobus de Voragine, a novelty that brought salvation.[4] The Dominicans are often represented as essentially intellectuals. And this quite wrongly. For the most part, they were simple friars, devoted to preaching and to informing themselves as much as that mission required. This was already the case in the thirteenth century. Intellectuals—and by his works, his ideas, and his influence, Jacobus de Voragine was incontestably an intellectual—were a minority within the Order.

His attachment to the Dominican Order can also be seen in the special influence on his literary activity, and in particular on the *Golden Legend*, of Dominican authors. In the early thirteenth century, which was marked by a renewal of preaching, in particular to the urban public, a new type of legendary was developed. These were in fact called "new legendaries" or "abbreviated legendaries" (the latter because they characteristically shorten the narration of saints' lives to avoid boring listeners). Before Jacobus de Voragine, two Dominicans had already redacted a "new legendary," and they became essential sources for the *Golden Legend*. The first of these figures was Jean de Mailly, who has already been mentioned and whose legendary was probably written and circulated after 1243. Jean de Mailly was a secular priest in the diocese of Auxerre, who at some unknown date between 1240 and 1250 entered the Dominican monastery of Metz.[5] Jacobus de Voragine's other Dominican source was the 1245 legendary of Bartholomew of Trent. The particular character of the *Golden Legend*, which is not an ordinary legendary, probably pushed the Dominican Order to continue to put new legendaries into circulation after Jacobus's death, the best known of which is that of the illustrious Bernard Gui, who died in 1331 and who was also the author of a much-admired manual for inquisitors. One indication of the exceptional success of Jacobus de Voragine's work is that we possess only one manuscript of Bernard Gui's legendary, as opposed to a thousand manuscripts of the *Golden Legend*.

Third, we need to measure what that work and its author owed to their times. For European Christianity, particularly in Northern Italy, the age was a turning point that saw Christian society move from the "beautiful thirteenth century" to the crises of the end of the thirteenth and early fourteenth centuries. Medieval Christianity had reached its zenith in the first half of the thirteenth century. The Gregorian reform had produced its full effects: the near independence of the Church and lay institutions from one another; a reform of the Church; the ascension of the laity; the rapid growth of cities; an acceleration of exchanges of both goods and ideas; the expansion of agriculture and animal husbandry, as well as of urban craft work; and the development of education, with a growing emphasis on calculation, reason, and debate. This was the time, as Father Marie-Dominique Chenu has demonstrated, when theology became a science and, as Alexander Murray explains in his fine book *Reason and Society in the Middle Ages*, when *ratio*, in its dual sense of calculation and reason, expanded in many domains. Although society remained profoundly religious, it recalled that God had made man in his own image and that man should make better use of the qualities and the strengths that God had placed within him. Some, Colin Morris and Aron J. Gurevich, for example, have spoken of the "birth of the individual." I have attempted to describe that great moment in "Du ciel sur la terre: La mutation des valeurs du XIIe au XVIIIe siècle dans l'Occident chrétien."[6] Jacobus de Voragine certainly made use of what these developments offered, and the *Golden Legend*, in a certain fashion, marks the high point of that expansion within Christianity.

However, the latter half of the thirteenth century was also a turning point when prosperity brought changes that were often painful and at times violent. (Indeed Jacobus de Voragine himself experienced these upheavals, especially in Genoa.) Internecine struggles peaked in the Italian cities: around 1280, the first urban workers' strikes took place; monetary difficulties brought the ancestors of bankers to the first financial failures; the last convulsions in the struggle against heretics led to the assassination of the Dominican preacher Peter of Verona, the saint of most recent date presented in the *Golden Legend*; apocalyptical fears arose of the end of the world; and there were early hints of confrontations within the Church that would lead to the popes' exile to Avignon. One might also argue that the glorious aspect of the medieval high point reflected in the *Golden Legend* was a prefiguration of the great Christian celebration that was to be the Roman jubilee of the year 1300. Alain Boureau has evoked the dual nature of the age—a time of festivity and confrontation, of order and disorder—in a fine article that focuses on Jacobus de Voragine's *Chronicle of Genoa*, but in which he evokes an atmosphere that applies to the *Golden Legend* as well.[7]

## 2

# The Major Inspirations for Jacobus de Voragine

A s a compiler, Jacobus de Voragine used an impressive number of texts, and one of the reasons for his success is certainly the multiplicity of his sources. But beyond that, his was a work of creation. Not only was the choice of the authors from whom he took inspiration (or, at times— though rarely—copied word for word) already a creative act, but also and above all, there was creativity in the way in which he reorganized his readings to produce a text that can be considered original.

Not surprisingly, Jacobus de Voragine often quotes from the Bible, in particular when he finds in it stories that accord with the largely narrative nature of the *Golden Legend*. It is striking, however, and might well surprise us, that he cites from and makes broad use of the apocryphal Gospels. Is this because they contain more narratives than the canonical Gospels? Perhaps, but we also need to explain why their apocryphal nature did not dissuade him from using them in a work that he conceived of as founded on truth and seeking truth. Nothing in either the *Golden Legend* or in Jacobus de Voragine's other works—nor in his activities as a responsible member of a religious order—manifests any opposition to or even distance from the papacy, which acted as the guardian of doctrine founded on the canonical Gospels. Among the cities mentioned in the *Golden Legend*, Rome is second only to Jerusalem in the number of times it appears. And the Rome that Jacobus cites is not only the ancient and pagan Rome, but, and especially, Christian Rome. I would suggest the hypothesis that for a work aspiring to lay the foundation for a Christian time, even Gospels that lacked official Church sanction might constitute a source. Jacobus de Voragine, who was by no means lacking in critical spirit, as we shall see, was above all guided by a desire to be inclusive. As he searched for everything that might be of help in sacralizing time, the apocryphal Gospels must have seemed to him purveyors of historical information and edifying narrations worthy of being integrated into his *summa*.

Like most medieval authors, Jacobus de Voragine only rarely indicates what we would call his "sources." But in his *sanctorale*, and even in the work as a whole, he is so intent on establishing the truth of what he writes that he does not hesitate to mention the superior minds from whom he borrowed and who serve as indisputable guarantees of that truth. Thus Christianity appears to him as a long and rich accumulation of sacralizing values. The apparent nostalgia for the past for which he has often been reproached responds in fact to an intention to emphasize origins and to insist on the decisive acts of the great doctors who pushed pagan time back into the shadows of antiquity in order to elaborate on the Christian time of which the *Golden Legend* was to be the illustration and prolongation.

Jacobus de Voragine had recourse to a small number of illustrious predecessors. In conformity with the structure of his work and with the orientation of his reflection on Christian time, these major sources of inspiration are sometimes important principally for liturgical or pastoral reasons, sometimes for influence of a more doctrinal nature.

The foremost master for Jacobus de Voragine in the *Golden Legend*, and indeed for all of medieval Christian thought, is Saint Augustine. Christianity celebrates Augustine on August 28, the official day of his death, but that date is not mentioned in the *Golden Legend*. The work follows calendar order, but it is by no means itself a calendar. Still, Jacobus de Voragine places the life of Saint Augustine within its proper liturgical period—that is, within the final part of the Christian year that he calls "the time of pilgrimage." Alain Boureau has noted that "Voragine consecrates a very long and very painstaking chapter to Augustine."[1] Jacobus states: "He was *augustinus* by his high rank, because, as Augustus the emperor had excelled above all kings, so Augustine . . . surpasses all doctors." He compares Augustine to "the sun" and insists: "Thus Augustine, that shining light of wisdom, that bulwark of the truth and rampart of the faith, incomparably surpassed all the doctors of the Church, both in native gifts and in acquired knowledge, excelling by the example of his virtues and the abundance of his teaching. Hence Saint Remy, commemorating Jerome and other doctors, concludes as follows: 'Augustine outdid them all in genius and in knowledge.'"[2] Saint Augustine must certainly have seduced Jacobus de Voragine not only by his doctrinal authority, but also through the intrinsic interest and the quality of the many narratives in the *Confessions*.[3]

Another profound influence was Saint Ambrose. Curiously, Jacobus de Voragine's greatest praise of Ambrose comes in a quotation from Saint Augustine, who says, "The blessed bishop Ambrose, in whose books the Roman faith shines, emerges like a flower among Latin writers." Jacobus de Voragine may have seen in Ambrose an ecclesiastical leader capable of resisting lay power, imperial power included, while at the same time remaining cognizant of the influence of the powerful of this world. Moreover, when Jacobus as archbishop of Genoa was rewriting the narration of his own life, he may have seen Ambrose as the exemplary figure of a bishop confronting civil power. He was probably also sensitive to Ambrose's desire to regulate the liturgy at a time when the Roman rite had not yet been imposed on all of Christianity. He also mentions Ambrose's talent as an author of moving hymns that fed his own tendency to emphasize sacred music. In the *Golden Legend* he devoted much more space and greater importance to the life of Saint Ambrose than did either Jean de Mailly or Bartholomew of Trent in their legendaries.

The third major inspiration for the *Golden Legend* among the founders of Christian spirituality and culture is clearly Saint Jerome, who was for Jacobus de Voragine the veritable creator of Christian liturgy. Jacobus describes in his life of Jerome how Emperor Theodosius and Pope Damasus asked Jerome to organize the ecclesiastical office. According to Jacobus, it was Jerome who distributed the Psalter over the annual liturgical calendar, as he also did the Epistles and the Gospels. Moreover, Saint Jerome's taming of a lion was one of the ancient tales of Christianity that Jacobus, always avid for striking anecdotes imbued with the marvelous, found the most appealing.

We might add to these three major inspirations, three other persons to whom Jacobus de Voragine did not devote a chapter, but whose works he used quite extensively. Two—the historian Petrus Comestor in the second half of the twelfth century and the liturgist John Beleth at the end of that century—were closer to him in time and had not yet been canonized, while the third, Isidore of Seville, who lived in the seventh century and was famous among the intellectuals of the Middle Ages, was proclaimed a saint only in 1598. The question is, What did the author of the *Golden Legend* find to admire in them?

Like many medieval thinkers, Jacobus de Voragine accorded great importance to the etymology of the names of the saints whose lives, virtues, and miracles he related. For him, the origin of a saint's name held the hidden meaning of the saint's profound Being, and each of his lives begins, accordingly, with a long etymological study. Later etymologists viewed these efforts as fanciful and their judgment contributed to discrediting Jacobus de Voragine in the seventeenth and eighteenth centuries. For me, however, these etymologies provide a key to his approach and to the structure of the *Golden Legend*. The vast compilation that Isidore of Seville left under the title *Etymologiae* earned him the title "the great schoolteacher of the Middle Ages." Jacobus de Voragine's passion for etymology led him also to use (though to a lesser extent) a specialist in etymology closer to his own day, Uguccio of Pisa.[4]

Jacobus de Voragine's greatest "modern" inspiration, however, was a university man. A student of Peter Lombard's in Paris and himself chancellor of the University of Paris, he wielded great influence through his teaching and through a work that was in wide use by the end of the twelfth century, his *Historia scholastica*, a kind of manual of biblical history. The highly visible presence of this author and this work in the *Golden Legend* shows, in my opinion, that Jacobus de Voragine, who has been accused of ignoring and scorning terrestrial history, was on the contrary greatly attracted by this discipline, on the condition that its content contribute to the sanctification of human time. This would explain his interest in this university professor, whose erudition was so great that he was called a devourer of books, "Petrus Comestor" or, in French, Pierre le Mangeur.

One surprising addition to these personalities of a more modern age is Saint Bernard, the great Cistercian saint of the twelfth century. Historians often contrast earlier monastic orders, whose members lived, in principle, in solitude, with the mendicant orders of the thirteenth century, the Dominicans and the Franciscans, whose members called themselves friars, not monks, and who lived in the cities. We know that Jacobus de Voragine was a prominent Dominican. In the life that he devotes to Bernard of Clairvaux, Jacobus praises him for "having wrought many miracles, . . . built 160 monasteries, and . . . compiled many books and treatises." There is nothing in this statement that distinguishes Saint Bernard in any fundamental way from the many other saints who figure in the *Golden Legend* or anything that would seem to validate such devotion on the part of Jacobus de Voragine. Despite the decline of the Cistercian Order in the thirteenth century, Saint Bernard certainly remained a celebrity. Jacobus de Voragine, who belonged to an order of preachers and was writing his great book especially for their use, saw in Saint Bernard something like a precursor, for the twelfth-century saint was indeed, in his own way, a famous preacher.

# 3

# The Prologue and the Temporale

## The Prologue

Prologues were usually important in the Middle Ages because they announce the plan, the intention of the work as a whole, and sometimes, when the work is a compilation, its sources. François Dolbeau has studied the prologues of Latin legendaries.[1] He notes the originality of the *Golden Legend* when compared with the other new legendaries that he examined, including those written by Dominican authors. Jacobus de Voragine does not speak of *brevitas*, of *utilitas*, or of *facultas praedicandi*. In fact, he does not aim at practical utilization for his work, but rather conceives of it in a universal perspective, combining the history of salvation, liturgical history, and saints' lives. This choice was favorable to the book's reception as it encouraged the work's distribution throughout Christendom. Jacobus opens by declaring this universal aim and announces that liturgical time, the time of the temporale, will set the pace for his work.[2]

In the two pages of this original prologue, Jacobus de Voragine does not speak of the saints nor, consequently, of the sanctorale. He limits himself to presenting, in condensed form, the liturgical time that would later be called the temporale, and to which he will later return in detail. The importance of liturgy in his age is not to be underestimated. As Father Pierre-Marie Gy writes, "In the Western Middle Ages, where the body of society and almost all of its members considered themselves Christians, liturgy occupied a central place."[3]

It took several centuries for Christian liturgy to become stabilized, but in its essence it had already taken shape by the early seventh century. Over the course of the eleventh century the various liturgies that had long defended their individuality—among them the Gallic, the Hispanic, and the Celtic in Ireland—were completely effaced by the Roman liturgy, which dominated the better part of Christendom in the thirteenth century. The Dominicans, whose Order had arisen at the beginning of that century, received their canonical organization from Saint Dominic and accepted the essence of the Roman liturgy. Humbert of Romans, the master general of the Order, was charged by the Dominican general council of Pest in 1254 with refashioning Dominican liturgy, a task that was completed in 1256.[4] Outside of the Dominican Order, the period was marked, above all, by the diffusion throughout the laity of the breviary and of silent reading. The increase in lay participation in certain aspects of the liturgy, while it had no specific impact on the *Golden Legend*, most certainly aided in its success, since it no longer needed to be read aloud collectively but could be read individually and silently.

Some historians of liturgy have stressed its importance in the construction of Christian time. Thus Monsignor Albert Houssiau, in a remarkable article, defined liturgy "as a manifestation of the time of God within the time of men." Although he does not refer to Jacobus de Voragine, Houssiau defines the relationship between time and liturgical action in a manner that can easily be applied to Jacobus's vision. He explains that liturgy is at once a remembrance of the resurrection of Christ, an expectation of his return, and communion with him.[5]

Jacobus de Voragine owed much to a work by the liturgist John Beleth, the *Summa de ecclesiasticis officiis*, a work written in the late twelfth century that had widespread influence until the late thirteenth century. On the other hand, Jacobus de Voragine seems not to have been aware of one of his own contemporaries, Guillaume Durand, the bishop of Mende (ca. 1230–1296), probably the greatest liturgist of the Middle Ages.[6]

Liturgy is closely connected with the calendar. The *Golden Legend* is by no means a calendar, but the temporale and the sanctorale unfold in chronological order, even if dates are rare in them. There are probably two reasons for the sort of difficulty that Jacobus de Voragine seems to have experienced with chronology and the calendar. The first of these is that the Christian calendar, which was still marked by its dual Jewish and Roman origins, was at base a solar calendar but was also subject to lunar influences. The result was the presence of movable feast days, first among them—or at least for a long time the most important within Christianity—Easter. A lover of constancy within movement, Jacobus de Voragine seems to have been bothered by this instability in certain dates, and in fact sought to neutralize the mobility of the date of Easter. Moreover, although he relies heavily on Pope Gregory the Great (590–604), another major source of his inspiration in liturgical matters, many problems inherent to the Christian calendar had not yet been completely resolved at the end of the thirteenth century. It was not until the Council of Trent, in the sixteenth century, that the calendar was definitively established. We should also keep in mind that Jacobus de Voragine was thinking, writing, and operating within a Christianity in which the lay calendar officially beginning with the first day of the year was neither uniform nor stable.

The strong presence of liturgical practices in the *Golden Legend* is shown (among other ways) by a number of elements to which its author lends particular emphasis, such as singing and vestments. If the spoken word was the essential instrument for the Dominicans as the Order of Preachers, the voice was even more forceful when it gave musical expression in chant. In the first chapter of his book, "The Advent of the Lord," Jacobus de Voragine emphasizes the attitude of the Church, which requires the singing of "joyful chants."[7] In the final chapter, "The Dedication of a Church," he not only recalls that "the Mass is sung in three languages, Greek, Hebrew, and Latin" and that, in particular, the *Kyrie eleison* "is repeated nine times, signifying that we are to enter the company of the nine orders of angels," but he develops as well a veritable apologetics of "the singing of the chant" in the consecration of the altar. Basing his argument on Ecclesiastes and on his fellow-Dominican, Hugh of Saint-Cher, a Parisian canonist and theologian who died in 1263, Jacobus distinguishes "three kinds of musical sounds, namely, those that are produced by striking, by blowing, and by singing." Moreover, "this harmony of sound may be applied not only to the offices of the church, but to the harmony of morals; the work of the hands is compared to the striking or plucking of the strings, the devotion of the mind to the blowing of the organ, and vocal prayer to the singing voice." He further states that "the offices of the church" consist of "Psalms, chant, and readings." Jacobus de Voragine does not forget that these chants must be inscribed within time, lending sacrality to time's unfolding and to its principal moments. In the same final chapter, "The Dedication of a Church," he recalls that, among other objectives, the Church uses liturgical chants to give a rhythm to time. These chants make up the seven canonical hours, condensation points of sacred time, which must not, however, cause us to forget that in all of time, even outside of its successive liturgical manifestations, "God should be praised at every hour of the day." Song is thus an essential instrument for the sacralization of time.

Still, when he places the feast days of the saints whom he mentions in his sanctorale into a chronological order defined by the periods of the liturgy, Jacobus de Voragine displays a great interest in the distribution through time of the calendar, which he senses is also one of the means for mastering and rendering that same time sacred—the overall objective of the *Golden Legend*. This is one demonstration (among others) of the importance of the inscription of the sanctorale within the temporale, a Dominican innovation imposed by the success and the wide distribution of the *Golden Legend*, and it also demonstrates once again, that the *Golden Legend* is not a legendary.[8]

Thus the meaning of the *Golden Legend*'s prologue becomes clear. The very first sentence, as we have already seen, gives its essence: "The whole time-span of this present life comprises four distinct periods."[9] Jacobus de Voragine declares that his aim is to construct a *summa* that explains the meaning of human time and makes it possible to experience it. The time in question in the *Golden Legend* is indeed the time of humanity but, as the author specifies, it is not chronological time. It is the time of the relations of humanity with the supreme God: time is subjected to God, and not the reverse. Still, not only does Jacobus de Voragine not reject chronological time, but he often refers to it, and the relations between the divine time of humanity that is real time and chronological time provide one of the themes of the work and of the reflection in which he engages. Thus he remarks that the time of the Church begins with "The Advent of the Lord," which stresses the primacy of Christmas. Morever, our Dominican explains the reasons behind that decision on the part of the Church, to which he himself conforms: "Although the time of turning away from the right way came before renewal, the Church begins the cycle of her offices with the time of renewal rather than with that of deviation—in other words, with Advent rather than Septuagesima—and this for two reasons. She does not wish to start from error, for she puts reality before the sequence of time. . . . And besides, the renewal of all things came with the coming of Christ."

Finally, from its opening sentence, the Prologue uses numeration, and the practice of quantification—of numeration—runs through the *Golden Legend*. Numbers, counting, and succession provide the very structure of human time, and in more general terms, the author divides his text by the use of "in the first place," "second," and "third." This is a characteristic of Christianity as a whole, and detailed studies of it would be welcome.[10] I might also note that in this prologue Jacobus de Voragine relates what he calls "this fourfold division of historic time" to the four seasons of the year and to the four parts of the day. This contradicts the view of the many commentators who claim that nature, so abundantly present in the encyclopedic works of the thirteenth century, is absent from the *Golden Legend*. Far from ignoring nature, Jacobus de Voragine accords it great importance, although his emphasis is on the marvelous manifested by God through the saints. When Jacobus, still in his prologue, evokes the feasts of the saints that are celebrated during the time of reconciliation, he stresses that a feast is a "time of rejoicing." Although he is a half-century younger than Saint Francis of Assisi, here Jacobus shows himself Francis's Dominican brother, and he too subscribes to a "beautiful" thirteenth century in search of joy.

## The Temporale

The four periods or times into which the *Golden Legend* is divided and that Jacobus de Voragine defines in his prologue are: the time of *deviation*, which goes from Adam to Moses; the time of *renewal* or *being called back*, which stretches from Moses to the Nativity of Christ; the time of *reconciliation*, celebrated between Easter and Pentecost; and the time of *pilgrimage*, which is "that of our life." There remains a hiatus between Christmas and the Pascal season that begins at Septuagesima (seventy days before the Saturday following Easter Sunday). Jacobus de Voragine divides that hiatus between a portion of the time of reconciliation from Christmas to the octave of Epiphany (or a week after Christmas) and the time of pilgrimage, during which "we are on pilgrimage and constantly engaged in warfare," which goes from the octave of Epiphany to Septuagesima.

The time of humanity thus begins with the appearance of humankind with Adam, but Christ stands firmly at its center. In the *Golden Legend* the feasts devoted to time are thus the most numerous. They include seven chapters: chapter 1, "The Advent of the Lord"; chapter 6, "The Birth of Our Lord Jesus Christ according to the Flesh"; chapter 13, "The Circumcision of the Lord"; chapter 14,

"The Epiphany of the Lord; chapter 53, "The Passion of the Lord"; chapter 52 [54], "The Resurrection of the Lord"; and chapter 72, "The Ascension of the Lord." One might add chapter 68, "The Finding of the Holy Cross" and chapter 137, "The Exaltation of the Holy Cross." In contrast, only three chapters are devoted to the Virgin Mary: chapter 37, "The Purification of the Blessed Virgin Mary"; chapter 119, "The Assumption of the Blessed Virgin Mary"; and chapter 131, "The Birth of the Blessed Virgin Mary." As for the Holy Ghost, Jacobus de Voragine devotes only one chapter to it: chapter 73, "The Holy Spirit."

Between the two feasts that mark the great event of the incarnation of Jesus, the *Golden Legend* displays a tendency common in its century to give increasing importance to Christmas over Easter. That tendency is clearly linked to the evolution of Christian spirituality, which, after having made of Christianity essentially the religion of a resuscitated God, began to accord more and more importance to the celebration of his incarnation.

The *Golden Legend* devotes a chapter each to the nativity of two figures besides Christ, the Blessed Virgin Mary and Saint John the Baptist, the precursor. The three nativities are tightly focused on that of Christ. The nativity of the Virgin Mary makes Christ's birth possible because she is his mother; that of Saint John the Baptist announces Christ's birth. The Nativity of the Lord, with all that the term promises in the way of novelty and life, places the birth of Christ at the dawn of sacred time, for that incarnation, by reconciling humanity with God, creates the time of reconciliation—and that of pilgrimage, which connect the four times of the *Golden Legend* and are themselves drawn by God, with the thread of eschatological time, toward the last days and Eternity. The temporale—or time of the liturgy, which is the dynamic structure essential to humanity is thus measured out by the feasts of Jesus incarnated and the three elements of salvation that accompanied him in his incarnation: the Virgin Mary, who bore him as a man; the Holy Ghost, the gift he left to his apostles and, through them, to humanity, before he returned to heaven in the ascension; and the cross, which was the instrument of his passion and his resurrection.

In addition to what might be called personalized feasts, Jacobus de Vorgine included Lent within the temporale (with chapters on Septuagesima, Sexagesima, Quinquagesima, and Quadragesima); the Ember Day fasts that recall, in a seasonal manner, the penitence that is required of humanity because of the deviation prompted by original sin; and, finally, the Major Litany of one day and the Minor Litany of three days, times of supplication that humanity be spared the calamities of terrestrial life—plague in the case of the Major Litany, and wars, failed harvests, and bodily ills in the Minor. The fact that two days of liturgical celebration are not included poses a problem, for which I can find no satisfactory explanation. There is no chapter on Ash Wednesday, nor one on Palm Sunday. They did not seem to Jacobus de Voragine sufficiently meaningful to figure in the unfolding of the four sacred times.

# The Sanctorale

Because the *Golden Legend* is not primarily a legendary—that is, a hagiographic catalogue—and because the time that Jacobus de Voragine seeks to sacralize combines liturgical time (the temporale) with a time of saints (the sanctorale), it follows that a large portion of the book recounts the lives of saints.

## Saintliness and Christianity

The figure of the saint is an integral part of the Christian religion. One of the greatest historians in this domain, Peter Brown, has emphasized that the Muslim venerables whom some have attempted to equate with saints really are not the same, and that those who most closely approach the saints are marginal figures venerated only on the periphery of the Islamic world, in the Atlas Mountains of Morocco and from Indonesia to the Maghreb.[1] Neither can the great Indian ascetics of Brahmanism or, more generally, sages and gurus be compared to Christian saints.

The main characteristic of the saint is that he or she was chosen by God to appear on Earth in his place as an instrument or an inter-

mediary, either by means of miracles or by virtue of an exceptionally religious comportment during terrestrial existence. That choice
takes the form of a vocation, a call that at a certain moment becomes
manifest in the life of the elect person, inhabits him or her until
death, and leads to sainthood.

Saintliness and the nature of the saint have evolved since the
early Christian era. The appearance of saints marked one of Christianity's first ruptures with Judaism, which sets apart only prophets
and patriarchs. After the apostles, those designated by Christianity
as "saints" were for the most part the martyrs who gave their lives
for the new faith as it gradually replaced ancient paganism and Judaism. Once Christianity, at first tolerated, then recognized, became
the official religion within Christendom, the saints were only rarely
martyrs—with the exception of the Dominican preacher Peter of
Verona, who was massacred by heretics. Henceforth they were confessors, monks, hermits, or bishops, identifications that are usually
attached to their names and that, in fact, Jacobus de Voragine cites,
though not in the section titles of his text (with the exception of the
apostles).

The saints of the post-Carolingian Middle Ages were essentially
sacralized as a result of God's perception of their virtues. Only one
category among them was truly distinct: that of the hermits who,
confronted with an increasingly frenetic life in the cities and on the
roads, preferred the relative sacrality of the forests. These hermits
were rarely reclusive, however; they received many visitors or themselves often left their hermitages.

What is more, in the late twelfth century the papacy reserved
to itself the privilege of attributing the qualification of sainthood,
a status obtained after what was usually a long and painstaking ex-
amination known as the process of canonization. Jacobus de Voragine respects both tradition, as confirmed by trustworthy sources
(including, as we have seen, the apocryphal Gospels), and Roman
orthodoxy. The number of saints that he selects and to whom he
devotes a chapter varies slightly according to the manuscript of the

work and according to whether the reader counts as one saint or several the multiple saints that he treats together in one chapter. The great majority of historians arrive at the figure of 153 saints in the *Golden Legend*. The reason is clear. The Gospel of John (21:11) states: "Simon Peter went aboard and hauled ashore the net loaded with sizable fish—one hundred fifty-three of them!" This is the famous episode of the miraculous catch, and it reveals much about Jacobus de Voragine's method: he counts often and everything, including time, beginning with Jesus, who renewed time.[2] Christ made those men who were fishing in the Sea of Tiberias "fishers of men," as the first three evangelists put it. The time of the *Golden Legend* is a time for fishing for men to be transformed into Christians devoted to God and to salvation, and it is the person of Christ that gives a new start to the time of men.

## Saints in the *Golden Legend*

The definition of saintliness has not only evolved during the course of time; it also depends on which Christian author is using the term. Does this mean that there is a particular conception of the saint for Jacobus de Voragine that serves as the basis and the framework for the sanctorale of the *Golden Legend*?

It has been said that Christian sainthood began with the cult of the martyrs and was usually focused on their tombs, which meant that at first the saints were, as Peter Brown puts it, "the very special dead." After the Christianization of Europe, when fewer martyrs were canonized, the connection between saintliness and death weakened. Most Christian authors, and probably the faithful in general, were aware of the location of saints' tombs within the space of Christianity, where they constituted a major spiritual network, and the mortal remains of the saints came to occupy an increasingly large place within the Christian cult—Jacobus de Voragine himself displays a high degree of sensitivity to the cult of relics. The prevailing current in the cult of the saints seems, however, to have gone in the opposite direction, moving from death toward an emphasis on life. The time of the saints was profoundly changed as a result. In the Christian calendar that change took place slowly and with great difficulty, as the cult of the saints became fixed in space to the tomb and in time to the day of the saint's death. Indeed, the birthdates of even powerful and famous personages of the Middle Ages were almost always unknown before the fourteenth century. Thus the saint's cult day was that of his death, which was more apt to be known, and that cult was defined as an act of memory. It was a commemoration. When the cult of the saints shifted from death to life, the day of their cult—even if it remained fixed on the death day in the liturgical vocabulary—ceased to be a commemoration and became instead a feast (*festivitas*). It seems to me that this change in the temporal conception of the cult of the saints corresponds well with Jacobus de Voragine's spirituality and with the aims of the *Golden Legend*. Certainly, and I repeat, Jacobus did not neglect periods of sadness, but the time of the world that he conceived as a movement carrying men toward God and salvation was primarily a time of festivity.

One characteristic of the sanctorale of the *Golden Legend* that has surprised many of the scholars who have studied the work is the high number of saints from the ancient periods of Christianity as compared with a smaller number of "modern" saints. There are six in all of the latter: for the twelfth century, Bernard of Clairvaux, a great preacher, and Thomas à Beckett, the famous archbishop of Canterbury assassinated and promoted to the rank of martyr; for the thirteenth century, the two founders of the mendicant orders, Francis of Assisi and Dominic, the Dominican preacher Peter of Verona, assassinated in 1252 by heretics, and Elizabeth of Hungary, who died in 1231 and was canonized in 1235. In addition to the apostles and evangelists, Jacobus de Voragine chose many saints who had undergone martyrdom under the Roman Empire, in particular under the emperor Diocletian (284–305). The explanation for this choice seems obvious. Jacobus de Voragine wanted to show two things: first, that as new markers of time, the earliest saints were the first workers of Christian times; second, that the shift from paganism to Christianity was an essential moment in the coming of a Christian time that regenerated time in its essence, just as Christ had done by his incarnation. He then was content to treat some of the saints that manifest the continued appearance of new actors in the drama of the sacralization of that time.

The Israeli historian Aviad Kleinberg has devoted a chapter to Jacobus de Voragine's saints, in which he explains, with great acuity, that the sanctorale of the *Golden Legend* proved so attractive because it responded to the cultural needs of many Christian men and women of the latter half of the thirteenth century.[3] He judiciously invited a comparison between the hagiographic narratives of the *Golden Legend* and works in the plastic arts, in poetry, and in the literature of that same age. According to Kleinberg, the importance that Jacobus accords to narrative episodes in the lives of the saints,[4] at the expense of purely psychological and spiritual developments, led to a success comparable to the one that adventure films enjoy with the public of our own day. Aside from individual saints, some of whose lives I shall discuss, I think that chapter 162 of the *Golden Legend* on "All Saints" gives a good indication of the motivations —or at least the admitted ones—that guided Jacobus de Voragine in his conception of the saints and in his choice of those whose lives he examines.

## All Saints Day

In the commentary to his bilingual critical edition of the *Legenda aurea*, Giovanni Paolo Maggioni rightly remarks that Jacobus's chapter on All Saints Day is "quite complex."[5] Alain Boureau and his colleagues state in the commentary to their excellent French edition of *La Légende dorée* that this chapter would not have been very well received in the Middle Ages: "The feast of All Saints encountered little cultic success among the faithful."[6] They give as the primary reason for this that the faithful "were perhaps too attached to the singular relation of devotion to one saint, one protector or one patron." I think they were hypnotized by the idea that the *Golden Legend* should be categorized as hagiographic literature, relying for its success on Jacobus de Voragine's talent as a narrator, which is above all apparent in the little stories (*exempla*) contained in the lives of the saints, whereas there is only one *exemplum* in the chapter on All Saints.[7] To the contrary, I believe that Jacobus de Voragine had a higher ambition and that, despite its lack of picturesque elements, he accorded great importance to this chapter on All Saints—a feast day to which he also devoted six sermons. What he was interested in showing was that the saints were "markers of time" and contributed to its sacralization. Moreover, there are no persuasive proofs of auditors' and readers' lack of interest in this chapter, which brings to a general and higher level the devotion that they might manifest toward one particular saint or another.

In his constant focus on organizing his materials numerically, Jacobus de Voragine declares that Christianity had four reasons for creating a feast of all the saints.

The first of these was that the popes of the early centuries wished to dedicate a church to all of the saints to replace the temple that the Romans had devoted to the pagan gods in an attempt—an aim to which Jacobus de Voragine was particularly receptive—to eclipse the old pagan time by means of the new Christian time. That church was the Pantheon, which became in 615 the church of Saint Mary of the Martyrs, on the order of Pope Boniface IV.

Jacobus's second reason was a desire not to deprive any saint, no matter how little-known or neglected, of a cult. In his fondness for multiplying enumerations, Jacobus gives the six reasons that had been suggested for the existence of a feast of all the saints by William of Auxerre, bishop of Paris, who died in 1231, in his *Summa de officiis*, a work that, between the *summa* of John Beleth (between 1160 and 1164) and that of Guillaume Durand of Mende, the author, after 1285, of a *Rational des divins offices*, became the most prominent liturgical manual of the late Middle Ages. One hundred twenty manuscript copies of this work have come down to us, and Guillaume was one of Jacobus de Voragine's favorite authors. Both men were shining lights in the thirteenth century, which was perhaps the most creative and richest century of the Middle Ages, since it benefitted from the profound changes that took effect in the period between 1150 and 1250, a turning point in the cultural, social, and political order of society. It has been said of Guillaume of Auxerre, "From the methodological point of view . . . Guillaume perfected for the generation that followed his own apologetic schema that legitimated the use of reason in sacred doctrine."[8] Jacobus de Voragine, who was more rational and critical than has been claimed, is one of his heirs. In later enumerations of the reasons for celebrating a feast for all the saints, he also cites the four reasons cited by John of Damascus, who insisted above all on the power of saints' relics. Jacobus de Voragine adds to this the reasons given by Saint Augustine, who made the bodies of the saints the instrument of the Holy Ghost, and by Saint Ambrose, who heard the voice of God himself in their voices. Clearly, Jacobus de Voragine was intent on bringing together a wealth of references.

The third rationale for instituting a feast of All Saints was the need to atone for our own neglect in failing to celebrate the saints, whom, according to his custom, Jacobus arranges into four traditional categories: apostles, martyrs, confessors, and virgins. And here again he lists four reasons for celebrating them.

When it comes to the virgins, it is worth remarking that the essential element in female sanctity continued to be the female body, even among the thinkers of the new mendicant orders and even when sanctity was clearly a consequence of the virtues and the pious lives of the women and no longer depended on their martyrdom. Jacobus de Voragine nonetheless seeks beyond the body for determining criteria. In speaking of the feast of All Saints, he gives several reasons for the sanctification of virgins, which are over and above the fact of virginity. First, the holy virgins are the spouses of God. Then, they are super-angels, for they triumph in the flesh while angels live without flesh. They are also "more illustrious than all the faithful,"[9] which supports the idea of a superiority of women in lay society. I might note that women (with the astonishing exception of nuns) are abundantly present in the *Golden Legend*.

Finally, Jacobus's fourth reason for a feast of All Saints is that it was instituted in order to "make it easier for us to have our prayers heard," because thanks to their merits and their affection for us, when the saints pray together for the faithful, they give our prayers a weight that God cannot ignore, whereas he can accord only a limited weight to prayers supported by only one saint. Number is thus a central argument in the sacralization of time that is the aim of the *Golden Legend*.

In the sanctorale of Jacobus de Voragine the feast of All Saints thus represents the concentration in one day of what divine time can bring humanity that is most sacralizing. It is a day of excellence in which all of the perspectives for salvation that time offers humanity are found united in precisely those beings whom God has chosen to be the models for human time. Jacobus de Voragine, following the example of the great Carolingian theologian Rabanus Maurus, likens the four types of saints—apostles, martyrs, confessors, and virgins—to the four divisions of the world: Orient, South, North, and Occident. These permit him to connect space and time, for to make time sacred is also to sacralize the world.

Already in the thirteenth century, Christian liturgy customarily drew a close connection between the feast of all the saints—All Saints or, in French, Toussaint—on November 1, and the commemoration of all the faithful who had died, which had been established in the eleventh century as the day after Toussaint, November 2 (All Souls Day). As dictated by the liturgical calendar, Jacobus de Voragine places his chapter on the commemoration of all the faithful dead immediately after his chapter on all the saints. I shall not follow suit, however, as the point of the present essay is to show how Jacobus de Voragine inscribes the temporale within liturgical time and the sanctorale within that of the saints. Although the chapter on All Saints clarifies Jacobus's conception of the identity and the role of the saints, it only presents one *exemplum*, an element characteristic of saints' lives and a narrative kernel regularly introduced into preaching in order to provide a concrete illustration and to entertain the listening public or the reader. *Exempla* constitute part of the richness of spiritual literature in the Middle Ages, and if for some scholars they accentuate the popular, even the coarse side of that period, the medievalist conscious of their originality will see in them one of the treasures of moral imagination that the age created and brought together. To repeat a definition of the *exemplum* that I gave in 1982, it is "a brief narrative given as true and destined to be inserted in a discourse (usually a sermon) in order to persuade listeners by means of a salutary lesson." I want to insist on the veracity of the *exemplum*: Jacobus de Voragine, who is often presented as a spinner of tales ready to swallow and to make others swallow the wildest fantasies, takes great care, on the contrary, to persuade his listener or his reader by the use of stories, even extraordinary or disconcerting ones. The marvelous that inhabits the *exempla* (among other things) is a moment of truth, the very truth that, even if it is not completely our truth, men and women sought ardently, as it led to salvation. Already used—notably by such Cistercians as Caesarius of Heisterbach, the author of the *Dialogus miraculorum* (ca. 1220) and by the Augustinian canon Jacques de Vitry (d. 1240)—the *exemplum* was favorite tool of preachers of the mendicant orders. The first important collection of *exempla* was the mid-thirteenth-century *Tractatus de diversis materiis praedicabilibus* of Stephanus de Borbone (Étienne de Bourbon). Compilers of *exempla* sometimes found it useful to alphabetize their entries. The masterpiece in this regard is the *Alphabetum narrationum*, written by the Dominican Arnold de Liège between 1292 and 1308. Like the *Golden Legend*, several collections of *exempla* were made during the Middle Ages in various vernacular languages. Finally, the *exempla* often contained cultural elements related to folklore. Thus Jacobus de Voragine can be situated within the movement for the teaching and the formation of knowledge and faith in which the Dominicans played an important role and which made of the late thirteenth and the early fourteenth centuries the prolongation of an age that saw the popular milieus of medieval culture enriched and broadened by contributions from three essential sources: the Roman heritage, popular culture, and the rich products of Christian learning.[10]

The *exemplum* that Jacobus de Voragine presents in his chapter "All Saints Day" tells of a vision that the guardian of the basilica of Saint Peter's was reported to have had after the inauguration of this feast day. As he stood before the altar of Saint Peter's he is said to have had a vision of God on a throne surrounded by all the angels, of the Blessed Virgin, and of the crowd of all the saints, who were thanking God for the honor that had been shown to them on this day by all the faithful, who were inciting them to pray for all the nations of the entire world. In one corner of this vision the poor begged for help: this was Purgatory and, given that the souls in Purgatory could not be helped by intercessory prayers, God ordered all of the saints to pray for those poor people so as to free them from their place of misery and solitude and gain entry for them to the corner of space inhabited by the souls of the saved, which was Paradise. This pictorial *exemplum* was meant to show that the saints were called to save all humanity and that Purgatory was but a place to pass through and from which the prayers of the saints would extract mankind. Jacobus de Voragine thus communicated that the time of Purgatory was only provisory in expectation of Paradise.[11]

Finally, the chapter on All Saints was aimed at putting order into the sanctorale. Jacobus de Voragine in fact constructs his sanctorale in a somewhat composite manner, according to a variety of criteria. He chose one hundred fifty-three saints, corresponding to the 153 large fish of the miraculous catch, striving to include among them the saints who were important for the Church and in the devotions of his time, but also following criteria of his own. Usually each chapter is devoted to only one saint, but there are times when he pairs two saints (Saints Gervasius and Protasius, Saints John and Paul, Saints Cosmas and Damian, for example), or writes of groups of saints. Three saints have two chapters dedicated to them, given that the Church had decided to commemorate not only their special feast day but also to sanctify a day of the calendar marking an exceptional event in their lives. These were: "Saint Paul, Apostle" (June 19) and "The Conversion of Saint Paul, Apostle" (June 25); "Saint Peter, Apostle" (June 29) and "The Chair of Saint Peter" (February 22); and "Saint Stephen, Pope" (December 26) and "The Finding of Saint Stephen, the First Martyr" (August 2). And finally, it is not always easy to distinguish between the feast days of saints with the same name, in particular, Saints John, Paul, Peter, and James.[12]

And now the time has come to enter into the *Golden Legend*, following the order established by Jacobus de Voragine.

# 5

# The Time of Renewal

## Advent

Following a long-established tradition, Jacobus de Voragine opens his treatment of sacred human time with the period in which the coming of Christ was announced. There are five chapters in this section: one on Advent itself and four on the saints whose feast days he does not cite but who were already placed within the period of Advent on the calendars most commonly used. These four are: Andrew, Nicholas, Lucy, and Thomas. In most manuscripts of the *Golden Legend*, and quite conceivably in the manuscripts that he himself dictated, Jacobus de Voragine does not usually specify in his chapter title the category—apostles, martyrs, confessors, or virgins—to which the saint, as we have already seen, was assigned by the Church of the High Middle Ages. He makes an exception for Andrew and Thomas, however, by specifying that they are holy apostles. Proximity to Jesus always dictated extra respect. As was his habit, Jacobus de Voragine begins his discussion of the Advent of the Lord with a numerical division. He considers the period of four weeks preceding Christmas important for four reasons: The Lord "came to us in the flesh, he comes into our hearts, he comes to us at death, and he will come to judge us."[1] With characteristic attentiveness to the expression of sentiments, which he plainly considers an important part of spirituality,[2] Jacobus embraces the balance between joy and affliction that marks this period. He announces at the start that the time renewed by Jesus, which is thus a time of joy, will end with the Last Judgment and the end of humanity, a time of sadness before eternity, hence a time of tears.[3] The spirituality of the gift of tears accorded by God to men who know how to feel sadness and show it in times of painful trials—in particular the trials in the life of Jesus—is illustrated by Saint Ambrose, one of Jacobus de Voragine's major inspirations, but also by a series of saints whose lives he recounts. This is the case, for example, of Saint Andrew, of Mary Magdalene, that saint of tears, and of Saint Augustine himself. Creators of festive times, the saints are in a general manner great wipers of tears. Jacobus de Voragine did not give eschatological time the place within the *Golden Legend* that it often occupied in his age as a period of apocalyptical passion marked by exaggerated penitential manifestations, such as flagellation. He shies away from the inevitable evocation of the Last Days with its woes and terrors, including the arrival of the Antichrist. It is as if he wanted to leave the way free for the enterprise that he was about to take on of sacralizing time, placed under the invocation of *festivitas*.

On the other hand, in his presentation of Advent, Jacobus insists on opportunity, necessity, and utility, the three reasons that explain the incarnation of Christ. An idea that he holds dear and that is one of the elements of his deep faith in Jesus is that his coming manifests, as Saint Augustine put it, "the fullness of time." Jesus is thus not only the essential object of the *Golden Legend* in his role of sacralizing time. He also, and even more, serves in some ways to create and realize the perfection of time. Thus the *Golden Legend* invites the faithful to follow Jesus in order to attain, with him, that perfection of the time of humanity.

This first chapter on Advent also introduces a certain number of themes and personages that we will find again in the body of the

*Legend*, such as the devil and the guardian angels. That universe of supernatural beings is in fact inserted into nature, since the sun and the stars illuminate this chapter, just as the seasons and the divisions of the day illuminated the prologue. One point merits an investigation that cannot be undertaken here: Jacobus de Voragine seems to express a conception of justice that encompasses both the desired reign of divine justice (given that he recalls Jesus's title as *Sol justitiae*, the "sun of justice") and the political and judiciary realities of chronological time (for he takes into account the progress of royal justice as a superior form of human justice whose sentences are not open to appeal). Just when we think that he has flown off to the heaven of the divine, we find Jacobus de Voragine with his feet planted on the ground, engaged in the affairs of his times, doing in fact just what the prior of the Dominicans of Lombardy and the archbishop of Genoa ought to be doing.

## The Saints of Advent

Though Jacobus de Voragine never mentions the calendar date on which the feast of the saint whose life he recounts falls, the order in which he presents his one hundred fifty-three saints shows clearly that he respected their place in the common Christian calendar. For the period of Advent he chose four saints: Andrew, whose feast is November 30, Nicholas (December 6), Lucy (December 13), and Thomas (December 21). He uses the same outline for all of his accounts of the saints. He begins with etymologies of the saint's name, and given that these are usually plural, they are meant to be possible but not certain. Detractors of the *Golden Legend* have made much of what they deem the whimsical nature of these etymologies. They are wrong to do so, because although, for Jacobus, etymology was what we today would call "scientific" and, in medieval terms, corresponded to the idea that it could access the deep meaning of a personage, it could not provide an absolutely certain result, because it was a science of probabilities, not of absolutes. It seems to me an indication of a truly scientific and critical mind. Jacobus de Voragine goes on, following a basically chronological order, to evoke the life of the saint, emphasizing, at the beginning, his or her eventual conversion and, toward the end, the moment and the nature of death, which is often martyrdom. Between these two moments he inserts a series of edifying stories, almost like news items, that marked the saint's life. For Jacobus, narration is an instrument for edification that combines the religious lesson with the pleasure of the tale.

Although Jacobus de Voragine does not cite all of his sources for a saint's history and achievements, he does mention many of them, like a true historian intent on showing the importance and the value of documentation. In fact, he introduces chronological references to a year or a historical period that includes the time-span of the individual human's life.

## Saint Andrew, Apostle

The lengthy etymological paragraph that opens the chapter on Saint Andrew reflects a reliance on Latin and, even more, Greek words to connect the name *Andreas* with beauty, virility, and all that is turned toward what is on high. In all of Jacobus de Voragine's accounts of the saints we encounter this same tendency to retain only the etymologies that highlight the exceptional characteristics of the saint. Here the paragraph ends with the assertion: "The Presbyters and deacons of Achaia wrote an account of his martyrdom, which they had witnessed with their own eyes."[4] We see here Jacobus's effort to give a "scientific" dimension to his work by the mention of the many sources he had consulted, among which he privileges the statements of eye witnesses.

He goes on to recount the life of Saint Andrew, insisting on the essential fact that he was an apostle, followed Christ and his teaching, and was among the first to propagate that teaching. With his usual fondness for numbers, he notes that Andrew was called by Jesus three times: first to be known by him; second, to become a part of his familiar circle; and third, to be one of his disciples.

Continuing in chronological order, Jacobus next retraces Andrew's voyages in his mission of conversion, and in doing so he lays out a veritable geography of the conversion of pagans to Christianity. The area of his evangelization was Scythia, then Margondia.[5] Here our author introduces a critical remark. Whereas certain texts mention as a fact that in Antioch Andrew is supposed to have restored the sight of the apostle Matthew after the pagans put out his eyes, Jacobus comments, "I find the story very hard to believe," and he justifies this criticism by noting how unlikely it was that as great an apostle as Matthew would have been unable to do for himself "what Andrew secured for him so easily." The anecdotes that follow tell of the apostle putting out a fire; of the fate of a woman in a difficult labor who, with the aid of the apostle, was delivered, but of a stillborn child; of his curing an old man of his addiction to brothels; of bringing on an earthquake that swallowed up an incestuous mother; and of demons who were ravaging the city of Nicaea being transformed into dogs, which he then chased away.

Jacobus de Voragine also repeats a story about a rescue of sailors or voyagers from shipwreck that can be found in one form or another in a number of the *Golden Legend*'s lives. The many texts on this theme remind us that Jacobus was born and died in a port city and that, even after the progress brought to navigation in the early thirteenth century by the compass and the stern-post rudder, for the men and women of the Middle Ages the sea was and remained the most terrifying part of nature.

Next Andrew tells a story that seems to evoke a situation frequent in the period of the conversion of pagans in Europe to Christianity, in which Christians seek to convert a powerful man whose wife has either been converted or was already a Christian at the time of their marriage. Clovis provided one example. The case that Andrew relates is that of Aegeus, proconsul of Achaia. Aegeus had attacked Christianity on the grounds that it was founded on Judas's wickedness in betraying Christ, which led Andrew to explain to him why Jesus voluntarily underwent the passion. This provides Jacobus de Voragine with an opportunity to use a saint's life to speak of Jesus, the central figure in the *Golden Legend*, who, by his incarnation, sacralized time and is thus the protagonist of Jacobus's *summa* on time. With his usual fondness for enumeration, Jacobus has Andrew put forward five arguments (which are of little importance here), and when he fails to persuade Aegeus, the proconsul condemns him to martyrdom. Jacobus uses this condemnation to emphasize a symbol of great importance in Christianity and one characteristic of the memory of Saint Andrew, which is his crucifixion on an X-shaped cross. Thus Andrew, who, though a saint, was only a man, was crucified on a cross different from and in several ways less significant than the Holy Cross of Jesus. At this point our Dominican introduces a long quotation from Saint Augustine, a figure to whom he accords a truly dominant place in his culture, his faith, and the redaction of his work. This text, which is taken from a work on penance falsely attributed to Augustine, makes the cross the symbol of terrestrial human life. Man's body is a cross, and death is thus a deliverance from that cross, which permits flight into the arms of Christ and into the "inexhaustible source of life and joy."[6]

One passage in the life of Saint Andrew shows that in the *Golden Legend* Jacobus de Voragine did not simply string together a series of miracles, but also gave importance to instants of amazement, visions of the kind that charm human beings through their blending of natural phenomena, human virtues, and the grace of God. Accounts of such moments are intended to serve his central objective of sacralizing and enchanting time. He writes, "As Andrew finished his prayer, a dazzling light shone out of heaven and enveloped him for the space of a half hour, hiding him from sight; and as the light faded, he breathed his last."[7] For the exemplary person who is a saint, the time of death, far from being dismal, is thus a luminous apotheosis.

Jacobus de Voragine's life of Saint Andrew ends with his *post mortem* miracles, thereby once again making use of a saint as a marker of time. By his acts, the saint first sacralizes the segment of linear time that is his life as a terrestrial man, but his contribution to the sacralization of time continues in the miracles that he accomplishes after his death, so that in theory his miraculous power prolongs indefinitely the worth of his human lifetime, extending to the Last Judgment. The grace granted to the saint to continue to sacralize time after his death also lies in the fact that at any moment God can send the saint back to earth on a particular mission or to perform a miracle. In the most significant of Saint Andrew's *post mortem* miracles, he returns to earth as a pilgrim in order to save a bishop from the temptation of seduction.

Clearly, time is complex in the *Golden Legend*. For those exceptional people who are saints, terrestrial time cannot be limited to the period of their actual lifetime, but may extend to include moments, long or short, when they return to earth. There is thus a future in the terrestrial life of the saints. Not only is eternal God the master of time, but his creatures, when they become nontemporal, can leave their mark on time by intervening on behalf of humans in ways that are beneficent when realized by the saints.

## Saint Nicholas

Jacobus de Voragine very probably chose to include Saint Nicholas because, since the end of the eleventh century, he had become one of the most popular saints in Italy and throughout Christendom. The special protection granted by one saint or another to a certain category of people was not yet as clearly defined as it later came to be, but Nicholas was beginning to be seen as the special saint protector of young people, thanks to his powers as an intermediary with God. And Jacobus de Voragine, as a member of a new and conquering Order, put young people at the head of his target groups for proselytism.

The etymology of the name "Nicholas," placed of course at the head of the chapter dedicated to him, is mainly founded on Greek words, given that Christianity began its spread in the East and Saint

Nicholas was a saint of Eastern origin. Jacobus de Voragine offers three principal possible etymologies: a Greek one, which came from *nicos*, or "victory"; a Latin one, *laus*, signifying "praise"; and *nitor*, or "shining whiteness", followed by *laos*, "the people," to form "the bright cleanness of the people."[8] Jacobus wanted to show that Nicholas was, on the one hand, a glorious and victorious saint and, on the other, a "popular" saint. Finally, Jacobus takes care to indicate the importance of his sources, which were first Greek, with Latin translations dating to the late ninth century by John the Deacon, who made many additions to the tradition and whose information on Saint Nicholas was notably enriched in the thirteenth century by both Jean de Mailly and Bartholomew of Trent, Jacobus de Voragine's two major Dominican sources.

According to Jacobus de Voragine, Saint Nicholas was born in Patras of wealthy parents. This social origin, which he shares with many early Christian saints, is doubly interesting. First because it often corresponds to reality, as simple people, peasants in particular, remained within paganism much longer than those in the upper levels of society, who were more rapidly affected by Christianity. In addition, far from being a glorification of wealth, his situation allowed the saint to abandon his patrimony and share his riches with the poor. This would have been all the more appreciated by a member of a "mendicant" order that emphasized the spiritual glory of poverty in its thirteenth-century preaching and stressed acting to reduce it in real society.

To what purpose did the young Nicholas, once a Christian, put his family wealth? The first marvelous act that is reported (it is not a miracle, properly speaking) sees Nicholas combating poverty by aiding to a poor neighbor obliged by his indigence to prostitute his three virgin daughters. Jacobus de Voragine here scores a double coup, if I may be permitted the image. He uses a concrete and spectacular act of generosity to further the struggle against a poverty that leads to sin, and he stigmatizes the social sin of prostitution. Finally, the beneficiaries of this first exceptional gesture are very young women, which bears witness to Nicholas's interest in the young.

The second phase of Nicholas's life as recounted by Jacobus de Voragine is that of his elevation to a bishop's throne. Although Jacobus holds that faith and piety make all Christians equal, he nevertheless respects the situation and the prestige of prominent figures in the Church, and in particular that of a bishop, a man who becomes the head of a Christian community. It should be unnecessary to recall that although he was and remained a Dominican, at the end of his life Jacobus served as archbishop of Genoa. The episode he relates is the story of the election of a bishop who, in the early days of Christianity, was not chosen by a secular prince or by the pope, but by a provincial college of bishops. The vacant bishopric was that of Myra, in Lycia (Asia Minor). The most influential bishop in the province hears in a dream (and here we have an echo of the importance of dreams in Christian spirituality) the voice of the Lord telling him that the best candidate for the bishopric will be the first man named Nicholas who enters a certain church. And this of course turns out to be our Nicholas. Jacobus de Voragine, who was always sensitive to concrete history and never hesitated to express a critical doubt when his sources seemed to him unsure, ends this episode with a statement destined to reinforce the importance of the figure of Saint Nicholas: "A chronicle also states that Nicholas took part in the Council of Nicaea."[9]

Two other stories follow. The first revisits the visceral fear of the sea common to men of the Middle Ages, showing Nicholas calming a storm and saving sailors. Here, rather than simply evoking a miracle detached from human life, Jacobus describes the actual daily work of the sailors, whom he had watched at their tasks. How does Nicholas get the sailors out of danger? "He began to assist them with the sails and ropes and other rigging of the ship."

A second intervention pictures the saint confronting one of the structural woes that faced men and women of the Middle Ages—on land this time, and concerning agriculture, the basic occupation of medieval people. A famine is raging, a chronic misfortune in Europe (and beyond, including Russia) up to the time of the French

Revolution. Here again, Nicholas intervenes more as an exceptional man than as a miracle worker, and through him our Dominican sketches a critique of the organization of medieval society. In a port there are ships loaded with grain. Nicholas wants the crew to unload part of the grain for distribution to a population threatened with famine. This would be to oppose the authority of the emperor and the authority of the state, the sailors tell him. But Nicholas believes that the life of the poor is worth more than the satisfaction of the powerful.

Yet another short tale reflects events that took place in Europe as Christianity was eradicating paganism. Nicholas brings to an end a popular cult of the ancient goddess Diana by cutting down the tree under which certain rites dedicated to the goddess took place, and eventually he brings about the disappearance of all pagan cults by chasing away the devil, who had come to the region disguised as a monk. The tale that follows is an encomium to justice as it should be rendered by the powers that be. In it we are shown examples of what was the essential duty of a powerful layman of the Middle Ages; namely, the obligation to respect justice and to see that others respect it as well. In the Life of Saint Nicholas this duty takes the form of two rescues. In each case innocent persons are delivered from the injustice of a secular power. First Nicholas obtains the liberation of three innocent soldiers whom a consul wanted to have executed; then he frees three innocent princes facing an unjust condemnation by the Emperor Constantine.

Jacobus de Voragine next turns to the terrestrial death of Saint Nicholas, which he evokes in a blending of the marvelous with the real. The marvelous is made manifest by the presence of a cohort of angels who surround Nicholas's deathbed, and reality both by the indication of the year of his death (343), which Jacobus borrows from the normal, chronological calendar, and by his burial in a marble tomb, marking the beginning of the cult of saints connected with death and the tomb, the first location for the occurrence of miracles. Still, Jacobus de Voragine maintains the marvelous by having "a fountain of oil" flow from the end of the tomb nearest to his head and "a fountain of water" from the end near his feet.[10] The oil stops flowing when a misdeed has been committed and begins to flow once again when the wrong-doing ceases. Jacobus de Voragine ends his paragraph on the death of the saint with a recital of the greatest event in his posthumous history, which, once again, he ties to actual events, this time with the Turks' infiltration of Asia Minor. At issue was how to prevent the Muslims, the worst enemies of Christ, from getting their hands on the relics of a man who was well on his way to sainthood. Soldiers from the Italian city of Bari, on the Adriatic coast in Puglia, took command. They opened the tomb of Saint Nicholas and brought his bones (which were immersed in oil) back to Bari. Jacobus, as always attentive to the lay calendar (despite what some have said), notes that this act took place in 1087, which is historically correct. Belief in this translation earned for Bari a promotion to the rank of Saint Nicholas's burial place, which led to the construction of a superb cathedral over his tomb that would attract many pilgrims. That pilgrimage helped to make Nicholas one of the most popular saints of Christendom, in particular when the custom of giving Christmas presents to children began and Nicholas earned the distinction of having them distributed on his feast day, December 6, in the regions where he was best known.

But Nicholas does not yet disappear from the *Golden Legend*. As we saw with Saint Andrew, one of the principal characteristics of the saints (and a characteristic that, after the thirteenth century, became exclusive to them) was an ability to perform miracles after their death in their role as intermediaries for God. The first miracle that Jacobus reports centers on a quite characteristic situation in medieval Western Europe: a Christian who borrows money from a Jew. In this case the Christian is in fact a swindler, and he dies by being crushed on the roadside by a speeding coach (thus showing us that accidents were not unknown on medieval roads). Nicholas resuscitates the dead man, who lost his money in the accident, and the Jew, amazed by this resurrection, converts to Christianity. We can see here all the anxieties that beset people in the Middle Ages regarding the management of money and usury, along with the problem of relations between Christians and Jews, and the Christian obsession with converting Jews. The story that follows this one also turns on the conversion of Jews, but it contains two extra elements. One consists in Jacobus de Voragine's extraordinary talent for storytelling; the other is the role of the image in medieval society. A wealthy Jew has the riches heaped up in his house guarded by an image of Saint Nicholas that is supposed to be the saint himself, thus illustrating the power of the image. However, thieves break into the Jew's house and steal his money. Furious that Nicholas's image has not protected him, the Jew scolds him violently, with the result that the saint goes to admonish the thieves, who return to the straight and narrow path, while the Jew converts to Christianity. In only a few lines, Jacobus uses his art to keep his listener or his reader in suspense, while he also shows how situations in human life can be reversed through a combination of human free will and God's intervention via the intercession of a saint.

Next comes the story that is one of the main sources of Saint Nicholas's popularity: the saint's resurrection of a schoolboy strangled by the devil. This story later earned Saint Nicholas his position as patron saint of schoolchildren, which, within the *longue durée* of history, became his principal title, if not to glory, at least to notoriety.

Another miracle has a child as its protagonist. A father and his son are bringing a gold cup to Saint Nicholas in his church in Bari. While attempting to fill the cup with water, the child falls into the sea and drowns. Saint Nicholas of course saves him.

A final episode that also concerns a child is given in two versions. In both of these the child is kidnapped by the Saracens; in the first version by the king of a group of Saracens from Asia Minor; in the second by the sultan, who is en route to the Holy Land to fight in the crusades. Jacobus de Voragine seems to have borrowed this second version from Jean de Mailly, given that the *Golden Legend* hardly ever mentions the crusades.[11]

# Saint Lucy, Virgin

The presence of Saint Lucy in the *Golden Legend* might seem surprising, as she was not one of the most popular female saints during the Middle Ages. In the first centuries of Christianity, however she did play an important liturgical role, and it is likely that Jacobus de Voragine wanted to present a woman early in his work, and she of course must be a female of the status so revered by traditional Christianity—a virgin. Lucy's name may also have influenced Jacobus's choice, as it had but one etymology, thus sparing him the need to hesitate between several or any combination of them. The name "Lucy" comes from *lux*, which makes Lucy, as Jacobus states, a "way of light."[12] If we also take into account Jacobus de Voragine's reference to Saint Ambrose, who was, as we have seen, one of his major inspirations, it is easy to explain Lucy's presence in the *Golden Legend*. The Latin legendaries of the twelfth and thirteenth centuries (and probably the *Golden Legend* even more) did much to elevate Lucy from her status as a local saint (she was long the patron saint of Syracuse, the city of her birth) to become a saint honored throughout Christendom. She then benefitted from the brilliance of Saint Agatha, a saint whose protégée she might be considered to have been.

Saint Lucy, to whom Jacobus de Voragine devotes only a short chapter, does not appear alone, for he uses multiple persons both as a narrative technique in the work as a whole and in order to create a setting in which the saintliness of the hero or heroine may be made manifest. The life of a saint, male or female, is therefore often shown within the theater of the family, the city or the region, and in public institutions. Lucy lived in close proximity to her mother, and their common life permits us to distinguish between the behavior of the saint and behavior that might seem similar but does not present the characteristics or the degree of engagement in the faith offered by a saint. Lucy and her mother are differentiated, to begin with, by their attitudes toward what was a highly important matter for the

Church: persuading the rich to give their fortunes to the poor—that is, to the Church. In the thirteenth century the mendicant orders gave particular emphasis to such donations, and their insistence on obtaining a part or all of the goods of a wealthy family was one reason some bourgeois were hostile to them. Lucy wanted to make an immediate gift to the poor of the family fortune, controlled by her mother. Her mother wanted the gift to be deferred until their death. Jacobus de Voragine presents here a quite special form of time, one that is highly interesting from the historical point of view and that I would call "the time of alms." The possibility open to the wealthy in the thirteenth century to make gifts to the poor either during their lifetimes or by testament underscores the multiplicity and the importance of particular times.

Lucy's desire to give away the family wealth without delay had a further consequence that would certainly interest many people in the Middle Ages, beginning with those who heard or read the *Golden Legend*. They would have seen an unlovely aspect of life in society in the behavior of Lucy's fiancé. Visibly attracted by her family's wealth (which she had already begun to inherit) and seeing his hopes for a rich marriage evaporate, he not only breaks their engagement, but denounces Lucy to the public authorities. We might be reading a Balzac novel.

From the virtue of giving gifts to the poor as a step toward the acquisition of sainthood, Jacobus de Voragine passes on to another common theme—and a dramatic one—the path to sainthood. It has to do with a refusal of prostitution, but what the listeners and the readers of the *Golden Legend* most likely would retain would be not only the malediction of prostitution, but the fact that Saint Lucy was ready to accept it because of the essential distinction that the Christian makes between the body and the soul. The body can be raped. If the victim does not abandon her body to the rapists, however, she remains a virgin in her soul. This line of reasoning was at times taken as a toleration of prostitution in medieval society. This conception of the separation between the soul and the body, which seems to lead to virtuous practice, might actually be used to justify acts that were less than virtuous.[13]

Finally we see something that will be more specifically stressed in other lives: the devotion that develops around the place of execution and the tomb of a saint. I remind the reader that Saint Lucy was first the patron saint of Syracuse (the Sicilian city of Siracusa), where she lived and where she was martyred, before her cult became widespread throughout Christianity.

Jacobus de Voragine, who has been accused of being indifferent to chronology, ends his life of Saint Lucy by indicating that her martyrdom took place "in the time of the emperors Constantine and Maxentius, around the year of our Lord 300."[14]

## Saint Thomas, Apostle

It is quite obviously his status as an apostle that led Jacobus de Voragine to write about Thomas. However, he very cleverly makes use of the episode—a none too glorious moment for Thomas—of his doubt regarding the reality of the crucifixion and resurrection of Jesus, when he put his fingers into Jesus's wounds, an act which Jacobus finds reason to praise.

As for the etymology of the name "Thomas," Jacobus states that it means "a dividing or separating." Thomas is "twofold," he explains, because he knew the resurrection in two ways, by vision and by touch. He was called "abyss" because more than the other apostles, he "was granted insight into the depths of God's being." Jacobus, for whom etymology was a science with somewhat equivocal results, also derives "Thomas" from "my God," because the apostle, touching Christ's wounds, is reported to have saluted him, calling him "My Lord and my God."[15]

Jacobus de Voragine takes as a historic truth the story, very probably a legend, that Thomas made a voyage to India, having been sent by Jesus to convert the population. Many have believed in this voyage, for even today the decoration of the Catholic cathedral in Madras depicts it. The recital of the life of Saint Thomas in India, where he converted many Indians under a variety of circumstances and where he did many miracles, reflects several of the general characteristics of the *Golden Legend*. The first is Jacobus's recourse to Saint Augustine, whose treatise, *Contra Faustus*, he quotes at length. He takes advantage of the opportunity to express, through his great master, his conception of source criticism. It is a conception much more complex and more subtle than the free and easy manner generally attributed to Jacobus would indicate. In the passage he quotes, Augustine is talking about an act of the apostle-saint Thomas. This quotation and the opinion that Jacobus de Voragine expresses regarding it is all the more interesting because it involves Gospels that the Church considered apocryphal, but which Jacobus used widely. In the episode in question Saint Thomas is slapped by a pagan cupbearer during a wedding feast, and he takes his revenge by having the man devoured by a lion. To quote Jacobus:

Augustine, in his book *Against Faustus*, will have none of this act of vengeance and declares that the incident is apocryphal, for which reason it is regarded as suspect on more than one point. It may, however, be surmised that what the apostle said to the steward was not intended as seeking revenge but as teaching a lesson: if Augustine's words are weighed carefully, they do not seem to express outright disapproval. In the book quoted he says: "The Manicheans read apocryphal books that were written under apostles' names by unknown fablemongers. At the time these books were written, they might well have been received by [the] holy Church as authoritative, if saintly and learned men then living were able to examine them and found elements of truth in them."[16]

Jacobus de Voragine's borrowing from Augustine clearly expresses, it seems to me, his personal attitude toward the apocryphal Gospels and, in a general manner, his notion of source criticism. He makes the partial trustworthiness of sources depend upon the period in which they were made public and upon the quality of the persons who utilized them. All in all, he concludes that, present certain guarantees, the sources known as apocryphal possess a basis of truth and can, within that perspective, be utilized as sure sources. This process, which takes into account the stage of elaboration of such sources and the way in which they are accessed, is worthy of a true historian.

What is more, Saint Thomas is supposed to have received from Jesus not only a commission to convert the inhabitants of India but also to learn the marvelous arts of that land and, in particular, the architecture of Indian palaces. Medieval Christianity, as is known, considered India to be a great reservoir of marvels. Jacobus de Voragine thus does his best to introduce into Christianity, which remained somewhat savage, the marvels that Christianity situated in the East, a place of fascination. Christ himself is supposed to have gone there.[17] With his usual fondness for enumeration, Jacobus relates how Thomas showed the Indians the twelve degrees of the virtues, one of the most interesting expressions of Dominican doctrine and preaching in the thirteenth century. I shall limit myself to noting the praise of the powers that God has given to man: wisdom, which is composed of "understanding, memory, and reason." He adds praise of the human body and of man's powers, the chief of which reside in the head. As is known, Christian thinkers of the thirteenth century vacillated between giving preeminence to the head or the heart among the qualities of man, made in the image of God. Jacobus, whose detractors have stated that unlike Saint Thomas Aquinas, a fellow Dominican, he was no intellectual, gives primacy to the head.

Following his habit of making frequent appeals to chronology when it interests him, Jacobus de Voragine indicates in his chapter on Saint Thomas the date of an event of great importance for the cult of Christian saints and one that occasionally contributes to their role as markers of time. This was not the year of their death, but rather the year of the translation of their relics, which, for Thomas, was "around the year of our Lord 230."[18] Christianity, which, as I am attempting to show (as have many others) gave great importance to the concept of time and its use, displayed an interest in space as well. Here again, Jacobus de Voragine shows that the translations that interested Christianity the most were those that brought the initial location of the burial and the cult of the saints closer to the West. For Saint Thomas, Jacobus insists on the fact that around the year 230 Emperor Alexander, at the request of the Syrians, had Thomas's body transported from India to the city of Edessa in Syria.[19]

Finally, Jacobus de Voragine, basing his remarks on Saint John Chrysostom, mentions an event of that had enormous repercussions, as Richard Trexler has shown in a fine book translated into French after his death.[20] Saint Thomas, it is thought, converted the Magi to Christianity and baptized them, after which they helped him to convert many people in India.

# 6

# The Time of Reconciliation and Pilgrimage

ollowing Advent, which forms something like a prelude to it, Jacobus de Voragine enters into the period that "falls partly within the time of reconciliation" and "partly in the time of pilgrimage" and runs from Christmas to Septuagesima.[1] I shall only discuss the saints whose lives seem to me to offer the best explanation of the intent and the method of the author of the *Golden Legend*. The time of reconciliation is the time in which Christ, through his incarnation, has reconciled us with God, and it is accordingly a time of joy. The time of pilgrimage is the current time, when "we are on pilgrimage and constantly engaged in warfare." We should keep in mind that, his intention being to enchant the world by emphasizing the sacralization of time, Jacobus de Voragine did not choose to begin his work with the creation of the world and the beginning of time, because that era was marked by Adam's fall, followed by a period of bewilderment. In his optimistic conception of a world and a humanity dedicated to eternal salvation, Jacobus preferred—as did the Church itself —the order of reality to chronological order. Faced with the terrestrial, concrete, and perishable nature of chronological time, which he was aware of but does not focus on, Jacobus de Voragine seeks to evoke a sublime time, the time of reality. The entire project of the *Golden Legend* thus consists in what might be viewed as a transmutation, an aim that we should never lose sight of. I have given the title "In Search of Sacred Time" to the present essay, but I could easily have called it "In Search of True Time."

The sacralization of human time is brought on by a decisive moment, the birth of Christ, and it is with that moment that Jacobus de Voragine opens this segment of the *Golden Legend*.

## The Birth of Our Lord Jesus According to the Flesh

Jacobus de Voragine first presents the dates proposed for the Nativity of Christ, which, since it is a historical phenomenon, is part of chronological order. He speaks of 5,228 or 5,199 years after Adam, and settles on the round figure of 6,000 years, proposed in the late third century by Methodius, the bishop of Olympus in Lycia. Thus Jacobus, who needs no etymological explanation of the name of Jesus, begins by situating him within history. The date of Jesus's birth remains uncertain, and Jacobus declares that "Methodius seems to have arrived at the figure 6,000 by mystical rather than chronological calculation,"[2] thus demonstrating his own attention to history. Next he notes that it was Jesus's will, in becoming incarnate, to "give us peace in time and in eternity," and he stresses that, in his own way, the Roman emperor had established an earthly peace over all of the known world, the famous *Pax romana*. It is worth noting that Jacobus de Voragine, along with many other Christian thinkers and preachers who lived in the medieval world known for its wars, its revolts, and its violence, held peace as an ideal. This is demonstrated by the movements around the year 1000 that called the "Peace of God" or the "Peace of the Prince." It is undeniable that the Middle Ages was a troubled world. And I might add that without a doubt peace was the greatest goal sought by its governments and by its faithful.[3] That demand, which I see as deeply rooted in medieval spirituality, permits me to repeat that in my opinion the crusades preached in the name of the Holy See and the Church were profound deviations from the Christian ideal.

In this chapter Jacobus de Voragine mentions on several occasions the *Historia scholastica* of Petrus Comestor, the director of the school of Notre-Dame-de-Paris in the late twelfth century, who was a prominent figure in the university and an important inspiration for our Dominican.

Jacobus notes that the birth of Christ came about in "a marvelous manner" and, despite hostile readings to the contrary by ancient authors, he carefully distinguishes the "marvelous" from the "miraculous." He makes full use as well of his customary enumeration to stress the importance of the Nativity, citing for example five proofs that Mary conserved her virginity after the birth of Jesus.[4] In these proofs he combines the marvelous and the miraculous and distinguishes between them. The person of Christ *is*, however, the result of a miracle. Returning to a text of Saint Bernard of Clairvaux, Jacobus de Voragine stresses that Christ was a miraculous combination, because God combined "in the one and the same person the eternal, the ancient, and the new."[5] The eternal is divinity; the ancient is the human body, sprung from Adam and continuing through successive generations over the course of the centuries. What is new is that the soul of Jesus transfigures the human soul.

The study of man through the great model that is Christ incarnate also permits us to enumerate what makes up life and to situate man on that scale. Certain creatures have only existence; they are simple material bodies. Others—such as vegetation—possess existence and life; still others possess existence, life, and sensation, as do the animals. And finally there are other beings who share existence, life, sensations, and reason, and these are men. At the top of the scale are the angels who add intellection to the four qualities of mankind. Thus for Jacobus de Voragine man is characterized by the fact that at the summit of his four gifts sits reason. This means that Jacobus is one among those intellectuals—I do not hesitate to use the term—of the thirteenth century who, far from having the obscurantist tendencies stigmatized by the philosophers of the Renaissance and the eighteenth century, sought instead (as historians as different as Father Chenu and the English medievalist Alexander Murray have shown) to develop the rational faculties of man by education, by preaching, and by theology considered as a science.

I might note in passing one interesting remark that Jacobus de Voragine makes: he notes that the Jews adopted certain pagan feasts as a result of cultural contact (*ex usu cohabitantium*).

Finally, it is in Jacobus de Voragine's treatment of the Nativity that the devil, the great enemy of humanity and the great disturber of time, appears for the first time in the *Golden Legend*. In a highly picturesque narrative, Jacobus (basing what he says on Peter the Venerable, the famous abbot of Cluny in the twelfth century) relates how, on the eve of Christmas, the devil sought to prevent the event from being celebrated as a great feast, but sacred time—that is, the feast of the Nativity—proved stronger than he and "so, confounded, he vanished."[6]

Jacobus de Voragine ends his chapter on the Birth of Christ with a definition of the relations between Jesus and man that conforms to Christian orthodoxy. Citing John of Damascus, he declares that Jesus "humbled himself for the sake of mankind, not against us; his humility reached man's level and above man. It was for men's sake because it was for their welfare and salvation; it reached men's level because the mode of birth was similar, and it was above them by the dissimilarity of the birth."[7] Thus, being born of a woman and by the operation of the Holy Spirit, Jesus teaches men at one and the same time about the humility, the equality, and the superiority of a God who voluntarily lowered himself to the level of man. Jacobus thus expresses in a highly concrete fashion what there is in man of both the human and the divine, since man is in a way the terrestrial image of Christ, who, from his height, lowered himself to the level of man.

In this section of his work, which moves from the birth of Christ to Septuagesima, Jacobus places six saints, including one female and one (the Holy Innocents) collective, between the Nativity of the

Lord, his circumcision, and Epiphany. Following the chronology of the liturgical calendar, which he does not name but obviously consults, he discusses Saint Anastasia (whose feast, originally set at December 25, was overshadowed when the Nativity of Jesus was fixed at that date), Saint Stephen (December 26), Saint John the Evangelist (December 27), the Holy Innocents (December 28), Saint Thomas of Canterbury (December 29), and, skipping December 30, the feast of Saint Sylvester (December 31).

## Saint Anastasia

The etymology of the name "Anastasia" makes the saint a model of verticality. By her name, she invites Christians to stand tall, "raised above vice and sin to virtue."[8]

What is special about Saint Anastasia from the viewpoint of history is that she lived during the period of the slow conversion of Romans to Christianity and, although the daughter of a Christian mother, she was married to a powerful pagan. This immediately poses the question of sexuality. Anastasia tries to avoid sex by refusing to consummate her marriage, pleading illness. Her husband, however, finds out that Anastasia, being a wealthy woman in her own right, has gone off, in the company of a servant woman, to give alms to Christians imprisoned in the dungeons. Saint Anastasia thus offers Jacobus de Voragine the opportunity to stress two behaviors held to be characteristic of the Christian: the safeguarding of virginity, even in marriage if the spouse is not Christian, and almsgiving. Our Dominican, always ready to lend a more novelistic texture to the edifying anecdote he is relating, imagines that the husband decides to have her put to death not only because she is Christian but also because, since she is the daughter of wealthy parents, he stands to inherit her immense fortune. A thriller is thus grafted onto the edifying anecdote. The story of Anastasia then takes another turn because although the wicked pagan husband dies before he can achieve his black designs, he is immediately replaced by another equally wicked man, the prefect, a pagan chief who does not dare attack Anastasia directly but turns his evil intentions to three very beautiful sisters, servants of Anastasia's, whom he attempts to rape. At this point a sudden plot twist has the prefect going mad. Believing that he is surrounded by the three servants whom he desires, he caresses pots, platters, and kitchen utensils. It is a tragicomic scene that shows the full extent of Jacobus de Voragine's literary talent. The prefect's madness gives rise to a series of similar episodes, ending only when, after an attempt to disrobe the servants that leads to their martyrdom, the prefect goes to eternal sleep in what seems to be a form of suicide. The plot continues to churn. In a new episode the emperor delivers Anastasia over to another prefect, who tries to starve her to death in prison, then deports her to a small island transformed into a kind of penal colony for Christians. There he executes the deported Christians by fire or other tortures, beginning with Anastasia. One of the deported Christian women escapes, however, and buries Anastasia in a church built in her honor.

Jacobus de Voragine, wishing to persuade his listeners and readers of the historical veracity of this saint and her life, ends his chapter by indicating that she underwent martyrdom in the reign of Diocletian, the last great pagan emperor and a great killer of Christians, who, according to Jacobus, "began his reign about the year of the Lord 287."[9] It is a known fact that Diocletian was made emperor in the year 284, but the statement nevertheless reflects Jacobus's attention to chronology.

## Saint Stephen

Saint Stephen occupies a prominent place in Christian devotion. Tradition makes him the protomartyr, that is, the first Christian martyr, killed on December 26, the day after the day of the Nativity. Although Jacobus de Voragine accepts that tradition, he does not make it the essential point of the lengthy passage that he devotes to Stephen. He treats Stephen to his usual and quite complex discussion of chronology, indicating that December 26 celebrates the translation of his body rather than his martyrdom. Thus, as always, Jacobus makes his saints markers of time. He is well aware that in his own time most birth dates were unknown, including those of saints and great figures. The feast day devoted to them is that of their death. In the case of Jesus, this is Good Friday, the day of his crucifixion; for the saints, it is the day of their martyrdom. With the coming of the thirteenth century, however, someone like Jacobus de Voragine who, while remaining faithful to orthodoxy and obedient to the Holy See, belongs to a new order and takes the renewal of the Christian faith as his mission, follows the growing trend to make saints' feast days correspond not to the day of their death or even of their martyrdom, but rather to the historical day on which they entered Christian ritual. This was the day of the discovery or the translation of their bodies, now become relics or, as we saw with Saint Nicholas, the day of their translation from a location outside of the Christian world to a place where the faithful honor the saint and pray to him or her while remaining within the Christian sphere.

The chapter dedicated to Saint Stephen begins with two possible etymologies of his name. The first and most usual is the Greek *stephanos*, which means "crown," the sign of the martyrdom that Stephen incarnates in spectacular fashion. But Jacobus de Voragine also suggests the Latin expressions *strenue stans*—that is, he who speaks vigorously, which makes of Stephen the preacher *par excellence*. How could a Dominican not evoke that etymology, when his Order defined itself as that of the *predicatorum*, the "Order of Preachers"? Jacobus de Voragine thus adds to the traditional and exceptional prestige of Saint Stephen a new reason to honor him by presenting him, via the etymology of his name, as the first example of excellence in predication.

Next, Jacobus situates Stephen within history by associating him directly with the group closest to Jesus the man: the apostles. Stephen is presented as one of the seven deacons whom the apostles ordained to the ministry. He soon arouses hostility among the Jews, who attempt to defeat him in three ways, one after the other (and here we see again Jacobus de Voragine's fondness for enumeration). First they attempt to break down popular admiration for him by besting him in a public debate. When the debate takes place, however, the Holy Spirit enters into Stephen and gives him the gift of eloquence, so that he comes out the winner in the verbal joust. In a second combat his Jewish enemies call up false witnesses who accuse him of various vices and misdeeds, but an advocate (who turns out to be an angel) appears at Stephen's side and confounds them. Finally, the Jews condemn him to a martyr's death, but Stephen undergoes its tortures in full mastery of himself and of his persecutors, because Christ appears to him to comfort him. Jacobus de Voragine next relates in detail the three-part trial Stephen had to endure. Of particular interest is the way in which he defends himself against false witnesses with the help of his angelic advocate. He stands accused of four blasphemies: against God, Moses, the Law, and the Tabernacle. He argues that he is innocent of blasphemy against God by expounding his belief in a God of glory, explaining the nature of God with the aid of a number of extracts from the Bible. He defends himself against the charge of blasphemy against Moses by praising him for three reasons: the fervor of his zeal, the miracles that he made in Egypt, and his access to God, who entered into familiar conversation with him on several occasions. In order to refute the accusation of blasphemy against the Law, he commends the Law for three reasons: "by reason of the giver, God himself"; by the prestige of the one who applied it; and by its purpose, "because the Law gives life."[10] Stephen then defends himself against the charge of blaspheming against the Tabernacle by demonstrating that the Tabernacle had been the first form of the Temple, the greatest monument built to God.

Jacobus de Voragine relates the stoning of Saint Stephen (the means of his martyrdom) at length. At the end of his account he attempts to show that Saint Stephen died in imitation of Jesus in his earthly death. Like Christ on the cross, who gives himself over to God the Father, saying "Into thy hands I commend my spirit," Stephen "called upon God and said, 'Lord Jesus, receive my spirit.'" He then begs forgiveness for those who put him to death. Finally, Jacobus's gloss comments on the final moment of Stephen's death, not with the words "He died," but by suggesting a relaxation into an expectation of resurrection: with the words, "He fell asleep in the hope of resurrection."

In what follows, Jacobus de Voragine returns to his primary master, Saint Augustine. It is true that Augustine often speaks of Stephen in his writings. We too return to the dating of the feast of Saint Stephen, because Jacobus not only repeats the hypothesis that the feast day was fixed not on the day of Stephen's death, but on that of the finding of his body, but also suggests another problem regarding the date of his stoning. In fact, in addition to the day after the Nativity of Jesus that the Church eventually retained as the date of Stephen's martyrdom, Jacobus says that one can also interpret Matthew 10:23 as situating it within the year of the Ascension of the Lord, in the month of August at the beginning of the third day. Finally, in his celebration of Stephen Jacobus de Voragine turns to an extract from the Song of Songs in which Christ the bridegroom is led to the Church by three companions: "My beloved is white and ruddy, chosen out of thousands" (Song of Songs, 5:10B). Jacobus judges that in this phrase Jesus combines attributes of the three most illustrious sorts of martyrs: there is John the Evangelist, the confessor who enlightens; Saint Stephen, the protomartyr, who is "ruddy"; and the thousands of martyrs who stand out collectively among the virginal multitude of the Holy Innocents.

All in all, this treatment of Saint Stephen shows that through the exercise of his imagination and his talent, Jacobus de Voragine was capable of adding to the prestige of a saint whom the Church had already brought to the highest level of hagiography.

## Saint John, Apostle and Evangelist

In this life of Saint John, who belongs to a quite different category of saints—the Evangelists—Jacobus de Voragine introduces a new element to his treatment of etymology by giving four meanings to the name "John": "grace of God"; "one in whom is God's grace"; "one to whom a gift is given"; and one "to whom a particular grace is given by God."[11] This time, rather than leaving open a choice between possible etymologies or piling them up one on top of the other, he joins them, declaring at the head of his section on John: "By these we understand four privileges which God bestowed upon Saint John." In what follows, Jacobus gives free rein to his passion for enumeration. The first list pertains to the four privileges that he had just proclaimed, which came to John thanks to the particular love that Christ bore him. John is in fact a well-beloved apostle. The second of the privileges is "freedom from fleshly corruption" because, according to Jacobus, Jesus called John to him and created a bond between them as John was about to be married. The third gift was "the revelation of secrets," for John was the companion to whom Jesus confided his greatest secrets, such as those concerning the "divinity of the Word and the end of the world." The fourth privilege was to have received from Christ during the passion the special mission of caring for his mother, the Virgin Mary, after his death.

According to Jacobus de Voragine, condemnation of wealth was the principal object of Saint John's preaching, and he presents John as giving six reasons for that condemnation. He draws the first from the New Testament, in particular from the story of the gluttonous rich man and Lazarus, the poor man. The second reason comes from nature, as man is born naked and dies without wealth: human life unravels between two states of utter poverty. The third is the example of Creation, for the sun, the moon, the stars, rain, and air are given free to all. It seems to me that this passage has a certain Franciscan tone, and I think that the mendicant orders were the receivers and the transmitters of the discovery that Christians seem to have made in the thirteenth century of the gifts of nature. The fourth reason for man's turning away from wealth is that it makes the rich man a slave of the devil. Here we return to the Gospel, which presents man with the choice between God and Mammon, who represents diabolic wealth. The fifth reason lies in the constant worries that beset the rich, who are tortured by the thought of losing their wealth. The sixth states that riches are in fact the source of two vital losses: the loss of grace in terrestrial life and the loss of eternal glory in the life to come.

In his treatment of Saint John the Evangelist, Jacobus de Voragine expresses once again his desire to extend the sacralization of time beyond the frontiers of Christianity, and in particular toward the East, for the Orient remained in people's imaginations a source of life as much as of riches. Asia was a place of marvels, which were, as we have seen, what Saint Thomas went to seek in India. This time Jacobus tells us: "Saint John had preached throughout the region of Asia."[12]

In order to show the broad range of points of view that Jacobus de Voragine offers in the stories contained in the *Golden Legend*, it should suffice to note only one episode in the many pages peopled with miracles with which the life of Saint John continues. It is an episode, what is more, that has nothing miraculous about it. Jacobus shows Saint John caressing a live partridge before a group of children who are laughing at him. One child, who is holding a bow for hunting birds, sees John and has contact with the apostle, whereupon he abandons his bow and his aggressive attitude, and instead reconnects with those fragile beings and opts for a contemplation that, better than arrows, permits an approach to celestial things. Toward the end of his chapter on John, Jacobus presents John as the last companion of Christ on earth, since he returned to heaven at the age of ninety-eight, under the reign of Trajan. Jesus himself appears to him and invites him to rejoin his fellow disciples at his table, set not on earth for the limited time of human life, but in heaven for eternity. Finally, showing that a saint can make a return voyage in the direction opposite to the one that took him from earth to heaven, Saint John returns to earth to give back to Saint Edmund, the king of England, the precious ring that Edmund had given to a poor pilgrim. In the *Golden Legend*, the sacralization of the conditions of human life always encompass space as well as time.

# The Holy Innocents

In this chapter Jacobus de Voragine draws a striking contrast between the Innocents, whom Christianity venerates, and the wicked, whom it curses. There is not much to say about the Innocents, who died soon after their birth. Jacobus limits himself to invoking the importance of baptism, stating that these unbaptized newborns merited, by their precocious martyrdom, to be assimilated into the baptized. He focuses his attack on the man who ordered the massacre and sketches a slice of comparative history by indicating—with his usual lively sensitivity to the meaning of proper nouns—that three of the cruelest non-Christian sovereigns were named Herod. Herod of Ashkelon (known as the Great) was the Herod who had the Holy Innocents massacred and under whose reign Christ was crucified. The second, Herod Antipas, had John the Baptist beheaded. The third, Herod Agrippa, put Saint James to death and imprisoned Saint Peter. One might have expected that Jacobus de Voragine would use this stigmatization of the Herods to sketch out a critique of terrestrial monarchical power, but he does nothing of the sort. Instead, the Holy Innocents give him an opportunity to compare the Herods with good kings. According to Jacobus, it was when Herod, frightened by the birth of Jesus, ordered the massacre of the Holy Innocents that three good kings, legitimate kings who, unlike Herod, were not usurpers, arrived in Jerusalem, guided by the Star, to seek the divine child. These were the Magi.

Above all, Jacobus de Voragine seeks to use the episode of the Holy Innocents to make a precise point about time. For somewhat complicated reasons, he interprets Herod's supposed meeting with the Three Kings in the light of an attempt to date Jesus's birth. Because Herod draws false conclusions from what the Magi tell him about when they were great rulers in the East, he ordered the decapitation of two-year-olds rather than newborns. Relying on connections that had already been established in the early centuries of Christianity between the Holy Innocents and the Three Kings, Jacobus de Voragine seems to have accorded something like a "scientific" status to the Holy Innocents thanks to their prominent place in one of Jacobus's major sources, Petrus Comestor in his *Historia scholastica.*

## Saint Thomas of Canterbury

The figure who follows the Holy Innocents, with his feast day on December 29, is the first saint of modern times whom we encounter in the *Golden Legend*. It is, of course, a work that does not abound in names from recent times, as Jacobus de Voragine was particularly interested in the older saints who contributed to the Christianization of the human world—which meant Europe and its surrounding territories, the only domain devoted to the one true God—and in a new human time of divine origin that began with the incarnation of Jesus at Christmas. The life of Thomas of Canterbury is well known. It belongs to history proper, in which the saint figures prominently as chancellor to the king of England, and a man whose assassination at the king's command had far-flung consequences. In his short article on the saint, Jacobus concentrates on the relations between Thomas and the king and on the martyrdom to which those relations led. It is obvious that Jacobus de Voragine's interest in this saint depends on the fact that he restores, within modern times, the early and elemental image of the martyr, a common figure in the era of the Roman Empire and one frequently linked to Christianization. Our Dominican was probably even more attuned to this particular case of martyrdom because it found an echo in Jacobus's own lifetime in the assassination of Peter of Verona, like himself a preacher and a Dominican. Jacobus had already discussed the etymology of the name "Thomas" in connection with Saint Thomas the Apostle; and he returns to the same analysis for his treatment of his homonym, the archbishop of Canterbury, but he adjusts the etymology to better fit Thomas of Canterbury. In its origin, the word "Thomas" had several meanings, among them "abyss," "twofold," and a "dividing" or "separating." "Abyss" refers to the comportment of a humble prelate who carries a chalice and frequently washes the feet of the poor. Thomas is "twofold" in that he was the shepherd of his flock by word and by example. The term "dividing" or "separating"—the etymology that best suits this Thomas—refers to his assassination.[13]

The assassination of Thomas à Becket by the order of the king of England because Thomas opposed him concerning relations between the ecclesiastical power and the royal power had immediate and major repercussions throughout Christianity in the latter half of the twelfth century. The act was a rare one, and Church propaganda to make the most of it was frenetic. Given that many lives of the saint had already been written recounting the drama, Jacobus de Voragine had available more sources than for the older saints. If he manipulates historical truth to some extent, he was probably not the first to do so, and the sources that he relies on the most, because they were contemporary to the event, had in fact been quick to transfigure the history of the archbishop to serve the propaganda purposes of the Church. Indeed, hagiographies showed him, even from the very beginning of his ecclesiastical career, as a prelate whose essential objective was to defend ecclesiastical rights against royal encroachment and who only accepted the archbishopric of Canterbury—selected for the post by King Henry II Plantagenet himself—in order to profit from the power that position would give him to control and limit the power of the king. The historical truth is that Thomas accepted the honor in order to dispose of the power and prestige attached to the archbishop's seat, and it was only during the course of his evolving relations with the king, whose chancellor he agreed to become, that conflict arose and developed between him, as the head of the Church in England, and the monarch. It is known, what is more, that these relations were strained, that Thomas sought exile in France for a time, and that it was only after his return to Canterbury that he was assassinated.

Jacobus de Voragine attributes to Thomas of Canterbury one of the visions, more marvelous than miraculous, of which he was so fond. He relates, in a narration calculated to keep his listeners or readers in suspense, that several days before Thomas's martyrdom, a young man whose spirit had departed from his body returned to life miraculously to report that he had seen in heaven an empty chair among those of the apostles, and that an angel had revealed to him that God had reserved that chair for Thomas. The anecdote is typical of the *Golden Legend*: it recounts a marvelous event; it shows the close relations between heaven and Earth; and it permits Jacobus de Voragine to set himself off from his sources by according to Thomas of Canterbury a rank among the saints even higher than that of the martyrs—that of an apostle. Nor does our Dominican hold back when he recounts the scene of horror that was the martyrdom of Thomas. The description is worthy of a thriller: "He bowed his venerable head to the swords of the wicked, and they split his skull and spilled his brains over the pavement of the church."[14] Showing special care to date this martyrdom historically because it was relatively recent, Jacobus indicates the year of the assassination of the archbishop, but, demonstrating that chronology was far from precise in the late twelfth century, even among cultivated people with an interest is such matters, his date is off by four years. He places Thomas à Becket's martyrdom in 1174, whereas it took place in 1170.

## Saint Sylvester

Sylvester does not owe the interest that he inspired within Christian literature, and in the *Golden Legend* in particular, to his place on the Church calendar because, as is known, there was no one date that marked the beginning of the year within Christianity, and the days most often chosen were usually in the early spring. Rather, Sylvester owes a notoriety that was already well established in the thirteenth century to a series of false documents, one of which figures among the most famous of history. Jacobus de Voragine cannot be blamed for this, however, as the documents' falsity was not demonstrated until later, in the fifteenth-century *Donation of Constantine*, a famous treatise by the Italian philologist Lorenzo Valla. Sylvester was traditionally held to have been the bishop of Rome in 313, the year in which ancient historians situate the "conversion" of Constantine. Until the eighth century little was known about Sylvester and he played only a very modest role in Christianization, whereas Constantine occupied center stage. However, it is known that the false donation of Constantine, forged in the offices of the Holy See in the eighth century, mentions sizeable Italian territories that the emperor is reported to have given to Pope Sylvester and which justified the temporal power of the pope over the Papal States up to the secular unification of Italy in 1870.

Jacobus de Voragine displays a particularly lush imagination when it comes to the etymology of "Sylvester." First he derives the name from *sile* or "light" and *terra*, "earth," thus linking Sylvester to the light of the earth that is the Church. Somewhat closer to reality, his second etymology derives "Sylvester" from *silva*, or "forest" and *theos*, "God," because Sylvester is supposed to have attracted woodsmen to the faith. More interesting is a third etymology, which associates "Sylvester" with "verdant" and the color green, which would imply a special reference to Christian spirituality.[15] It seems to me that this association manifests something particularly Gothic and luminous in Jacobus de Voragine, for whom sacred time was fundamentally a time of clarity. Curiously, he attributes importance of the first rank to Saint Sylvester for the establishment of a special unit of time: the week. He is also credited with seeking to sanctify Thursdays as well as Sundays, but he encountered opposition from Greek Christians. He apparently triumphed over that opposition, however, as even in Jacobus's day in the second half of the thirteenth century, Thursdays continued to be specially honored. Whether this story is true or not, Jacobus's seeking to trace the evolution of the week to actions taken by the first pope after the conversion of the emperor to Christianity shows that it is indeed all manner of time that he intends to illustrate and to sacralize in the *Golden Legend*.

Jacobus de Voragine does not make use of Saint Sylvester to draw a contrast between the nascent Christian world and the pagan world that the bishop of Rome and the converted Constantine were combating. He instead sought to show, through the example of Sylvester, how Christianity in its efforts to wipe out paganism detached itself from Judaism and sought to advance further than Judaism along the road to truth. Thus Jacobus's account of Saint Sylvester devotes a good deal of space to discussions between Jews and Christians. First he argues that the true God, the Christian God, although unique, is distinct from the Jewish God because he is God in three persons. Sylvester then offers an interpretation of the circumcision of Jesus that distances it from the meaning that this ceremony had for the Jews: Abraham had been saved in receiving his circumcision from God; Jesus, however, was the son of God before circumcision, and so that event did not sanctify him, though it did set him apart from others. Sylvester is reported to have responded to the Jews who rejected some of the miracles and the virtues attributed to Jesus that a new rite—baptism—had given Jesus the power to sanctify, and that the same rite, as it spread among future Christians, would offer all a chance for salvation. Another Jewish critic based his arguments on the defeat of the Christian God in the face of Satan, who had succeeded in leading Adam, the creature beloved by the Christian God, to fall into sin. Sylvester is reported to have responded that this was for humanity only a temporary fall, and that humanity had been redeemed by God, who sent his own son, Jesus, to restore to man the hope of salvation. In a passage of particular importance for my interpretation of the *Golden Legend* as a *summa* on time, Jacobus shows Sylvester arguing that Jesus existed before time, but that his human birth was inserted into time, and that the Word that God gave to Jesus as his principal mission was to repair time, brought to ruin by Adam's sin. The long chapter on Saint Sylvester is thus an occasion for Jacobus de Voragine to propose something like a summary of a Christian theology that brings to humanity a time of liberation. At the end of this chapter, he stresses that this first official pope saved the Roman people from a double death, that of the cult of the devil and that of the poison of the dragon. Moreover, Jacobus fixes Sylvester's happy dormition—"After that he fell asleep happily in the Lord"[16]—in the year 330, whereas the historical pope died in 335. In spite of the inexact date, we see here another instance of Jacobus's attention to chronology.

## The Circumcision of the Lord and the Epiphany of the Lord

In the following two chapters, Jacobus de Voragine discusses the Feast of the Circumcision (January 1) and Epiphany (January 6). As Alain Boureau and his colleagues have noted, Jacobus here tries in various ways to eliminate an ancient pagan observation of an exceptional period known as the "period of the twelve days." This period had in fact left a strong imprint since it was in essence reconstituted when Christmas was fixed on December 25, the circumcision of Jesus on January 1, and Epiphany on January 6 (to use the later dates), even though its unity was well obscured by the establishment of three separate feast days. We have already spoken of the Nativity; we now encounter the circumcision as viewed by Jacobus de Voragine, an event to which we have already alluded, because it was linked with the human life of Jesus, both as God and as a newborn human being.[17] Jacobus declares that four circumstances make the day of Jesus's circumcision worthy of celebration and solemnity.

The first of these circumstances is that the feast falls within the octave of the Nativity; an octave being one of the periods of eight days that in Christian liturgical time mark off the time from an important feast day to the solemn end of its observance. It bears repeating that one of the characteristics of human time, according to Jacobus de Voragine, consists in the combination of the liturgical temporale with the sanctorale of the saints, who are drawn along by eschatological time toward the end of time. There exist various segments of time that make that divine creation a universe of great diversity with a wide variety of celebrations.

The second reason for the importance of the feast of the circumcision is the assignment of a name to the newborn Jesus—or rather of three names, since from that moment on he could be called "the Son of God," "Christ," or "Jesus," the three names being three different ways of expressing the connection that he establishes between God and man. According to Jacobus de Voragine, those three names also have a special source and a special meaning. "Son of God" is the foundation of faith and certitude; "Christ" expresses the power to spread out like the oil used for unction; while for the name "Jesus" Jacobus calls on one of his major (and somewhat astonishing) sources, Saint Bernard of Clairvaux, for whom "Jesus" signifies "food, a fountain, a remedy, and a light."

The third circumstance that lends importance to the circumcision is "the shedding of Christ's blood,"[18] one of the great gifts that Jesus brought to humanity. He bled for humanity on five occasions: at his circumcision; when he wept tears of blood in the Garden of Gethsemane; in the flagellation; when he was crucified; and, finally, on the cross, when the soldier opened his side with a spear.

A fourth circumstance has to do with the very meaning of circumcision, which Christ accepted as an example and a demonstration of piety.

According to Jacobus de Voragine, Jesus had six reasons for allowing himself to be circumcised: first, to show that he was of true flesh; second, so that all could be brought to understand that a spiritual circumcision must accompany the circumcision of the flesh; third, to show the Jews that in the beginning he was one of theirs and that they should follow him in the foundation of the true religion; fourth, in order to fool the devil, who would think that a circumcised man could not be divine in nature; fifth, because it was an act of great humility; and sixth, in order to accomplish the Law, as Paul states in the Epistle to the Romans.

At this point, Jacobus de Voragine inserts a reflection on time, his real subject, as he does in nearly every chapter. He asks himself why the circumcision took place on the eighth day of Jesus's life on earth—thus marking off once again a segment of time. A first reason is that, according to medical science, the flesh of a newborn remains delicate for seven days. A second reason is that the eight days represent the eight ages of time: from Adam to Noah; from Noah to Abraham; from Abraham to Moses; from Moses to David; from David to Christ; from Christ to the end of the world; a seventh age that will bring the death of humanity; and an eighth age that will witness its resurrection. In short, Jacobus de Voragine summarizes the six reasons for the circumcision of Jesus in a couplet, the meaning of which remains obscure:

> Cautery, sign, merit, remedy, figure,
> Example: This is what the *circumcision dure* once was.[19]

This long chapter comes to a close with two developments that concern time. The first refers to history in the traditional sense. Jacobus de Voragine retraces the diachronic history (from Aix-la-Chapelle to Rome) of a relic, the foreskin of Christ. For many liturgists, Jacobus de Voragine among them, the dates of the translation of relics and of their movement through space by means of commerce, piety, or theft are, as we have seen, the dates that mark human history as it is rendered sacred by the cult of saints' relics. The second development, Jacobus tells us, concerns the date of the feast of Saint Sylvester, which for the pagans was a holiday marking the end of the year, a celebration characterized by amusements that Jacobus describes in great detail, emphasizing their shamelessness and even their diabolical nature. He hopes to reinforce the fatal blow that the Church struck to the repugnant celebration of the day, citing his favorite source, Augustine, in a sermon that was in fact delivered by Caesarius of Arles. Pagan celebrations of the end and beginning of the year threatened to turn the feast day into a secular celebration, whereas for Jacobus de Voragine time consisted only of feast days.

Jacobus de Voragine gives to Epiphany, which closely follows the feast of the circumcision, a special treatment that once again shows him to be a great manipulator of time. For him, Epiphany celebrates two essential moments in the life of Christ that are separated by twenty-nine or thirty years. First, Epiphany is the sixth day of January, as it is for all Christians. But since January 1 was not seen as the first day of the year in Jacobus's day, he situates Epiphany on the thirteenth day after the birth of Christ, thereby avoiding any specific allusion to the pagan cycle of twelve days. The etymology of "Epiphany," he states, is normally explained by the Greek words *epi*, or "above," and *phanos*, or "appearance."[20] These can be explained in either of two ways, either as an allusion to the Star that guided the Three Kings, or as the revelation to those same Magi of the Infant Jesus as true God. But Jacobus, as always in search of the "scientific" truth and unafraid of showing that some uncertainty remains, notes that the second important event of the Epiphany took place either when Jesus was twenty-nine years and thirteen days old; when (according to the Gospel of Saint Luke) he was in his thirtieth year; or else, following Bede, on whom the Roman Church based its calendar, when Jesus had completed his thirtieth year. Since Jacobus explains the feast as taking place on the traditional date of the Three Kings' visitation, the second Epiphany, which occurred with the baptism of Jesus by John the Baptist, would have taken place when Jesus was thirty years old. That event was truly an epiphany, an apparition, because during the baptism, the Trinity appeared: God the Father represented by his voice, Jesus the son in the flesh, and the Holy Spirit in the form of a dove. But Jacobus de Voragine does not stop there. He envisions commemorating on the same day two miracles of Jesus that took place on January 6, one when he was thirty-one, the other when he was thirty-two. These, which date to the period of Jesus's earthly teaching, were the miracle of the water turned to wine at the wedding feast in Cana and, one year later, that of the multiplication of the loaves to feed the faithful who had followed Jesus into the desert. Thus for Jacobus de Voragine, time is marked by exceptional days that are not limited to commemorating one great religious event, but can instead superimpose several events in one day, even events that took place in different years, sometimes far apart one from the others.

Jacobus's lengthy remarks regarding the Magi provide a sort of summary of what had been written about them before the second half of the thirteenth century.[21] He arranges his account so that the Kings serve his purposes in several ways. First, by having them come, as in tradition, from the Orient, the land of marvels, he makes them the markers of a time that was unknown to the Jews, but that the Magi recognized by the appearance of the Star. Jacobus de Voragine clearly states: "The Magi showed the Jews the time."[22] He also wonders (as did all Christian writers) who the Magi were. The usual response tends to see the Three Kings as sorcerers of a kind who converted to Christianity after they had seen and adored Jesus. Although Jacobus de Voragine juggles with etymologies of the term "Magi" in a variety of languages and preserves the story of their conversion, he makes it clear that they are wise men (*sapientes*). He is so obsessed by changes due to time that as the Star of the Magi travels toward Bethlehem he transforms it into five different stars, supporting his spiritual interpretation of the five times of the Star by the astronomic characteristics of stars. Here again Jacobus de Voragine seeks to attach time to nature, but also to sacralize nature by giving it a spiritual dimension. The first and purely natural star of the Magi was followed by a second star, one that entered into their hearts and inspired them with faith, but Jacobus stresses that it was the first and natural star that permitted that metamorphosis into a star of faith, which was followed by the intellectual star whose sacrality came from the angel who put it into their minds. The fourth star, which becomes a star of reason, corresponded to the Virgin in the flesh at the cradle, an indication of the great richness that the cult of Mary still had in the thirteenth century. The final star is the Infant Jesus, a star that was "supersubstantial"—beyond the material, the spiritual, the intellectual, and the rational."[23] I might note that Jacobus de Voragine, like many other commentators, takes the occasion of the Three Kings episode to include a hymn to childhood in which he invokes several of his principal masters: Saint Augustine, Saint Bernard, Saint Hilary, and Saint Jerome. No, the Middle Ages did not neglect children. Attention to the child was widespread in the century of Jacobus de Voragine, the century that saw the creation of the Feast of the Infant Jesus.

Finally, Jacobus de Voragine, who—and I repeat myself—was not unaware of contemporary things when they seemed to him meaningful within time, notes that the relics of the Three Kings first reposed in Milan, but were transported by Emperor Frederick Barbarossa to Cologne, where they still remain.

Between Epiphany and Septuagesima, Jacobus de Voragine presents sixteen saints, among whom I shall only speak of those who seems to me of particular importance for his treatment of time, noting the relevant liturgical dates. These will include Saint Paul the Hermit and Saint Anthony, who were tightly linked to one another and who mark the beginning of a new time in Christianity, the time of hermitism; Saint John the Almsgiver, because of the importance of giving alms for the mendicant orders, which considered it one of the fundamental activities of Christianity; and finally, Saint Paul the Apostle, in one of the exceptional instances of two chapters dedicated to a single saint—one of which treats him as an individual and the other as he appears at the very special moment of his conversion, celebrated in the Roman calendar on January 25.

## Saint Paul, Hermit, and Saint Anthony

Saint Paul the Hermit (feast day, January 10) is closely connected with Saint Anthony (feast day, January 17). The *Golden Legend* devotes only a short passage to Paul, and a passage not much longer to Anthony. Here Jacobus de Voragine takes inspiration from one of his major sources, Saint Jerome. He begins by stating, "This Paul was the first hermit."[24] He then connects Paul historically to the reigns of the emperors Decius and Gallienus, and by introducing the date 256, once again displays his attention to terrestrial chronology. That year marked a critical moment in the Roman persecutions of the late Empire that preceded the "conversion" of Constantine in the early fourth century. Historians generally consider that the hermit movement arose in the Orient and only spread to the West through the imitation of this Eastern Christian practice, which is thought to have continued the pagan custom of spiritual retreat to the desert. It is known that with the growing separation of Latin and Greek Christianity, the Latin West found itself with fewer and fewer desert places. Western religious instead sought solitude in the forest, which can thus be considered the "desert" of the West.[25] According to the *Golden Legend*, Saint Paul became a hermit, called not by the spirituality of the desert, but in order to flee the terrible persecutions of Christians under the pagan Roman emperors.

To associate Paul and Anthony, Jacobus de Voragine uses the rhetorical figure of the dream, which makes the story more picturesque. Saint Anthony had already retired into the desert and thought himself the first Christian hermit, but he learned, thanks to a dream, of another, "holier than he," who lived in the desert.[26] The path that Anthony took to meet Paul makes for a particularly fantastic tale. He is supposed to have met a hippocentaur, then a goat-man (or satyr), and finally a wolf, who guided him to Paul's cell, only to find that Paul had locked his door, wishing to preserve his solitude even from Anthony. But Anthony knocked so persistently that Paul opened his door "and they fell into a warm embrace." Their exchange continues in an atmosphere of marvels. A crow comes every day to bring them a loaf of bread that, after polite demurrals, the two hermits share. After Paul had left to return to his hermitage, Anthony saw Paul's soul being carried to heaven by angels. Rushing to Paul's hermitage he found him dead, "kneeling upright in the attitude of prayer." Two lions then appear who dig a tomb in which Anthony buries Paul, after taking his tunic of woven palm leaves, which he later wore "on solemn occasions." Paul is thought to have died around the year of Our Lord 287. One can see from this that hermitism, far from drying up Jacobus de Voragine's imagination, fills it with the miraculous, though Jacobus never leaves the realm of historical and chronological time.

The earliest of the hermits Jacobus de Voragine considers is really Saint Anthony, to whom he devotes a somewhat longer chapter, crediting him with a very long life. With Anthony, Jacobus returns to etymology (which he had left aside in speaking of Paul), and begins by deconstructing his name into *ana*, "above," and *tenens*, "holding," to arrive at "one who holds on to higher things and despises worldly things."[27]

Jacobus de Voragine takes advantage of the opportunity to allude to the many temptations that made Anthony famous, but he does not dwell on them as much as might be expected. A man of enormous imagination, with a passion for the marvelous, Jacobus found little to inspire him in Saint Anthony. He grants Anthony only a banal history in which a fervent young Christian, aged twenty, hears the call to Jesus in church, sells all his goods, distributes the proceeds to the poor, and goes off to live a hermit's life. He does not mention (as he does in his treatment of Saint Paul the Hermit) that Anthony may have been the first hermit or one of the first hermits. Jacobus hints that Anthony did not live as a solitary hermit but rather as a cenobite in community with other brothers. It is worth noting, however, that although he gives tempered praise to the eremitical life, he makes Anthony, after some time spent in the desert, fall victim to an attack of that form of sinful ennui known in the Middle Ages as *acedia*. In point of fact, Jacobus de Voragine does not use that word, but speaks only of *tedium*. In this episode Jacobus seems to give expression to two of his principal preoccupations. For him as a Dominican and a member of an urban order, city time was perhaps a more interesting kind of time to offer to God. Then too, he has an angel respond to Saint Anthony's expression of his ennui, telling him that in order to chase away sadness one must do two things: work (*operare*) and pray. In my eyes this is supplementary proof that the Middle Ages, and in particular the central Middle Ages of the twelfth and thirteenth centuries, thought highly of work, and that time devoted to it was of equal weight in the divine scales to the time of prayer.

Next we shall see how, in certain instances, Jacobus de Voragine devoted two chapters to the same saint or to two different saints who bore the same name. This means that the human time that Jacobus sacralizes can include doublings, real ones in the case of one of these saints and imagined ones in the case of two others with the same name.

## Saint Paul

The case of Saint Paul brings into play three different commemorations, fixed on three different dates. As we have just seen, in addition to Saint Paul the Apostle, there was a second Paul who was associated with Saint Anthony because the two of them were considered to have been the first hermits, were connected during their terrestrial life, and had feast days seven days apart. There is yet another Saint Paul, however, who is part of another pair, who are not celebrated independently but on the same day. That day is far from Saint Paul the Hermit's on the liturgical calendar, as it falls not in the time of reconciliation but in that of pilgrimage—that is, not between the Nativity and Lent, but after Easter. This second Saint Paul is connected with a Saint John, a saint who also has homonyms on the calendar and in the *Golden Legend* and to whom I shall return. The Saints Paul and John commemorated together share celebrations on June 16. Historians of hagiography consider the pair to be imaginary, the result of a faulty reading of an obscure dedication found in a church on Monte Celio in Rome.[28] In the *Golden Legend* the two saints are closely connected on two occasions: first, they are supposed to have converted to Christianity the head of the Roman army sent by Constantine against the pagan Scythians; second, they are thought to have been martyred at the same time under Emperor Julian the Apostate, who is known to have instituted a brief return to paganism in the Roman Empire in the fourth century. To justify the chapter he devotes to Paul and John, Jacobus de Voragine cites Saint Ambrose, who says of them, "These were brothers . . . bound together in their common faith, equal to each other in their martyrdom, and forever glorious in the one Lord."[29] Thus for Jacobus de Voragine, time can be sanctified on one date by two different saints united by the joint effect of their life and their martyrdom. He can also accept marking one saint on different dates, if that saint had accomplished a solemn act worthy of a special day of commemoration over and above the day dedicated to his life as a whole.

This was the case of a third Paul, the most important of that name, whose conversion to Christianity was commemorated separately in the Roman liturgical calendar on January 25, an event so important that Jacobus felt it merited a special chapter, which he titled "The Conversion of Saint Paul, Apostle." Here Jacobus de Voragine of course alludes to the future saint's being struck down on the road to Damascus, after which he abandoned paganism and became a Christian convert. In the chapter he dedicates to this event, Jacobus de Voragine accords Paul an exceptionally important place in the unfolding of time. He is the perfect antithesis to Adam, which makes him akin to a first man. Jacobus places the conversion of Saint Paul within the same calendar year as the passion of Christ and the lapidation of Saint Stephen. This Paul also offers Jacobus an opportunity to raise the problems that the calendar posed for Christians, who hesitated for centuries between the year that was called *naturalis*, which began on January 1 and was essentially lunar, and the Jewish calendar year, which was *emergens*, beginning with the Jews' flight from Egypt. Despite his tendency to rationalize the sacred time of Christian humanity, Jacobus finds it difficult to reconcile a question about measuring time that had bothered Christians throughout most of the Middle Ages. This had to do with the pressure exerted on an essentially solar calendar by what remained of the lunar calendar and the difficulties it caused in fixing the date of the first day of the year and settling how to handle movable feasts such as those that fell around Easter, the Passion, and the Resurrection of Christ within a time that was at once cyclical, linear, and eschatological.

In this short chapter, Jacobus de Voragine also speaks of how the conversion of "he who previously spent his fury in persecuting" Christians led the man who became Saint Paul to consider "tyrants and peoples breathing fury" to be like "so many gnats" and to state that "he felt more adorned when bound with chains than crowned with a royal diadem;"[30] in other words that he would choose martyrdom and sainthood over the splendid trappings of a purely terrestrial power. Kings and emperors (whom Jacobus de Voragine often has difficulty keeping straight) are on earth the masters of a time dedicated to death, while those who oppose them and suffer martyrdom as a consequence are the masters and the teachers of a time that leads to life eternal. This notion is inscribed within a more general theme of the *Golden Legend* that is political in nature: a critique of power, once pagan, now secular, and a glorification of the sacred power expressed by the ecclesiastical liturgy and the commemoration of exemplary saints.

In addition to the day dedicated to his conversion, the Saint Paul of the Acts of the Apostles reappears in another chapter that is dedicated to him but is to some extent coupled with a chapter on Saint Peter, as it immediately follows a chapter dedicated to the latter and refers to the same liturgical day, June 29. Although this feast day is situated in a period of the liturgical year quite distant from that of the chapter I have just examined, I invoke it here in order to speak of the two days dedicated to Saint Paul. The chapter on "Saint Paul, Apostle" is one of the longest in the *Golden Legend*. After discussing an etymology that leads him to "mouth of a trumpet" and "miracle of election,"[31] Jacobus de Voragine attributes to Saint Paul six "privileges" that exceed those of the other apostles." The first is "fruitful speech," its priority indicating that (in the opinion of an eminent member of the Order of Preachers) predication is the finest human activity. The second is his profound charity, and Jacobus specifies that "charity" here bears its essential Christian meaning of "love," since after calling Saint Paul the "mouth of a trumpet" he calls him "the mouth of the heart." Paul's third special gift is his miraculous conversion. Although Paul was not born into a Christian milieu and had not received baptism at his birth or in his childhood, the real birth into time for a Christian is conversion, and the conversion of Paul was the most spectacular of all those mentioned in ancient Christianity. Paul's fourth gift was the "hands of a workman," and here we see once more how well Jacobus de Voragine represents the moment in human history, at the heart of the Middle Ages, when labor came to be honored instead of viewed, as it had been previously, as a punishment for original sin. Paul's fifth privilege was that of "blissful contemplation." Although Jacobus de Voragine encourages devotion to all manner of work from manual labor to the exercise of reason, a very important part of time had to be dedicated also to contemplation, for the man who makes himself worthy in that manner can be elevated by God to the third heaven. Thus, even on earth the Christian can sometimes attain to the time of life eternal, which may explain why Jacobus de Voragine insists less on eschatological time and the end of time than do some of his contemporaries. Saint Paul's sixth privilege is the "virtue of humility," for he is reported to have said of himself, "I am the least of the apostles."

In his long chapter on Saint Paul, Jacobus de Voragine focuses, as well he should, on the many voyages that Paul undertook and on the geographical extent of his preaching, a topic that brings Jacobus back to the essential theme in the *Golden Legend*, the union of space and time. He also lingers over the tortures inflicted on Paul by Nero and on the latter's wickedness, returning to the theme of hostility toward imperial and royal power. Finally, although Jacobus de Voragine stresses the close connection between Saint Peter and Saint Paul, who are celebrated on the same day and were both sent to their martyrdom in Rome, he grants primacy in Christian virtue to Peter and seems to balance that primacy by attributing to Paul a superiority over the greatest figures of the Old Testament. He implies that Paul is greater than Abel, greater than Noah, greater than Abraham, greater than Isaac, greater than Jacob, greater than Job, greater than Moses, and greater than Saint John the Baptist. Thus it seems certain that God had already raised him to the rank of an angel.

This chapter gives us an opportunity to admire the narrative talents of Jacobus de Vorgine, which seem to blossom more when describing the horrible than the marvelous. The time of humanity is not only a time of feasts and festive commemoration, but also a time of horrors. I am of the opinion that Jacobus de Voragine was trying to "enchant" human time. But he sensed that the time of man's peregrinations would be long. Human time still had many horrors to dispose of (with the help of Jesus, Mary, the Holy Spirit, and the saints), and this was the task of the Church and in particular of the Dominicans. Although the recital of Paul's martyrdom resembles that of many other figures in the *Golden Legend*, it contains an extraordinary page worthy of a modern thriller in which Jacobus recounts the odyssey of the decapitated saint's head. A bishop and a crowd of Christians tried in vain to reunite the saint's head with his body, both of which had been rescued from a trench full of other bodies and heads, but they gave up. They left the head at the feet of the body, whereupon it miraculously regained its rightful place. This account points to one of the reasons for the prodigious success that the *Golden Legend* enjoyed from the late thirteenth century on: beyond the force of Jacobus's ideas on time, there was the power of his narration, in particular, his narratives on what one might call dramatic and fantastic deeds. Time in the *Golden Legend* is an extraordinary combination of adventure tales and marvelous events that were long denigrated but that provide a brilliant illustration of the logic and profundity of Jacobus de Voragine's thought as he employs his narrative talents to persuade his listeners and readers.

To remain within the time of reconciliation (which I will conclude with Saint John the Almsgiver), let me note that in his short chapter on Saint Remy (or Remigius; feast day January 13), Jacobus de Voragine gives specific details about the saint's conversion, the baptism of Clovis, and the importance of the church of Reims, where the phial containing the sacred chrism with which the new king of France was anointed on the day of his coronation is still preserved. I might also note that Jacobus de Voragine, on this occasion, does not call Clovis the "king of the French," as he had long been known, but the "king of France," using an expression that became official only in the early thirteenth century under Philip Augustus.

## Saint John the Almsgiver

This saint seems to have been an invention of the Dominican hagiographers. He in fact appears for the first time in the works of Jacobus de Voragine's predecessors, Jean de Mailly and Bartholomew of Trent, but they are very vague in their rapid treatment of him. It seems that it was Jacobus de Voragine who assured the Almsgiver's presence in the sanctorale, thanks to the attention that he accords to him in the *Golden Legend*, and the reputation with which he credits him. Jacobus cites no source for his information on this saint, although, as was his wont, he indicates a historical date for his lifetime by ending his account of the Almsgiver with the information that he lived around the year of Our Lord 605, in the time of the Byzantine emperor Phocas.

It is easy to understand why the Dominicans, if they did not invent this saint outright, at least drew him out of obscurity. Presented with no etymology (which can be explained both by the fact that there are other saints named John and because the essential character of this Dominican creation is incorporated in his title), this Saint John was, *par excellence*, a giver of alms. The mendicant orders, with the Dominicans at their head, praise alms as a primordial act of piety.

We have arrived at Jacobus de Voragine's own age, the thirteenth century. This was a high point in the of the exaltation of alms and of the practice of almsgiving, both by the new mendicant orders and by all the faithful who followed them in this gesture, including the king of France, for Saint Louis was himself a renowned giver of alms. By proposing John as an example to those who consulted the *Golden Legend*, Jacobus de Voragine was obliged to confer on him an existence and traits that made him a saint. He thus presents him as the patriarch of Alexandria and attributes to him, as the keynote of his spirituality and his charity, the statement: "Those whom you call the poor, the beggars, they are the ones I declare masters, and helpers."[32] Thus, although Jacobus de Voragine did not step outside the bounds of a feudal society dominated by lords, he nonetheless replaces those lords—at least ideally—with the poor. Jacobus also has Saint John the Almsgiver say to his servants: "Go through the city and make me a list of my masters, down to the last one." In order to justify the introduction of this previously unknown saint into his *Legend*, Jacobus describes John's practice of giving alms in a variety of circumstances, each of which gives rise to a little story in which Jacobus demonstrates his wonted skill at narration. In these tales Jacobus de Voragine emphasizes the giving of clothing, thus recalling to his listeners and readers the importance of clothing in everyday life. Here again, he proves himself a man of his times, for it was in the thirteenth century that fashion seems to have made its first appearance, prompting the revival of ancient sumptuary laws condemning luxurious dress. It might be amusing to compare Saint John the Almsgiver with Saint Martin, about whom Jacobus speaks later on, when he reaches Martin's place in the chronology of the sanctorale, November 11. From the late fourth century on, Saint Martin was famous for cutting his mantle in two and giving half of it to a poor man. Saint John the Almsgiver goes him one better: he gives all of his clothing to the poor and dresses himself in rags and tatters. This gives Jacobus de Voragine a chance to use one of those stories for which he had a special gift. The anecdote is all the more amusing for presenting John the Almsgiver as a kind of saintly con man. A rich man, seeing John in tatters, offers him a luxurious quilt. The saint sells it and gives the money to the poor. The rich man is astonished by this behavior and puts up a fuss, but John explains to him that the quilt was too fine for him. The rich man then goes and buys him another, less costly, but Saint John the Almsgiver sells that one as well. There follows an entire series of sales, with each coverlet costing less than the last, until at last John succeeds in transferring all of the rich man's money to the poor, making him into an almsgiver in spite of himself.

Saint John the Almsgiver compares himself to Saint Serapion, who gave first his cloak, then his tunic to a poor man, until he himself was left nearly naked. When people asked him who had robbed him, he pointed to the Gospel and said, "That did."[33] Obviously the giving of alms in the form of clothing had taken a radical turn since Saint Martin's day. Like all members of the mendicant orders, Jacobus de Voragine had heard the saying that had been spreading since the late twelfth century in those Christian circles where a new spirituality was taking form: "Follow naked the naked Christ." Jacobus de Voragine places the feast of Saint John the Almsgiver on January 23.

# 7

# The Time of Deviation

As he had announced in his prologue, after covering the feast days that are grouped together in a time of mixed reconciliation and pilgrimage after the Nativity, Jacobus de Voragine now turns to the feasts of deviation that fill the time from Septuagesima to Easter, that is, from Lent to the Passion of Christ. Starting at the date of the Nativity, by now fixed at December 25, he expresses a degree of embarrassment at the mobility of the liturgical feasts in this time of deviation that leads through Lent to the crucifixion, then turns to the time of reconciliation that begins with the Resurrection of the Lord. Thus he arrives at Easter Day, the movable feast that creates the mobility of the liturgical time of deviation that precedes it.

Jacobus de Voragine begins by recalling that the time of deviation or turning away from the right way corresponds, historically, to the period from Adam to Moses, because the original sin, committed by Adam, brings on a deviation that Moses brings to an end, albeit only a preliminary end, because it is Jesus, by his incarnation, who will end it definitively.

The time of deviation is essentially the period of Lent, which, despite the very important place that Jacobus de Voragine gives to those forty days, he extends to include the three Sundays preceding Lent itself, in keeping with Roman liturgical practice as it had developed in the eighth century. The first chapters of the *Golden Legend* covering the time of deviation thus concern Septuagesima, Sexagesima, Quinquagesima, and Quadragesima, the latter leading to the Passion of Christ. Among these feasts centered on Christ incarnate there are also two dedicated to the Blessed Virgin, his mother— the Purification of the Blessed Virgin Mary and the Annunciation of the Lord—and another on the institution that advances Christ's teachings on earth, the Chair of Saint Peter. In this section of his work, Jacobus de Voragine deals with twelve saints: Saint Ignatius, Saint Blaise, Saint Agatha, Saint Vaast, Saint Amand, Saint Valentine, Saint Juliana, Saint Matthew the Apostle, Saint Gregory, Saint Longinus, Saint Benedict, and Saint Patrick. In these pages I shall discuss Saint Gregory, given his importance in the history of the medieval Church; Saint Benedict, for having been the principal creator of monasticism in the West; and Saint Patrick, for reasons that will become clear.

Jacobus de Voragine extended Lent, the period that begins on the ninth Sunday before Easter, to include the three feast days preceding Lent proper, a forty-day period known as Quadragesima. Septuagesima begins the time of deviation; Sexagesima, the time of widowhood; Quinquagesima, the time of remission; and Quadragesima, the time of spiritual penance. Septuagesima, which opens on the ninth Sunday before Easter, ends, according to Jacobus, on the Saturday after Easter, as the week after Easter is included in Lent. Jacobus does not discuss that Saturday; for him, Easter Sunday ends the time of deviation and opens a new phase, the time of reconciliation. Jacobus de Voragine seems somewhat troubled by the fact that the two feasts in this period, Easter and Lent, are movable. Perhaps his apparent attachment to stability, which he valued as a divine virtue, led him to find them disturbing; perhaps he was baffled by the complex calculations used by earlier liturgists to fix the dates of these feasts. Once more, this highlights a characteristic of the

*Golden Legend* that my readers have undoubtedly already noticed, which is the importance, complexity, and subtlety of thirteenth-century thinkers, and Jacobus de Voragine in particular, when dealing with numbers.[1] Not only was sacred time divided into divine time and human time for Jacobus de Voragine, but although the essential point concerning time in the *Golden Legend* is the combination of liturgical time, the temporale, with the time of the saints, the sanctorale, both of which are oriented toward the end of time (or to put it differently, both are in accord with eschatological time), each of these three principal times can itself also be divided into several segments. This demonstrates the degree to which time was complex and open to manipulation. Moreover, there is all the less oneness in time because it is, as we have seen, united with space, which also is not unified. Given that the place where a saint's relics reposed was the most important center of attraction for his or her cult, that cult could occur in different locations; for example, a saint's relics could be scattered among places, their location might be unknown (in rare cases), or they could be moved, as when Saint Benedict's relics were divided between Monte Cassino and Saint-Benoît-sur-Loire.

## From Septuagesima to Quadragesima

Septuagesima was instituted for three reasons.

First, it is a time of redemption that had its origin in a curious readjustment of days. Because of the veneration due to Ascension Day, which is on a Thursday, the primitive Church established Thursday as a day of solemnity equal to Sunday. When the seven-day week was imposed on this week burdened with two solemn days, Thursday retreated before Sunday, which became more important. But in recompense and to make up for that effacement, the Church is supposed to have added a week to the commemoration of Christ's fasting, with the result that Septuagesima, according to Jacobus de Voragine, ended on the Saturday after Easter. Thus, somewhat oddly, in the *Golden Legend* Lent is inscribed within a longer time of fasting that begins on the ninth Sunday before Easter and ends on the Saturday following Easter, which is, however, the first feast of the next time, that of reconciliation.

Second, Septuagesima was instituted as a symbol. In order to explain this, Jacobus de Voragine combines the sacred time of humanity that structures the *Golden Legend* with the chronological time of human history, which is also structured around Christ, but in a different manner. Septuagesima thus symbolizes the wandering, the exile, and the tribulations of all humankind after Adam within a cycle of seven thousand years, six thousand of which took place before the Ascension. That sixth age of the world is the one in which Christ is incarnated to lead humanity into the seventh millennium, the end of which is known only to God and where the world, humanity, and time will end and enter into eternity. This is one of the rare allusions in the *Golden Legend* to a final eschatological time, existing within the combined framework of time.

Finally, Septuagesima was instituted as a representation, and Jacobus de Voragine ends this article stressing, more than his predecessors had done, the numerical symbolism of the time that is expressed in the very name of the feast day. This was a way to emphasize not only the symbolism of the number seven, but also the historical significance of its multiplication by ten, given that the sons of Israel spent seventy years in Babylonian captivity. Because the end of that exile was marked by many songs of joy and thanks to God, Jacobus insists on the idea that contemporary Christians should continue to sing Alleluias. The *Golden Legend* often marks Christian time by music and songs, which though they can be sad are more often festive. For Jacobus de Voragine, music was another marker of time, both because of its repetitive character, which expresses the time of remembering, and by its duration, thanks to which it occupies an important part of terrestrial life and announces an eternity of song.

Sexagesima begins with music, thanks to the canticle sung on the Sunday that opens this period. Jacobus places considerable stress on the numerical symbolism that gave its name to Sexagesima, a name that signifies "6 times 10," the 6 standing for "the six works of mercy" and the 10 for the Decalogue. Six also refers to the six mysteries that marked Christ's life on earth: "Christ's incarnation, birth, passion, descent into Hell, resurrection, and ascension into heaven."[2]

Jacobus de Voragine connects Quinquagesima with an ancient pagan tradition, something he rarely does. It is supposed to have been the day of the liberation of slaves, then to have become the day on which the Law was given, and, finally, in Christianity, the day on which the Holy Spirit was sent. Whereas Septuagesima ended on the Saturday after Easter and Sexagesima on the Wednesday after Easter, Quinquagesima ended on Easter Sunday itself. According to Jacobus de Voragine, who speculates on the symbolism of the number fifty, Quinquagesima is considered to be one of the sources for the Roman Christian Church's return to the Judaic Jubilee. In 1300 Pope Boniface VIII instituted the new Christian Jubilee, which was to be held every fifty years and brought an influx of pilgrims to Rome. That jubilee, which persists to this day, was seriously disrupted fifty years after the Roman Jubilee of 1300 when the papacy found itself in exile in Avignon.

Quadragesima Sunday leads Jacobus de Voragine to speak in more precise terms about the time of Lent, since it corresponded to the time that Jesus fasted during his incarnation. Jesus is supposed to have explicitly adopted "forty" as a sacred number. This time of Lent seems to have posed particular problems, numerical and symbolic, for Jacobus, who piles questions, suppositions, and references one on top of the other to explain two essential things that illuminate this particular time: the choice of the number forty, a multiple of four, and the decision of the Church to situate this period of fasting within the Roman calendar, whereas, according to tradition, Jesus fasted in the desert soon after his baptism. As for the number "forty," Jacobus insists on the symbolic meaning of the number four, which is its root. The world has four parts, and there are four seasons and four Gospels. Man's body is formed of the four elements, which have four "seats" in us: "fire is predominantly in the eyes, air on the tongue and in the ears, water in the genitals, and earth in the hands and the other members."[3] If I am not mistaken, this is the first time that Jacobus de Voragine mentions the five senses, to which he will return later. Above all, Jacobus strives to explain this time of penance that leads to a time of beatitude (Easter and the Resurrection of the Lord) by bringing in the entire world with its four parts, all of meteorological time by evoking the four seasons, and the whole of the human body through its physical composition. We return here to Jacobus de Voragine's propensity—one he shared with many of his contemporaries—for showing and explaining totality. The thirteenth century developed a thought that was encyclopedic and universal, that attempted to display and explain all of divine creation. It is within this context that I seek to define the *Golden Legend* as a *summa* on time.

## The Ember Day Fasts

Reflection on Lent, a time of fasting, and on the number four, which lies at the heart of Lent, leads Jacobus de Voragine to devote the next chapter of the *Golden Legend* to the Ember Day fasts. He gives the practice of the feasts of the four seasons an origin that is neither divine, nor Judaic, nor evangelical, but rather human. According to Jacobus, Callistus (pope from 217 to 222) instituted this fast. Historians believe that its creation came much later, probably under Siricius (pope from 384 to 399), who is credited with having Christianized several old pagan feasts, a harvest feast in June, a feast of the grape harvest in September, a feast of the olive harvest in December, and a feast of the sowing of seeds in early spring. Jacobus, whose practice was to avoid any hint at the pagan heritage of Christianity, tended instead to place the origins of Christian feasts at as early a date as possible.

Jacobus gives eight reasons for the institution of the Ember Day fasts, most of which either draw their meaning from the four seasons, or refer to times when mankind should punish such sins as arise from climatic and environmental sources. In the spring there were sins brought on by warmth and humidity; hot and dry summers caused others; in autumn punishment was called for "to temper the aridity of pride," and in winter "to overcome the coldness of malice and lack of faith."[4] Each of these four seasonal fasts lasts three days, a number that is not linked to climate or to human sins but rather to Christ's Passion, as they recall the Thursday of Holy Week, when Judas betrayed Jesus, Good Friday, when Jesus was crucified, and Holy Saturday, when Jesus lay in the tomb.

## The Passion of the Lord

The material in the time of deviation that directly concerns Jesus and Lent ends with a final chapter on the passion of the Lord.

For Jacobus de Voragine, the passion has three essential characteristics. It is bitter, subject to contempt (*despecta*), and fruitful. The passion was painful, first, because of its shamefulness: it "happened in a place of shame, on Calvary, where malefactors were punished;" and it put Jesus on the cross, "the instrument of punishment for thieves," thus placing him in the company of criminals.[5] It was also painful because it was brought on by unjust accusations, and even more painful because it was brought on by friends. This last fact leads Jacobus to apply to Jesus the situation of Job in the Old Testament. It was painful because Jesus had a very tender body, which was much mistreated by the soldiers who crucified him. Finally, the passion "penetrated every part of his body, it smote all his senses." Jacobus enumerates all of Jesus's sufferings: he suffered with his eyes when he wept; with his hearing, struck by "insults and blasphemies," with his sense of smell, from the "strong odor of decay" that "pervaded the place of Calvary, where dead bodies were left to rot." His sense of taste was assaulted when, on the cross, he was given vinegar to drink; and he suffered in his sense of touch, for "in every part of his body, from the soles of his feet to the top of his head there was no soundness."[6]

The Passion involved contempt because Jesus was the object of derision. He was spat upon, slapped, and a veil was placed over his eyes. He was "draped . . . in a white robe of a fool." A reed was placed in his hands to mimic a scepter, and a crown of thorns was placed on his head. He was mocked on the cross.

Finally, the Passion was fruitful, for unlike the ignominies just mentioned, it was a fertile sacrifice that served multiple purposes. Here Jacobus de Voragine cites Augustine (in a sermon that was really the work of Ambroise Autpert): "Let us wonder and rejoice, love and praise and adore, because through our redeemer's death we have been called from darkness to light, from death to life, from corruption to incorruption, from exile to fatherland, from grief to joy."

There were four reasons for the fruitfulness of the passion. It appeased the wrath of God; it cured man of sickness and death; it attracted humanity to God; and it made possible victory over the devil, the enemy of mankind.

Time was, according to Jacobus de Voragine, one of the great gifts of the Creator to humanity. Here he makes another use of time; he speaks of it as a commemoration that effaces. Adam committed the original sin one Friday in March at the sixth hour, and Jesus was crucified in March and died on the cross on a Friday at the sixth hour. This, for Jacobus de Voragine, was one of the virtues of time, that it can efface a bad moment in the past by superimposing on it a future good moment that makes the bad moment vanish.

Jacobus de Voragine ends his long chapter on the passion of the Lord in a quite original fashion, with a story concerning the end of one of the authorities most closely responsible for the crucifixion of Jesus, Pontius Pilate. When Pontius Pilate refuses further responsibility for events that led to the crucifixion of Jesus, he is supposed to have violently irritated the Roman emperor. Recalled to Rome, he is said to have been imprisoned and condemned to death, but he committed suicide in prison. Jacobus de Voragine, whose fondness for telling dramatic stories in the style of thrillers gives full play to this probably imaginary episode, which he admits he found in an apocryphal text. As a historian who (despite what has been said about him) does in fact care for truth, Jacobus confesses: "Thus far we have quoted the aforementioned apocryphal history: let the reader judge whether the story is worth the telling." He adds, however, that according to the best Christian sources, Eusebius and Bede, Pilate did "suffer many calamities and died by his own hand."[7]

After this review of the chapters of the *Golden Legend* that have to do with the time of deviation, a period consecrated to Jesus, who is the great master of time and who participated by his divine nature in the creation of divine time and by his incarnation in the practice of human time, I would like next to comment briefly on five chapters that, within this same time of deviation, furnish interesting arguments for my thesis that the *Golden Legend* constitutes a *summa* on time. Two of these chapters concern the Virgin Mary, the mother of Jesus. The others are dedicated to three saints who might be considered as particularly effective markers of time: Saint Gregory, who lived at a particularly significant point in history and left to the Church and Christianity some particularly important writings and customs; Saint Benedict, the founder of a Christian way of life, monasticism, that left a profound mark on several centuries of Christian history; and Saint Patrick, whom I shall discuss because of the ways in which, as presented by Jacobus de Voragine, he seems to me particularly interesting for the chronology of Christian time.

## The Purification of the Blessed Virgin Mary

The period of Lent was thus reduced, within the sacred time of the *Golden Legend*, to the four Sundays of Septuagesima, Sexagesima, Quinquagesima, and Quadragesima, a period, as Jacobus de Voragine stresses, of forty days of fasting before the passion and resurrection of the Lord. This time of Lent closes with the chapter on the passion of the Lord, which treats of Good Friday, Holy Saturday, and the portion of Easter Sunday preceding the resurrection of Jesus and his departure from the tomb. That period leaves out, as less significant within the unfolding of annual liturgical time, Ash Wednesday, Palm Sunday, and, except for its last three days, Holy Week, including Holy Thursday.[8]

As already stated, I shall indicate briefly what the two chapters of the temporale and the three chapters of the sanctorale concerning the Virgin Mary contribute to my study of time.

The first feast connected with the Blessed Virgin Mary is that of the Purification. The heavy promotion that the cult of Mary received in the twelfth and thirteenth century had, among its other effects, that of reducing this feast, which takes place forty days after the Nativity of the Lord, to the status of a strictly Marial feast. It must be pointed out, however, that Christ is strongly involved in this feast day, since it marks the presentation of the Infant Jesus in the Temple, an event that Jacobus de Voragine does indeed stress, but that does not appear in the chapter title, which alludes only to the Purification of the Virgin.

Jacobus de Voragine indicates that the term "purification" used in connection with this day can be replaced with *Hypopanti,* which "signifies a meeting," because it was on that day that Simeon and Anna met the Infant Jesus when he was brought to the Temple. The day also bears the name Candlemas, "because on this day candles are carried in the hand."[9] Jacobus de Voragine notes here, perhaps reluctantly but because his respect for historical and, in particular, chronological truth requires it, the fact that the Christian feast of Candlemas replaces a pagan Roman custom in which the city of Rome was illuminated every five years on the calends of February in honor of Februa, the mother of the war-god Mars, and as a petition for military victory. Jacobus admits that "it is hard to relinquish such customs," adding that Christians who had formerly been pagans were reluctant to give up their feast of lights. Still, he stresses that the Christian Candlemas has an entirely different meaning. It was devoted to Mary and it signaled the purity of the Virgin, "utterly pure and radiant," by bathing her in that light so glorified by Christianity, particularly in the Gothic age.

The feast of the Purification of the Blessed Virgin Mary was also marked, like the days of fasting and of Lent, by the use of the number forty in the sacred calendar, a number with a particularly powerful symbolic meaning for Christianity. Jacobus de Voragine explains the forty-day interval between the Nativity of the Lord and the Purification of the Blessed Virgin Mary not only in relation to Mary, who waited forty days until she was cleansed of the pollution that follows a childbirth, but also in relation to Jesus himself. Jacobus is aware that the day of the Presentation of the Infant Jesus at the Temple celebrates two events in one, and he goes to some lengths to explain this forty-day period in relation to both Mary and Jesus. Concerning Jesus, Jacobus argues that the soul enters into the body of a newborn child, as into a temple, forty days after birth. This chapter also presents him with an opportunity to speak of the inequality of the sexes in the context of time. The time of the purification of a young mother and the presentation of her baby in the Temple was, he explains, twice as long if the baby was a girl. This was because the soul needs not forty days, but eighty days, to make its way into the body of a female child. Hence we see that among the many meanings of time and the many instances of the use of time that make the *Golden Legend* such an extremely complex construction, there is also a distinction between the sexes that carries pejorative significance for the female sex. This is not, to pick but one example, the position of Thomas Aquinas, who demonstrates the equality of man and woman by noting the height on the male body of the part God used to create woman. She was made from the rib, in other words from the midsection rather than from the head, which would have signified superiority, or the feet, which would have signified inferiority.[10]

Finally, this chapter allows us to understand that the great devotion that Saint Bernard manifested toward the Virgin in the twelfth century, when her cult in Western Christianity was in full ascent, was no doubt one of the reasons why the Dominican Jacobus de Voragine, also a devotee of the Blessed Virgin, so often cites Bernard, a Cistercian.

Jacobus de Voragine closes his chapter by recounting, with habitual verve, two miracles connected with this feast day. Better yet, he shows how a candle lighted for Candlemas could become a relic. This little incident, which might seem insignificant, testifies to the energy that Jacobus devotes to sacralizing every phase and every day of time, through his use, in particular, of miracles, saintliness, and relics.

## The Annunciation of the Lord

The Annunciation is celebrated on March 25, during the month that lies at the heart of the time of deviation. Commentators of the *Golden Legend* have often stressed an aspect of this chapter that is at once quite original and quite important. In standard liturgical practice and in ordinary Christian literature, "the Annunciation" means the annunciation to the Virgin Mary, and I myself have connected it with her purification. But Jacobus de Voragine speaks of the Annunciation of the Lord. For him, Christ incarnate is truly the center of time. Jacobus devoted many sermons to the Annunciation, and the plausible hypothesis has been advanced that this was by way of compensation for the Dominican Order's hostility in the thirteenth century toward the doctrine of the Immaculate Conception of Mary. That doctrine did not of course become Roman Catholic orthodoxy until the nineteenth century, and Saint Bernard, who was devoted to Mary, was hostile toward it. This chapter on the Annunciation is an opportunity to stress also that the *Golden Legend* is full of angels. Indeed, when Satan and his devils succeeded in penetrating the marvelous creation that was for God the world and man, God moved to oppose them with an army devoted to the good. Jacobus de Voragine, always ready to borrow from Saint Bernard, completely upsets the birth traditions about Jesus and John the Baptist, the miraculous but purely human son of Elizabeth, who was not conceived, like Jesus, by a mother whose virginity remained intact, but was instead born of parents beyond the natural age for conceiving and bearing children. Jesus had no genuine youth nor any real coming into adulthood, since "from the very first day of his conception he had as much wisdom and as much power as he had in his thirtieth year."[11] As for Saint John the Baptist, his role as a precursor of Jesus began when he was but a fetus in the womb of his mother, and although his position as the precursor and baptizer of Jesus was given to him by God, the presence of the Virgin Mary next to Elizabeth during the final months of her pregnancy and the fact that Mary was present at the birth of John also contributed to his being born in spite of time and nature. The birth and baptism of Jesus required that God upset the natural time for pregnancy, birth, and youth for the sake of his incarnated son.

## Saint Gregory, Saint Benedict, and Saint Patrick

I have chosen to speak of Saint Gregory, whose feast falls on March 12, because of the importance of his papacy within both historical time and the sacred time of Jacobus de Voragine. He was pope from 590 to 604, but Jacobus de Voragine has him dying in 606 after thirteen years in office and coming to the pontifical throne one year after a great flood of the Tiber in Rome that was followed by a short but violent episode of the bubonic plague. Those events took place in 590, but if Gregory's death is set in 606, they would have taken place in 593. Once more, we see that Jacobus de Voragine's knowledge was approximate, but we note nonetheless his effort to furnish precise dates for historical events and for the lives of saints. Saint Gregory is also interesting because he left literary works that marked not only Christianity but also the history and the culture of Europe. Jacobus de Voragine clearly reserves special treatment for the four books of Gregory's *Dialogues on Miracles*, which is for him a source of exceptional importance. He also cites a work that served as a sort of manual of spirituality for all of Christianity throughout the High Middle Ages and that proposed to Christians the ideal of humility as the greatest of Christian virtues. This text, the *Moralia in Job*, was written, it should be noted, even before the thirteenth century had elevated poverty to its position at the pinnacle of Christian spirituality. Jacobus de Voragine, who gives great emphasis in both his sermons and in the *Golden Legend* to the spiritual efficacy of ceremonies, and in particular to music and chants, stresses Gregory the Great's importance as a liturgist and master of the ecclesiastical chant, as well as the founder of a school of cantors, thus making the coming to prominence of what was later known as Gregorian chant a historical event of prime importance. The sacred time of Jacobus de Voragine was a time set to music. He notes, finally, that Gregory the Great was the first to call the pope a "servant of the servants of God" in an official pronouncement, thus introducing a lasting custom into the history of the papal chancellery.

I have quite obviously picked Saint Benedict because, although in historical terms he was not the first monk in the West, he was the creator of what would become Western monasticism's most important rule and, after the Synod of Aniane (817), the only monastic rule until the Gregorian reform of the late eleventh century. Gregory the Great wrote a life of Saint Benedict that takes up all of Book II of his *Dialogues.* Jacobus de Voragine, in an attempt to move monasticism out of the desert, where it was to be found in the East, sends Benedict into the desert early in his life. He takes advantage of the occasion of speaking of Saint Benedict to show that a saint whose name remained attached to one feast day (for Benedict, March 21) could be attached to several localities if he had lived in several places. This was the case of Saint Benedict, who lived first in a grotto, then in a monastery in Latium (at Subiaco, not far from Rome), and then in the famous monastery of Monte Cassino between Rome and Naples. Jacobus also stresses the important part that manual labor played in the rule and in the practice of Saint Benedict and his fellow monks. He notes that Christianity promoted manual labor, long scorned, and that even though labor was considered a penance resulting from original sin, God had nonetheless sacralized human time as a time of labor.

Jacobus de Voragine, like Bartholomew of Trent before him (but not Jean de Mailly), devotes a chapter to Saint Patrick. Patrick gave him an opportunity to speak of a European country that had been converted to Christianity, Ireland, and in particular about another religious place situated within time, Purgatory. First, as concerns Ireland, Jacobus gives free range to frightening marvels presided over by ancient emperors and pagan chiefs or, at other times during the long span of human life, by the devil and his helpers. He speaks of the isle as a blissful place, thanks to blessings received from God and spread abroad by the beneficent works of Saint Patrick. There were in Ireland no poisonous animals, and the woods and the tree-bark of the region had the power to neutralize toxins. Next—and this was clearly more important for Jacobus de Voragine—he describes how one day Saint Patrick drew a large circle with his bishop's staff and "the earth opened within the circle and a very deep, wide pit emerged" leading to Purgatory.[12] I have demonstrated elsewhere that Christianity does not speak of Purgatory, the third region of the great beyond, until the second half of the twelfth century.[13]

By the latter half of the thirteenth century, Purgatory had been defined more precisely and had been accepted by the Dominican Order, but, curiously, the vision that Jacobus de Voragine presents of it is unclear. The Purgatory accepted as dogma by the Second Council of Lyon in 1274 was a temporary afterworld destined to hold Christians whom God would later welcome among the elect, after they had been purged of what remained of minor, venial sins, at which point Purgatory itself, having fulfilled its role, would disappear. Only the elect in Paradise and the damned in Hell would remain. The Church drew up a series of devotions to enable living Christians to help particular sufferers escape Purgatory in advance of the world's end. During the latter half of the thirteenth century several ecclesiastical authors tried to locate the earthly site of the mouth to Purgatory. They ended up not with the conception of one sole Purgatory for humanity but with several, for they determined that there were a number of mouths to Purgatory, scattered in various places and serving a variety of religious purposes. This is how the Purgatory of Saint Patrick came to be invented in the late twelfth century, and it soon became a pilgrimage site for people who were attracted also by the beauty of its setting on an island in an Irish lake. It is unclear whether Jacobus is describing this particular Purgatory that might be deemed Saint Patrick's or a more general Purgatory. He calls it the "place of purgation" or "the place of Purgatory" (*quidam Purgatorii locus*), an expression that seems to stand midway between the older term, *locus purgatorius*, which designated various separate spaces within the earth, and the one *locus purgatorius* that was supposed to be one of the entrances to a unified, single Purgatory. He also seems to waver between two destinations for the sinners sent to Purgatory. In a lengthy anecdote he has an Irishman named Nicholas pass through a number of places of torture before arriving at a "pleasant meadow redolent of the perfume of all sorts of flowers"[14] that stands before the city of Paradise. And indeed, according to a new dogma established in the late twelfth century, all the souls were in Purgatory only temporarily and would eventually pass on to Paradise. But Jacobus de Voragine also says that some of those condemned to Purgatory would not get out and, as we shall see in his chapter on the commemoration of All Souls, Purgatory was for him received doctrine, but at the same time a relatively vague notion.

Since we do not know exactly what a belief in Purgatory meant in the devotions of North Italian Christians in the latter half of the thirteenth century, the best we can do is to point out that Purgatory (which the Second Vatican Council removed from dogma in the twentieth century) was a new and still imprecise idea in the milieu where Jacobus de Voragine's thinking evolved. It is clear, however, that the concept interested him, for he seized the opportunity provided by the chapter on Saint Patrick to evoke the fluctuating temporality that was still connected with Purgatory. Purgatory would of course become firmly established—and in a particularly brilliant manner—by Dante in the *Divine Comedy*, a work written not long after the death of Jacobus de Voragine. That work contains three equal parts, one on each of three regions for which Dante shows equal interest: Hell, Purgatory, and Paradise.

# The Time of Reconciliation

The time of reconciliation is the glorious endpoint of time, deviated by the sin of Adam and Eve. Reconciliation between mankind and God was initiated by the incarnation of Christ; that is, by the Nativity. The time of reconciliation begins with the resurrection of the Lord—on Easter—and ends with his ascension. In the sanctorale covering the period, Jacobus de Voragine places it as running from the feast of Saint Secondus, March 30, to that of Saint Pancratius, May 12.

As he introduces the time of reconciliation, Jacobus de Voragine refers to the end of the preceding period, using a more vigorous expression than his usual "time of deviation," calling it "the time of turning from the right way."[1]

The resurrection offers no opportunity to deliver a detailed consideration of the celebration's date, as it is a movable feast. It does, however, give Jacobus a chance to voice some important thoughts on a limited but essential portion of sacred time. Because the resurrection took place on the third day of the Passion, he feels impelled to explain the meaning of that particularly rich time period. He poses a number of essential questions: 1. "How is it true to say that the

Lord lay in the tomb for three days and three nights and rose on the third day?" 2. "Why did he not come to life immediately after dying instead of waiting until the third day?"; 3. "How he rose"; 4. "Why he hurried his rising rather than wait for the general resurrection"; 5. "Why he rose"; 6. "How many times he appeared after the resurrection"; and 7. "How he brought out the holy fathers who were in limbo and what he did there."[2]

Citing Saint Augustine, Jacobus de Voragine makes use of a synecdoche. He explains that only the second day of the three, which is Holy Saturday, represents an entire day. The first day begins near the end of the day, as Jesus died on the cross in the evening of Good Friday, while the third includes only the early part of day, as Jesus rose on the morning of Easter Sunday. Jacobus de Voragine wants to consecrate time, but also to explain its nature, which means that this period is of critical importance because (and here he cites Bede) the resulting period of three "days" with a night preceding it "reversed the usual order of day and night, because previously day came first and night followed, but after Christ's passion this order was changed so that the nights came first and the days followed." For Jacobus de Voragine, this constitutes one of the great mysteries of time, since man once fell from "the daylight of grace into the night of sin," but now, by his passion and his resurrection, Jesus causes mankind to "come back from the night of sin to the daylight of grace."[3] Jacobus believed that he had thus arrived at the core of the concept of human time—the time in which he himself lived—and had shown that it is a positive time, illuminated by the marvelous and directed toward salvation. His conception of human time is more than positive. It possesses a kind of warmth.

Jacobus de Voragine has much to say about the seven questions that he asks at the beginning of the chapter. We will look only at what he says about time. The three days during which Christ lay dead represent the light of his sacrifice during the second complete day that he spends in the tomb between the two nights of his double mortal death, the death of original sin and natural death. The answer to his second question is that the length of the three days makes the reality of his death more sure. As chronological time unfolds, duration affirms and confirms. The response to the third question is that he rises again, thus asserting his power, bringing happiness, and showing the utility of escaping death—that is, escaping the devil—by offering the first marvel of time renewed, because he emerges out of a closed tomb and his resurrection was announced by an angel. On the fourth point, Jesus did not wait for the general resurrection in order to show the eminent dignity of his body and to fortify faith by choosing not to draw out the time of doubt that would follow his death, and also in order to present to mankind, as swiftly as possible, a model of its own resurrection. On the fifth point, he rises to present us with life as the goal of our mortal existence.

Jesus appeared five times on the day of his resurrection, and primarily to women (this in homage to the woman who gave him life, the Blessed Virgin Mary), an explanation that accords with the heightened importance of women after the Gregorian reforms, a rise in prominence that was confirmed and supported by the mendicant orders. Jesus appeared to his disciples to call on them to become apostles of charity. In particular, he appeared before Simon, calling him Peter, which means "obedient." Between his resurrection and his ascension, he appeared another five times: to the doubting Thomas, allowing him touch his sacred wounds; to a group of disciples whom he sent out to preach (I might note that here Jacobus de Voragine furnishes preaching, the mission of his own order, with its own divine origin); to a group of contemplatives on Mount Tabor; to a group of fishermen to incite them to penitence; and, finally, to the disciples on the Mount of Olives, where he urges them to practice mercy. The logical result of the resurrection of the Lord is thus a prefiguration of the essence of Christian faith, as indicated by Jesus himself. This is the time of the mission. The fairly lengthy discussion that follows is interesting, as in it Jacobus de Voragine affirms his belief, bolstered by Saint Ambrose and his *De Virginibus,* in the reality of another apparition, Jesus's appearance before his mother, the Virgin Mary,

which is not mentioned by the Evangelists but which Jacobus holds
to be necessarily true. Jacobus ends this long chapter with a lengthy
description of the descent of Jesus into Limbo after his resurrection,
from which he returns leading out not only the "holy fathers" of the
Old Testament and the good thief who died on the cross next to his
own, but also the ransomed Adam, whom he leads by the hand out
of Limbo and entrusts to the archangel Michael, who accompanies
him into Paradise. Thus the three days of the resurrection are extended until they contain all the men who lived in past times and
were in Limbo, who now will be led into eternal salvation. What
is more, all those marked by the sin of Adam are and will be, until
the end of time, reconciled and saved by Jesus, and even Adam is
allowed entrance into Paradise. The three days of the resurrection
of the Lord offer Jacobus de Voragine an opportunity to evoke the
promise of Paradise made to all men since their redemption by the
incarnation, the nativity, the passion, and the resurrection of Jesus.

   Jacobus de Voragine extends the time of reconciliation, which
for him begins with the resurrection of the Lord (Easter) and continues to Ascension, to Pentecost, and even a bit beyond, since it
ends with the commemorations of several saints just after Pentecost,
the last of them being Saint Pancratius, whose feast is celebrated on
May 12.

## The Ascension of the Lord

Contrary to his usual practice, Jacobus de Voragine discusses the
place in time of the Ascension and Pentecost without furnishing either liturgical details or stories connected with those days. He concentrates on the position and significance of the commemoration of
these events that mark the end of the Incarnation of the Lord and of
his stay on earth.

   As for the ascension of the Lord, he underlines in his very first
sentence the fact that that it took place forty days after Jesus's resurrection, thus returning once again to the number forty, which (as in

Lent) plays an important role in the rhythm of sacred time. He opens his chapter with the announcement that the ascension of the Lord poses seven essential questions: "where he ascended from; why he did not ascend immediately after the resurrection; . . . in what manner; with whom he ascended; by what merit he ascended; where he ascended to; and why he ascended."[4]

Jacobus de Voragine responds to the first of these questions by stating that Jesus rose to heaven from the Mount of Olives, "out toward Bethany," near Jerusalem, because that was where the apostles and the saintly women who accompanied Jesus were living. Thus Jacobus, who liked to tie people to a time and a place, inserts them into a society and a history. The ascension occurred in that place because it was where the society attached to Jesus lived and where he lived his earthly life. Jacobus gives three reasons for the forty-day period after the resurrection. First, it allowed the certitude of the Resurrection to be solidly established and it assured that the miracle of the Resurrection would be known to a larger number of human beings. Here we see one of the characteristics that Jacobus de Vorgine attached to time: time is a source of persuasion. The second reason was that Jesus wanted to bring consolation to the apostles over a period longer in duration than the three days of tribulation of his passion. Time, for Jacobus, is thus measured in terms of its affective connotation, and, as an optimist, he strives to arrange things in such a way that within sacred time (and in particular within the founding time of the incarnation of Christ on earth) periods of joy are longer than periods of sadness. Third, the forty days between Easter and Ascension can be explained, according to Jacobus de Voragine, by mystical means based on proportionality, an arithmetical practice that had developed within Christianity, along with the birth of Purgatory, in the late twelfth century. He states that "one day of trial yields a year of consolation"[5]; a day becomes an hour and an hour a moment: the duration of the perception of time was thus, for him, tied to the nature of an affective state. It might even be said that putting time in arithmetical terms in this manner accompanies the general trend within the Church to move from commemorating saints on the days of their martyrdom, thus associating the power of time with death, to the joyful transformation that turned these days of mourning into days of feasting. Jacobus de Voragine also adopts the arithmetic that the Christianity of his day tended to apply to religious life when he declares that, since Jesus remained dead for forty hours, the proportionality principle justifies the fact that his sojourn on earth after his Resurrection lasted forty days.

When he takes up the third problem—how Jesus ascended to heaven—Jacobus de Voragine stresses the rapidity of his rise and imagines men traveling through space in a prescientific utopian manner. He says:

Rabbi Moses [Moses Maimonides, 1135–1204], the great philosopher, tells us that each orbit or heaven of any of the planets is 500 years across, i.e., the distance from one side to the other is as far as someone could travel on a level road in 500 years, and the distance between one heaven and the next is also, he says, a journey of 500 years. Therefore, since there are seven heavens, from the center of the earth to the vault of the heaven of Saturn, the seventh heaven, there will be, according to Rabbi Moses, a journey that would take 7,000 years, and to the dome of the empyrean, 7,700; i.e., as far as one would go on a level road in 7,700 years if he lived that long, each year comprising 365 days and a day's march 40 kilometers, each kilometer being 2,000 paces or cubits long.[6]

Thus Christ returned to heaven in one leap, in the wink of an eye, and, given the logic of that miracle, Jacobus next cites Saint Ambrose, who states, "By a leap Christ came into this world,"[7] and concludes that in comparison to his eternity, his life on earth lasted only the time of one great leap. Here we again see Jacobus reconciling terrestrial time and divine time, one of the profound ideas that inspire the *Golden Legend*.

The rest of the *Golden Legend's* long chapter on the Ascension is little concerned with Jacobus de Voragine's reflections on time. He speaks at some length of heavens and angels. According to Christian doctrine, there are, it seems, several heavens piled up one on top of the other and inhabited by angels, who move about in them and can descend to earth for short or long visits. Thus the *Golden Legend* too is populated by a multitude of angels and demons who have relations with human time only during their descents to earth, which vary both in duration and in number. If angels and demons appear rarely in the present essay, it is because they are basically nontemporal beings. There is, however, a supreme heaven that Jacobus calls "supersubstantial" and that is the residence of God himself. That heaven, from which Christ came and to which he returns on Ascension Day, was accordingly connected with human time during the time of the Jesus's earthly incarnation, which is known to have lasted thirty-three years in human terms, from the nativity to the final resurrection, but which, in the scheme of divine time, was only a leap in time, just as the time of the ascension was but a leap in space.

## The Holy Spirit

Although Jacobus de Voragine places his chapter on Pentecost Sunday immediately after the chapter on the ascension, he does not use the term "Pentecost" in the title, even though the term was certainly known to him, given that he mentions the Pentecost sermon of Pope Leo I (440–41). Nor does he devote a chapter of the *Golden Legend* to the Trinity. The human time that he seeks to sacralize in this work centers on the incarnation of Christ. He may have found it impossible to exclude from his *summa* on time the Holy Spirit, who, using the apostles as intermediaries, came to earth to bring to mankind all the teachings that would fit them for salvation. Jacobus de Voragine may not have found a place in the *Golden Legend* to speak of the

Holy Trinity because the tripartite aspect of God did not seem to him to have any particular relation to time. But he did not want to leave the Holy Spirit out of his *summa*, because man's knowledge and use of time also depend on it, given that the divinity that renewed time was Jesus and that it was certainly not the Father alone who sent the Holy Spirit, but also Jesus, as John reports in his Gospel, where Jesus speaks to his disciples of the Paraclete—that is, of the Holy Spirit—telling them, "If I go, I will send him to you" (16:7).

As in his chapter on the ascension, Jacobus de Voragine does not talk about liturgy in this chapter on the Holy Spirit, nor does he include any narratives. For Jacobus, the two events that connect the inverse movements of the rising Christ and the descending Holy Spirit inspire no rites or events situated within terrestrial time. Still, he speaks in some detail about the number of times that the Holy Spirit has descended to earth (which implies a multiplicity of moments), and he indicates that Ascension and Pentecost together do define a specific time.

On the first point, Jacobus states that the Holy Spirit has descended to earth five times and in five forms, which show that it is able to enter time under different signs. Its first appearance was in the form of a dove that hovered over Christ on the day of his baptism. The second took the form of a luminous cloud that appeared above Christ on the day of his transfiguration. The third, according to John the Evangelist, was "in the visible form of breath" when Jesus appeared to his apostles on the day after his resurrection. In its fourth descent, the Holy Spirit came "in the appearance under fire" on a mountain to which the apostles had gone on Pentecost. Its fifth and most important descent was on Pentecost, when it appeared to the apostles as "parted tongues, as it were of fire."[8] This last appearance of the Holy Spirit laid the foundation for the mission subsequently taken on by the apostles and by all preachers. Jacobus de Voragine borrows here from Saint Bernard, the model preacher, noting that the ideal of Christian predication is preaching in which tongues of fire preach a law of fire in words of fire. Thus predication, the essential work of the Dominicans, is an activity that blazes fire. Among the periods of time, which vary greatly in their meaning and their objective, there thus exists a time of preaching that is also a time of fire. At the end of this chapter Jacobus de Voragine defines what he calls "the day of Pentecost," which he presents as a day of rest, love, and prayer.

## The Finding of the Holy Cross

The Finding of the Holy Cross, celebrated on May 3, is yet another historical time that Jacobus de Voragine includes in the time of reconciliation. Within Jacobus's sacralized time, there are feasts commemorating the discovery or translation dates of saints' relics, and there is no more sacred relic in Christianity than the cross of Christ. Jacobus de Voragine reviews several possible historical moments for its discovery, but Christians consider only the last of these to be the veritable and definitive finding date. The other possible moments of discovery are, in chronological order: by Adam's son Seth in the earthly paradise, by Solomon in Lebanon, by the queen of Sheba in Solomon's temple; by the Jews in the water of the pond,[9] and by Saint Helena on Mount Calvary on May 3. Hence Jacobus was willing to consider the notion that from the moment of Adam and Eve's creation in Paradise, their original sin could be foreseen and that, since the time of creation, there had existed wood destined to serve in another event that was also foreseeable, the incarnation of Christ come to earth to redeem original sin. But in his efforts to establish a calendar of these successive findings, Jacobus expresses doubt concerning these allegedly ancient dates. It is in the apocryphal Gospel of Nicodemus that the archangel Michael is reported to have told Seth that he would have to wait 5,500 years to obtain oil from the tree of mercy in order to restore the body of his father Adam to health. Jacobus adds skeptically, "this although it is believed that only 5,199 years elapsed from Adam's day to Christ's passion," plus the thirty-three years of Jesus's life. He further reports that the angel offered

Seth a shoot from the tree, to be planted on the Mount of Lebanon. Another text (which Jacobus suspects of being false) has this slip grow into a "great tree" that was still standing in Solomon's day. Jacobus de Voragine leaves it up to the reader to believe "any of this" or not, but he himself seems unconvinced.[10]

Jacobus de Voragine then turns to the historical version, which relates that after it has remained buried for over two hundred years, the true cross of Christ's passion was found by Saint Helena, the mother of Constantine. Thus he connects the discovery of the Holy Cross to the emperor Constantine's conversion to Christianity, an event that set off the rapid and sweeping conversion of the inhabitants of what is today Europe. This event, which remains historical, whether or not the cross that Helena discovered was the authentic cross on which Jesus suffered, illustrates the way in which Jacobus de Voragine emphasizes anything that might enhance the importance of the period from Christ's incarnation to his passion for the unfolding of time.

Given that the most important consequence of the incarnation and the resurrection was the appearance and development of Christianity, a necessary for condition for human salvation, Jacobus de Voragine takes advantage of the discovery of the Holy Cross to address another essential event, the conversion of Constantine. As was his wont when faced with multiple sources and traditions, he enumerates them, usually giving his opinion as he chooses the hypothesis that seems to him to have the most solid historical base and to be founded on the best sources. Thus he situates the conversion of Constantine at the battle near the Milvian bridge in 312, using as his principal source the *Historia ecclesiastica* of Eusebius of Caesarea, which serious scholars also consider the most reliable. Jacobus de Voragine then surveys the range of opinions regarding the date of Constantine's baptism. He does not state his preference, but he does indicate that the event took place during the pontificate of Pope Sylvester (314–335). What Jacobus considers of greater importance is the actual finding of Jesus's cross, because it provides material proof of his crucifixion and because it is, in a sense, the earliest and the most illustrious of the traces left on earth by the saints—that is, of their relics, given that the cross is an absolutely unique relic that gives witness not to a simple saint, but to God himself in the person of the incarnated Jesus. For Jacobus de Voragine, the time of the discovery of the True Cross is all the more important because it did not occur by chance, but resulted from the conversion of Constantine. It was in fact after receiving a vision that Constantine is reported to have sent his mother, Helena, to Jerusalem, with explicit instructions to search there for the remnants of the cross of Christ.

At this point Jacobus de Voragine feels the need to add something more about Helena, who was (admittedly, at the command of her son) the real discoverer of the True Cross. There are two reasons for this. First, Jacobus wants to show that this was a woman who was worthy of making such a discovery. And also because this gives him an excuse to tell an unusual story, his normal practice when he wants to move his audience or capture their interest. He subscribes to the tradition that Constantine's mother (who, after her death, became *Saint* Helena) was an innkeeper whom Constantine's father (also named Constantine) married on account of her beauty. Here Jacobus follows another of his principal sources, Saint Ambrose, in that he does not limit Helena's virtues to her beauty but indicates also that she was a woman of exceptional goodness. She cared for travelers who had fallen foul of robbers, and modeled her inn on the inn par excellence which was the manger in which the Lord was born.[11] What is more, she became a Christian before her son Constantine converted.

Jacobus de Voragine ends this long chapter on the finding of the Holy Cross, as he often does, with an *exemplum*, a morality tale that permits him to make full use of his talents as a narrator. The point of this particular *exemplum* is to show that the Holy Cross is a relic of such exceptional virtue and that when someone makes the sign of the cross in affirmation of their Christian faith, the cross is fully worthy of the gesture. The *exemplum* recounts the story of a good young notary deluded by a sorcerer who promises him great wealth if he will deny Christ. In order to impress the notary, the sorcerer surrounds him with demons and shows him Satan himself in the form of a "huge Ethiopian seated on a high throne." When the notary makes the sign of the cross, "the horde of demons vanished."[12] Later, when the notary goes into a church to pray before an image of Christ, the image's shining eyes follow him from left to right as he moves. This, Jacobus explains, is God's way of congratulating him and rewarding him for having resisted the demons by making the sign of the cross. Thus the chapter on the finding of the cross gives Jacobus de Voragine a chance to show how greatly the life and death of Jesus changed human time, which was henceforth endowed with a new defensive arm against the devil—the sign of the cross— that became to some extent a magical gesture sign, but one of good magic. This final *exemplum* also shows Jacobus de Voragine making full use of the images that Christianity admitted and validated within human time.

## The Greater and Lesser Litanies

As we have already seen, Jacobus de Voragine makes every effort to banish from Christian time all significant residues of earlier pagan time. But in a world in which even a citizen of Genoa such as himself had to recognize that most human labor takes place in the countryside, he was unable to erase from Christian time feast days dedicated to important liturgies that marked precise moments in the annual time cycle.

This chapter begins as follows: "The litanies occur twice in the year. The first time is on the feast of Saint Mark, and this is called the Greater Litany. The second, or Lesser Litany, falls on the three days before the feast of the Lord's ascension into heaven. The word 'litany' means prayer, supplication, rogation."[13] And indeed these are the offices and prayers that are usually called "rogations." They are invocations to God to provide fertility and abundance to the earth.

The first thing that Jacobus de Voragine does is to attach to Christian time these feast days, which are simply the remains of earlier pagan feasts dedicated to the same purposes. The Greater Litany is connected with the feast of Saint Mark and the Lesser with the Ascension of Christ. Jacobus does more, however. He assigns a date of origin in Christian history to these special temporal periods—a date that was in fact that of the era in which the Church solemnly ratified the maintenance of these pagan holidays under a Christian guise. According to him, one of the litanies was known as the "greater" for three reasons: because it was instituted by Pope Gregory the Great (590–604) in Rome, "mistress and head of the world"; because that was where both the body of Peter, the chief of the apostles, and the apostolic see were located; and, finally, it was established in 590 in the hope that it would drive away an epidemic of the black plague by persuading the faithful to give up the feasting, gaming, and voluptuous living that were the causes of "a widespread and deadly pestilence."[14]

The Lesser Litany was said to have been instituted by Saint Mamertus, bishop of Vienne, in the reign of the emperor Leo, clearly a reference to the Byzantine emperor Leo I, who, according to Jacobus began to reign in 458. This is quite close to the actual date of 457. Jacobus once again attempts to give the day a more Christian character by turning the meaning of "rogations" toward penance. Thus he calls the Greater Litany "the Black Crosses" because people wore the black garments of penitents on that day and in the churches the altars were shrouded with sackcloth, a coarse fabric that signifies penitence and mortification. Jacobus de Voragine, who so often speaks of joyous celebrations involving music and banners, here instead describes the processions with black crosses that marked these days and the ringing of mourning bells that evoked the time, between the original sin and the coming to earth of Christ, when the devil reigned over the world. Rather than an appeal to joy, then, rogations were an evocation of the end of terrors. Since we are viewing the *Golden Legend* as a *summa* on time, I should mention that

Jacobus de Voragine (in this chapter, explicitly) expresses a lack of enthusiasm for springtime, which is for him, as Alain Boureau and his collaborators have so rightly remarked,[15] a bad moment of the year, one that engenders war, famine, and fleshly urges. We can see how insistently Jacobus de Voragine strives to distance Christian time from pagan time, for if the pagan celebrations of rogations were indeed intended to chase away hunger with the help of the gods, Jacobus greatly broadens their functions.

The presentation of these two litanies as celebrations meant to chase away evil is also evident in Jacobus de Voragine's description of devils who take part in the processions. These demons in dragon shape were, in their successive representations, expressions of time: "The custom obtains of carrying a dragon with a long tail stuffed with straw or some such material: the first two days it is carried in front of the cross, and the third day, with the tail empty, behind the cross. The significance of this is that on the first day, before the Law, and on the second, under the Law, the devil reigned in this world, but on the third, the day of grace, he was expelled from his realm by the passion of Christ."[16]

## Saint Ambrose

Ambrose, as we have seen, was one of Jacobus de Voragine's major sources, thanks to his prominent role in the creation of Christian liturgy and, consequently, of liturgical time. Again our Dominican seeks to explain Ambrose's profundity by an etymology of his name. He proposes three possible meanings that are, as in fact often happens, rather close to one another. The first is that Ambrose comes from *ambra*, or amber, a highly fragrant and precious substance. Ambrose was "precious to the Church and spread a pleasing fragrance both in his speech and in his actions." A second etymology adds to "amber" *syos*, which means "God," which would make Ambrose "the amber of God" and "the good odor of Christ in every place." Finally, "Ambrose" can be derived from *ambrosia*, "the food of the angels," and from *ambrosium*, "the heavenly honeycomb."[17] As is evident, all of these etymologies turn on the notion of a good smell. Ambrose thus furthers Jacobus de Voragine's goal of giving the cyclical time of the liturgy a fragrance of perfume and incense. There follows a summary of the life of Ambrose, a segment of time marked by meaningful and symbolic moments. In the first of these, Ambrose's face and mouth was covered by a swarm of bees that then "soared upward to such a height that the human eye could barely follow them." Ambrose's father, seeing this, is reported to have said, "If this child lives, something great will come of him." The second symbolic moment came when Ambrose, now an adolescent, offered his own right hand to his sister to be kissed as he had seen her kiss the hands of priests. She refused, but the incident reflects Ambrose's instinctive sense that his would be a religious life. Indeed, Jacobus de Voragine reports later that four years after Ambrose had become a bishop, his sister came to see him and kissed his hand and he said to her, smiling, "See, I told you back then that you would kiss this bishop's hand!" A third critical juncture in his life was his election as bishop and the extraordinary manner in which it took place. A great commotion had arisen between Catholics and Arian heretics, and in the midst of the fracas a child's voice was heard crying, "Ambrose for bishop!" This event refers back to the etymological introduction to the chapter, in which Jacobus de Voragine stressed the fact that Ambrose had always been close to children. We might recall, in this connection, that the thirteenth century witnessed a rise of the importance of childhood in Christianity, a trend related to the official rise of the cult of the Infant Jesus.

Next Jacobus de Voragine summarizes the time of the young priest's initiation into his functions. Ambrose was baptized rather late, eight days before he became a bishop. Time is presented here in terms of age: in the early centuries of Christianity, it was common both for a man to be baptized late in life and for him to become a bishop at an early age. Both Christian time and Church time had evolved before Jacobus de Vorgine appeared on the scene. Jacobus goes on to relate several anecdotes in which Ambrose plays a part in his role as a bishop.

Finally, Jacobus writes at some length on the eight qualities that make Ambrose worthy of imitation. The first is his generosity, in particular toward the poor: Jacobus de Voragine belonged to a mendicant order of the thirteenth century, the great century of alms in the Middle Ages. The second is his purity, for he remained a virgin. The third, his firmness in the faith. The fourth, his eagerness for martyrdom. Fifth was his perseverance in prayer. Sixth, the abundance of his tears. Seventh, his unyielding courage. And his eighth quality was the purity of his doctrine. Here Jacobus de Voragine cites Augustine, who quotes Pelagius "the heresiarch" as having said, "The blessed bishop Ambrose, in whose books the Roman faith shines, emerges like a flower among Latin writers."[18] Jacobus adds that Ambrose was the greatest authority of his time, as such doctors of olden times as Augustine valued his teachings above all others. Here Jacobus de Voragine evokes the period of history that was probably for him the most important, which explains why certain modern authors have reproached this a man of a new religious order for being also a nostalgic admirer of ancient times. I see no nostalgia in Jacobus de Voragine. Admiration, yes, for the strength that the early Christians needed to have, but it seems to me that he sees in time, which is a gift of God, above all an instrument for explaining the march of humanity and a means whereby men, guided by the lessons of liturgical time and the exemplary character of the time of the saints, may achieve perfection.

## Saint George

The figure of Saint George also tells us about Jacobus de Voragine's interest in Christian time, a time within which Saint George commands Jacobus's attention but also poses some problems for him. Saint George came to prominence in Western Christian hagiography at a quite late date. He was rediscovered in the age of the crusades and, as Alain Boureau and his colleagues have rightly recognized, his cult owed much to Richard the Lionhearted and the kings of England. Given that the feast of Saint George (April 25) was not proclaimed until the Council of Oxford in 1222, the long chapter dedicated to him appears only in the version of the *Golden Legend* that Jacobus de Voragine reworked toward the end of his life. By then the most celebrated episode in the saint's history was his killing of the dragon who was holding a princess prisoner. Indeed the thirteenth century became the century of Saint George to some extent because of Jacobus's contribution to the saint's reputation. At the end of the century, Saint George, who had become the patron saint of knights (the most important lay figures in Western Christianity) and the patron saint of England (thanks to the efforts of England's kings), also became the patron saint of Genoa, the city that our Dominican served as archbishop. One might almost say that for Jacobus de Voragine, who has been reproached for concentrating too much on the saints of the earliest days of Christianity, Saint George was in fact a near contemporary.

At first Jacobus de Voragine seems hard pressed to establish the etymology of the saint's name. The basic sense, which comes from *geos* (earth) and *orge* (to work, to cultivate), does not have any particular connection with the holy warrior that George had become by the thirteenth century. Jacobus thus uses a text of Augustine's to draw a meaning out of that etymology that reflects honor on the saint. He stresses the predominance of the color green, the color of purity, and the fact that in order to supervise the cultivated lands put under his protection, George had to remain "on the heights" and scorn inferior things. Another etymology connects Saint George to pilgrimage and conciliation. Immediately after these etymological reflections, however, Jacobus de Voragine notes that there is no sure record of George's martyrdom, and that the Council of Nicaea therefore relegated accounts of his martyrdom to the apocryphal writings. He manages to find a place for George in historical time, however, by stating that he was born in Cappadocia.

One day, Jacobus relates, George arrived in a city that was being terrified by a dragon to which the city was obliged to make a yearly sacrifice of a young man or a young woman chosen by lot. The year when the victim's lot fell on the only daughter of the city's king, George promised to kill the dragon if the king and his people converted to Christianity. This indeed happened, and Jacobus de Voragine recounts several episodes marked by various miracles due to visions of God. Saint George was martyred soon after the year 296 by order of the prefect Dacian, who served under the emperors Diocletian and Maximian. Although he managed to connect George with his preferred sources, Augustine and Gregory of Tours, Jacobus ends his chapter on the saint by linking him with the real historical moment for which he is best known, the crusades. In order to do so, he relies on a *History of Antioch* written by a historian of the crusades. The most important episode shows Saint George clad in white armor and bearing a red cross, appearing before crusaders who were encountering difficulties in their assault on Jerusalem. George leads them up a ladder, helps them to scale the walls of Jerusalem, and they take the city. This brief narrative allows Jacobus de Voragine to place George (albeit by means of a miracle) within the unfolding of history and to justify his role as the patron saint of knights.

## Saint Mark, Evangelist

Since it is my claim that Jacobus de Voragine demonstrates, in the *Golden Legend*, a vigorous interest in historical and chronological truth, it is only fitting to furnish an example of the errors that he commits in this area, errors that, in my opinion, are not due to any lack of respect for historical time. A better explanation is that, despite the care that he takes to consult an abundance of dependable sources, he obviously did not have the benefit of the hagiographic scholarship that reached its peak only with the Bollandists and especially in the nineteenth century. The resulting text is not always free of errors, but a search for truth is always present. Thus, after giving the etymology of the name "Mark" as either *marchus*, "sublime by mandate," or *marcus*, "a heavy hammer,"[19] a reference to his Gospel, which crushes pagans and heretics, Jacobus describes the missions that Mark is supposed to have received from Saint Peter, in particular, his mission to Alexandria. Here Jacobus describes a real, historical event that left a profound mark on history: the purchase or theft by Venetian merchants (a theft considered legitimate because it was committed against pagans) of the relics of Saint Mark in Alexandria, where the evangelist is supposed to have met martyrdom at pagan hands. The Venetian merchants, men who had extensive commercial ties with the East, brought Saint Mark's relics back to Venice in 467, according to Jacobus de Voragine. It happens, however, to be an established fact that this highly important event took place in the year 828. Our Genoese renders homage to Venice, Genoa's rival, by noting that the Venetians built "a wondrously beautiful church" in honor of Saint Mark.[20]

Jacobus de Voragine ends his chapter on Saint Mark with a historical *exemplum* that involves the appearance of the saint at the bedside of a dying young Dominican in "the convent of the Order of Friars Preachers" in Pavia "about the year of the Lord 1212."[21] Let us repeat again then, that Jacobus de Voragine lived in his century and had a great interest in his century and, combining space and time as he always did, he knew that the Venetian saint had a broad resonance in Northern Italy.

## Saint Peter Martyr

The case of the first Dominican inquisitor to have been assassinated (on April 6, 1252, on the road from Como to Milan by paid killers in the service of certain Milanese notables devoted to the Cathar heresy) furnishes Jacobus de Voragine with an unexpected opportunity to devote to the date of that assassination a chapter on the first martyr of his order, declared a saint in 1253. In canonizing him the pope set the date of his feast at April 29. Even though Jacobus de Voragine redacted the first version of the *Golden Legend* in 1262–1264, he seems to have added the life of Saint Peter Martyr only in the final version that he wrote not long before his death. This means that he could use as a source not only the pontifical bull of canonization, but also the official life of the saint. This was redacted by the Dominican Thomas Agni de Lentino, at the request of the Order, and was a work that all the libraries of the Order of Preachers were obligated to acquire in 1275. That did not stop Jacobus de Voragine from producing a version of the saint's life that, while conforming to a recent and well-known reality, he nonetheless conceived in his own fashion. First he states that Peter, who is also called "Peter of Verona" after the city in which he was born, is a "new" martyr. That word is highly important for Jacobus's conception of time. It has often been said that the Middle Ages was a period hostile to the very idea of novelty, which was thought to be nearly heretical. In my opinion, that cast of mind was limited to a small segment of monastic society of the early centuries of the Middle Ages. As Father Marie-Humbert Vicaire has shown in his *Histoire de saint Dominique*, the mendicant orders born at the start of the thirteenth century claimed newness as a characteristic and almost as a title to glory. Jacobus de Voragine takes advantage of the occasion to indicate that his own era and his region had been strongly affected by heresy. Peter of Verona was born into a family of heretics. His entrance into the Order of Preachers and his behavior for the first thirty years of his life illustrate the difficulties facing the men who entered the Order and their strength of character, and our Genoese author emphasizes that Milan, because of the number of heretics there and the fact that they "occupied places of secular power,"[22] could be considered the capital of heresy. By the large number of miracles that Peter Martyr performed it could be said that Jacobus de Voragine connected the new Dominican saint to the saintly martyrs of earlier ages and, in particular, to those of the earliest times, all the while insisting on the fact that Saint Peter Martyr performed his miracles against contemporary heretics and in favor of the contemporary faithful. The character of several of his miracles shows that the efficacy of a saint can be translated in new ways from one time to another. Thus one miracle takes place while its recipient and his companions are looking at a painting. In another, which occurs in Utrecht in the milieu of the textile crafts, women sitting by the side of the street spinning cry out that they suspect the Dominicans of having invented a martyr to raise money, thus broaching the question of the relationship between money and alms that was so characteristic of the thirteenth century.[23] Another miracle concerns a student in Montpellier, which brings the new world of the universities into the universe of miracles. Another miracle bears witness to the importance for demography of multiple miscarriages. Yet another shows the passion for gambling that was developing within Christianity in the thirteenth century. And yet another brings doctors onto the scene and shows that medieval society was making some progress in the area of health care. There had always been miracles, but now a new society was profiting from them. Time also renews the domain of the miraculous.

# 9

# The Time
# of Pilgrimage

After the time of reconciliation, which stretches from the Resurrection to Ascension and Pentecost, when Christ, by his incarnation, his passion, and his resurrection, permitted time to reconcile humanity with God, comes the time of pilgrimage. Humanity, marching always in step with a time that has now become eschatological, leading to the end of time and the hope of salvation, is like a pilgrim on his way, for the end of time in eternity has not yet come.

This time of pilgrimage progresses from Saint Urbain and his feast on May 18 to Saints Barlaam and Josaphat on November 27, and it includes just under a hundred saints. Jesus, who has returned to heaven, does not appear in this time of pilgrimage, but his saintly mother, the Blessed Virgin Mary, both appears and disappears within it. She appears on the feast of her Nativity on September 8 and on that of her ascension (August 15), while the saints appear on November 1, All Saints Day, and on the feast (instituted in the eleventh and twelfth centuries) of all the deceased faithful on November 2. Finally, we shall see the *Golden Legend* coming to its end with two exceptional chapters, one of which, nominally about Saint Pelagius, is in fact an example of the construction of historical time, while the other and final chapter, "The Dedication of a Church," presents the buildings in which sacralization—of both the temporale and sanctorale—occurs, and which are the places within which sacred time can best be approached on earth.

Because the Blessed Virgin Mary outlived Jesus after his resurrection, two of the principal feasts that concern her are situated within the time of pilgrimage in which humanity lives, after the incarnation, the passion, and the resurrection of Jesus. Jacobus de Voragine had devoted a chapter to the Purification of the Blessed Virgin Mary in the section he dedicated to the time of deviation, but since that feast celebrates her churching after the birth of Christ, it also (and perhaps above all) celebrates a first important moment in the terrestrial life of the incarnated Infant Jesus. Although the Assumption of the Blessed Virgin Mary, celebrated on August 15, comes earlier in the calendar than the Birth of the Blessed Virgin Mary, celebrated on September 8, and is placed before it in the *Golden Legend*, I shall reverse my commentary on these two chapters to examine what these feasts contribute to our understanding of the sacred time of humanity.

## The Birth of the Blessed Virgin Mary

I will begin, then, with the birth of the Blessed Virgin Mary. Since the chapter that concerns her has no need to seek for the meaning of her name through etymology, Jacobus de Voragine opens it instead with a search for her ethnic, historical, and social origins, which is yet another way to value time. He strives to show that the Virgin Mary was born from "the tribe of Judah and the royal stock of David."[1] Clearly, even for a member of a mendicant order (although Jacobus was a Dominican, not a Franciscan), social rank and, even more, royal identity were determining factors in the evaluation of a human being. Next, Jacobus—probably influenced by problems of kinship and consanguinity, which were taking on growing importance in medieval society—does his best to show that Mary was a cousin of Elizabeth, the mother of Saint John the Baptist, even though one belonged to a royal tribe and the other to a priestly tribe, between which there could have been no possible kinship in ancient Israel. Citing Bede, Jacobus advances the hypothesis that in the more recent period of Jewish history when Mary lived and gave birth to Jesus, such an alliance was permitted. Thus we see that in his many-faceted conception of time, a conception in which he strives for totality, Jacobus de Voragine also takes into account the evolution of customs and of the rules of society as they function throughout history.

Jacobus de Voragine encounters another problem related to duration when he comes to the birth of the Blessed Virgin Mary, and this concerns the time period within which a woman is able to bear a child. He finds himself obliged to speak about questions of female sterility in sacred history. He underlines the fact that the Old Testament contains instances of childbearing late in life made possible by the will of God: Sarah waited until she was ninety years old to give birth to Isaac; Rachel was sterile for a long time before she gave birth to Joseph. Moreover, children conceived by an older mother were often among the strongest and healthiest. This was true of Samson and the saintly Samuel, both of whom had mothers who had long remained barren. Thus Elizabeth's birth to a mother who had long been sterile was not exceptional. Here Jacobus de Voragine intends to show that despite their terrestrial kinship, God did not consider Mary and Elizabeth as on the same plane. Elizabeth was not unique: as the daughter of a long-barren mother, she belongs to a category with Old Testament antecedents. Mary, whose Immaculate Conception was not proclaimed until the nineteenth century and was an extremely controversial idea in the Middle Ages, was, in spite of everything, a unique case in the history of humanity and in biblical history, for as the mother of Jesus she was the mother of God. Jacobus de Voragine turns next to the childhood of Mary to outline the time periods that governed the lives of the young virgins in the

Temple. This concerns both forms of time and uses of time. He states that the virgins were expected to remain in the Temple until they were fourteen, at which point they were considered to have come of age and might legitimately marry. He also states that the young Mary spent her days in alternating periods of prayer and manual work, thus serving, as we know, as a model for the monks of the early Middle Ages, though not for our Dominican, who was a member of an order of a different sort that was new in the thirteenth century. According to Jacobus de Voragine, who cites Saint Jerome, Mary devoted the time from dawn to the third hour to prayer, worked at weaving from the third to the ninth hour, then "she prayed without stopping"[2] until Vespers. She was the beneficiary of a rare favor, for she had an angel who acted as a clock, bringing her meal to her when the moment came to stop praying.

Jacobus de Voragine also shows how the commemoration of the segment of time that is the life of a person as exceptional as the Virgin Mary can change over the course of history. At first, the day of the birth of the Blessed Virgin was unknown to the faithful. Then one day (Jacobus does not specify just when) a holy man revealed to the pope that every year on September 8 he heard "choirs of angels chanting solemn paeans," and God told him that "on this day the glorious Virgin Mary had been born to the world." At that point (and Jacobus still does not specify exactly when this was), September 8 was instituted as the feast of the Birth of the Blessed Virgin Mary. This feast later underwent another historical reversal, and celebration of the octave of the Birth of the Blessed Virgin fell into disuse, but—and here Jacobus returns to history—Pope Innocent IV ("a native of Genoa" and hence Jacobus's compatriot) reinstated it. It soon fell into neglect again, only to be restored in yet another historical context which coincided with Jacobus's lifetime, a restitution that he hoped would be definitive. This occurred during the long conclave that followed the death of Gregory IX in 1241. The cardinals, who were divided among themselves, decided that whoever came out of the conclave as pope would definitively reestablish the feast of the

Birth of the Blessed Virgin Mary. Jacobus's own time thus witnessed troubles brought on by contingent events, and in treating this feast, Jacobus was so acutely aware of the importance and complexity of the problem of time for humanity that he felt obliged to recall that the Church solemnizes only three birthdays: those of Christ, the Virgin Mary, and John the Baptist, and that these three birthdays "mark three spiritual births." In doing so, Jacobus expresses the idea that a purely terrestrial birth (or one realized by incarnation in the case of Christ) depended on the nature of the newborn child for its lesser or greater spiritual force and symbolic value.

Next Jacobus de Voragine turns to two quite special liturgical times that frame major feast days. These are the vigil, or eve, of a feast and the octave, or eight days following a feast. Jacobus adds that these three birth days do have octaves "because they all look forward to the octave of the resurrection."[3] The feast of the Birth of Mary however has no vigil because it takes place during a period of penitence, and penitence takes the place of a vigil. Time finally makes its appearance in this chapter in little stories, *exempla*, and miracles of the kind that adorn the end of all the chapters of the *Golden Legend*. All of these are more or less historical in nature, and Jacobus de Voragine assigns more or less precise dates to them in order to persuade the listener or reader of their concrete reality. In one instance, a thief who had committed many robberies but "had deep devotion to Blessed Mary," was condemned to be hanged but Mary supported him, holding him up in mid-air for three days. Struck by this marvel, those who had condemned him cut him down and let him go free. Another example concerns a priest who knew no other Mass than that of the Blessed Virgin Mary and was reprimanded and forbidden by his bishop from saying Mary's Mass. The following night Mary appeared to the bishop, "rebuked him severely," and told him that "he would die within thirty days unless he reinstated the priest in his parish." Another story regards a figure who later became famous in art and literature, Theophilus, a fervent devotee of the Virgin. Theophilus gave himself to the devil, but, repenting that act, renounced his contract with him on the instigation of the Virgin, who appeared to him. He died in peace three days later. Jacobus gives this imaginary event as a real one that took place in Sicily in 537. Another story in which Jacobus shows his exceptional talent as a narrator of titillating tales is dated to around the year 1100 and located near Lyon. In it Jacobus tells of a woman who, because she was jealous of her daughter, arranged to have her son-in-law strangled by two peasants. Stricken with remorse, she prays to the Virgin and, thanks to her, emerges untouched from the flames into which she had been thrown as a punishment for her crime. Finally, "in the time of Theodosius the Elder" (346–395), the famous saint John of Damascus was the object of a miracle granted by the Virgin Mary. Unjustly accused, John's hand was cut off on the order of the emperor, but by a miracle the Virgin restored him to physical integrity.

## The Assumption of the Blessed Virgin Mary

The Assumption of the Blessed Virgin Mary, which Jacobus de Voragine presents before her birth because it is celebrated in the Roman calendar on August 15, before the celebration of her birth on September 8, is one of the longest chapters of the *Golden Legend*.[4] Jacobus states at the outset that the best description of this event can be found "in a small apocryphal book attributed to John the Evangelist."[5] This statement a good illustration of the way in which Jacobus de Voragine uses apocryphal texts, treating them as having a historical value equivalent to that of the canonical texts officially recognized by the Church. Since the life of Jesus incarnated is, as we have seen, the center of time and the force that propels time, the chapter on the Assumption of the Blessed Virgin Mary begins after the terrestrial life of Christ. It opens with a description of the life of Mary as it unfolded on earth during that period, as she moved from place to place, devoutly visiting all the sites sacred to the memory of her divine son: the places "where he had been baptized, had fasted, had prayed, had suffered, died, and been buried, rose, and ascended into heaven."[6] Citing Epiphanius, who translated the Greek chroniclers into Latin for Cassiodorus in the fifth century, Jacobus states that Mary lived on earth twenty-four years after the ascension of Jesus. She was fourteen when she conceived him, fifteen when she gave birth to him; she lived with him for thirty-three years and survived him for twenty-four years more. Hence she died at the age of seventy-two. Jacobus de Vorgine applied his always-critical intellect to this calculation, however, and began to doubt that she survived her son for such a long time and died at such an old age. Given that she died surrounded by the apostles, which seems irrefutable, it is probable that she did not live much longer than the time of their preaching in Judea and the nearby regions—which is to say, twelve years—and that she rose to heaven aged no more than about sixty. Our Dominican relies here on the *Ecclesiastical History* of Eusebius, who seems to him much more reliable and whom contemporary historiography also usually considers the best-informed and most serious source. Jacobus de Voragine dedicates several pages to the agony and the dormition of Mary, a major iconographic theme in the Middle Ages. This provides him with an opportunity to show an angel appearing to Mary to announce her coming ascent to heaven; to describe the dying Mary on her deathbed, surrounded by the apostles; and, after her death, to show the apostles deposing her in her tomb and seating themselves around her, a scene that is followed by an appearance of Jesus, surrounded by angels, and asking the apostles how they would like him to show his love and gratitude to his earthly mother. The apostles answer that they think he should bring his mother's body to life and enthrone her at his right hand for Eternity.[7] Jacobus de Voragine goes on to praise the Virgin, citing famous texts, Saint Jerome in particular. Then, as is his custom, he ends the chapter with stories, *exempla*, and accounts of miracles accomplished by Mary. The first of these is set in the city of Bourges and is dated to 707. A Jewish father throws his young son, who has taken communion with his schoolmates, into a "white-hot furnace."[8] The child implores the beautiful woman whose image he has seen for aid, and she saves him from the flames, for she is none other than the Virgin Mary. In another story the Virgin Mary chases devils away from the monastery of Saint-Gall and away from Ebroïn, the seventh-century mayor of the palace in Neustria. Finally, Jacobus reproduces a long passage from Augustine in praise of the most holy assumption of the Virgin. Hence, despite his evocations of the terrestrial life and the historical cult of the Virgin Mary, he ends this lengthy chapter with a quotation from his greatest master, Augustine. Above all, he insists on the eternity of the Virgin Mary, who thus seems placed in these pages on the same level as the Christ to whom she gave birth rather than being incarnated for only a limited terrestrial life. Jacobus de Voragine does not speak explicitly of the Immaculate Conception, but according to him, Mary did remain pure and untouched by corruption.[9]

## The Exaltation of the Holy Cross

The last chapter in the period of pilgrimage concerns the Exaltation of the Holy Cross and is thus connected with the incarnation of Jesus, the temporal event that stands at the center of the *Golden Legend*. The cross, the instrument of Jesus's passion, had already been the object of a chapter dedicated to its finding by Helena, the sainted mother of the emperor Constantine, the first Roman emperor who converted to Christianity. In this new chapter, which celebrates a commemoration that takes place on September 14, Jacobus de Voragine stresses above all the fact that the cross of the passion had a history within historical time, after the death and resurrection of the incarnated Jesus. We have seen how Helena accomplished the marvelous deed of finding the cross in the Orient. In this new chapter, Jacobus de Voragine clarifies other essential aspects of the history of the Holy Cross. In general, that history is one of a growing embellishment of the cross's story, that progressed as the Holy Cross itself lay buried. Originally a symbol and an instrument of death, it was on its way to becoming eternal throughout history, thus offering an opportunity—a rare occurrence in the *Golden Legend*—to recall that the time that dominates all others is eschatological time.

This chapter also makes it clear that the feast of the Exaltation of the Holy Cross commemorates a historical event. According to Jacobus de Voragine, when Chosroës, the king of the Persians, conquered "all the earth's kingdoms"[10] (most notably those in the Near East), he took away from Jerusalem a fragment of the Holy Cross. The Christian emperor, Heraclius, declared war on Chosroës, however, and, after vanquishing the Persian king and personally cutting off his head, he brought the piece of the Holy Cross back to Jerusalem. This is what the feast day celebrates. Always scrupulous when it came to his sources (or at least much more so than modern historians claim), Jacobus later gives a different version of events, one borrowed, he tells us, from chronicles to which he clearly gives little credence. Those sources state that Heraclius did not return the Holy Cross to Jerusalem, but rather took it to Constantinople. One of the miracles that Jacobus relates, as was his custom, takes on special importance because it dates an event that affects the order of liturgy and that is reported to have taken place in the city of Berith (modern Beirut) in Syria. An image of Jesus on the Cross that had been left in a house is reported to have been trampled by a group of Jews, who "thrust a lance into the image of his body," as had been done to Jesus himself on the cross. "A copious flow of blood and water" issued from the wound.[11] The Jews, terrified by this miracle, converted to Christianity and turned their synagogues into churches. What is more interesting to us is that Christians, who until then had consecrated only altars, in homage to this event (which occurred in the year 750) developed the habit of consecrating entire churches. This miraculous happening is reported by Jacobus de Voragine in a manner that emphasizes the critical importance that he gives to everything connected with liturgical time. Other narrations of marvelous or miraculous happenings attributed to the Holy Cross that Jacobus gives at the end of the chapter also have a temporal character and relate either to historical time or symbolic time. One of these adds a special richness to the significance that Jacobus assigns to the various forms of time in the *Golden Legend*. In a story toward the end of the chapter on the Exaltation of the Holy Cross, Jacobus describes a series of demons reporting back to their master, Satan, about the misdeeds they have done. Satan asks each of them, "How much time did this take you?"[12] Thus we see here that time, an essential creation of God and an essential object in the redemption of humanity by Jesus incarnated, is also a central preoccupation of the devil. When two of the demons report to Satan that their misdeeds took them thirty days to accomplish, Satan smartly reprimands them for having taken too long. A final demon, who admits that he spent forty years in a desert and finally got one monk to commit one sin of the flesh, is much praised by Satan. As is often the case in the *Golden Legend*, in the evocation of either good or bad periods of time "thirty" appears as an inauspicious number, while "forty"—particularly in relation to Lent—is auspicious.

What I intend to do now is to seek out, within the sanctorale of the time of pilgrimage, those saints whose history and nature, for a variety of reasons, Jacobus de Voragine particularly stresses and whose stories seem to me to contain elements that reinforce the description of the *Golden Legend* as the *summa* on time that I believe it to be. To this end, I have chosen twenty of the ninety-eight saints Jacobus writes about, and I shall begin with two of them, Saint Stephen and Saint John the Baptist, whose feast days commemorate a particularly important event that occurred during or after their own lifetimes.

## The Finding of Saint Stephen, the First Martyr, and the Beheading of Saint John the Baptist

Saint Stephen—as Jacobus de Voragine takes pains to emphasize in the chapter he devotes to him—possesses a degree of superiority over his colleagues in the sanctorale because he was, historically, the first Christian martyr. His feast day is December 26, the day after the Nativity of Christ. Stephen's body disappeared after his martyrdom, which explains the importance of its finding. During his life Stephen had been a part of the first Christian community in Jerusalem, which formed immediately after Jesus's sojourn on earth, hence in the first century. The finding, according to Jacobus, occurred in 417, a date that he takes to be the seventh year of the reign of the emperor Honorius (who in fact mounted the throne of Byzantium in 395). An account of the finding of the body of Saint Stephen was written soon after the event, allegedly by a priest named Lucian, who credits himself with the actual finding and whose text can be found in a number of works of the early Middle Ages. That original source claims that the finding took place in something resembling a cemetery near Jerusalem where, once disinterred, Stephen's remains gave out the "sweet odor" characteristic of saintly persons, the famous "odor of sanctity."

Jacobus de Voragine next offers an explanation having to do with the calendar that is interesting because it shows one of the ways in which time can be manipulated by man, especially by the Church, machinations that are tolerated by God and that can radically alter the order of the calendar. Jacobus states that the finding of the body of Saint Stephen took place on the same day as his martyrdom; that is, on December 26. He further claims that Saint Stephen's feast had taken place on August 2 until the tenth century, when the Church, thinking that the protomartyr should be commemorated right after the feast of the Nativity of Jesus, switched the date to December 26. The date of the feast of the finding of his body remained on August 2.[13]

Saint John the Baptist has a right to a chapter of his own within the time of pilgrimage, on June 24. The chapter of the *Golden Legend* that speaks of the beheading of Saint John, celebrated on August 29, is of special interest, however, due to its treatment of time. For one thing, the event is dated from the birth date of King Herod (*natalis sui dies*), a secular celebration that became widely established in the Christian West, but not until the late fifteenth century (as Jean-Claude Schmitt has recently shown[14]). Jacobus de Voragine next states that the decapitation of Saint John the Baptist actually took place during the Jewish feast of the Azymes (unleavened bread, hence Passover) preceding Easter. Moreover, it was in order to distinguish the feast of John the Baptist from the greater feast of the Resurrection of the Lord that Christians moved John's second feast to the heart of summer. As we can see, in the sanctorale in any event, Jacobus de Voragine permits calendar manipulations on the part of men or, more precisely, on the part of the Church.

## Multiple Saints

Of the twenty chapters from the sanctorale of the time of pilgrimage that I have chosen to discuss, some are devoted not to a single saint or a pair of saints, as is usually the case, but to a group of saints. The simple fact that there is only one feast day and only one date for these groups authorizes us to see these days as a particular kind of sacred time. The chapters in question are: "The Seven Brothers, Sons of Saint Felicity"; "The Seven Sleepers"; "Saint Maurice and His Companions"; "Saints Dionysius, Rusticus, and Eleutherius"; "The Eleven Thousand Virgins"; and "The Four Crowned Martyrs."

Jacobus de Voragine introduces the Seven Brothers (feast day July 10) as the seven sons of Saint Felicity. It is known that these seven saintly persons were placed in the catacombs during the same period (if not on the same day), but they were not blood relatives.[15] Jacobus de Voragine situates the common martyrdom of these seven putative brothers around the year 110. He seems to have brought them together for two reasons: first, because in ancient thought the number seven was a symbol of perfection; second, because this simultaneous martyrdom gives Jacobus an opportunity to present the "super-martyr," a type defined by the number of martyrs killed at once. Indeed, Saint Felicity declares that she wants her sons to be martyred before she was, and before her eyes, so as to add to her own suffering as she was dying the pain of watching the martyrdom of her beloved children. In doing so she manages to reverse the usual temporal sequence of the executioner's work. It seemed natural and, in a certain way, more humane to kill the mother before the sons. Jacobus concludes "Rightly therefore have I said that this woman was more than martyr."[16]

The Seven Sleepers were seven Christians who lived in Ephesus and held high-ranking offices in the palace that the emperor owned there for his stays in that city.[17] Decius (249–251), a notorious persecutor of Christians, wanted to subject them to martyrdom when he came to Ephesus, but God performed a miracle that he granted to certain believers: he put them to sleep. When Decius found he could not awaken the seven, he ordered the cave in which they lived walled up while they were still asleep in it. Three hundred seventy-two years after the death of Decius—according to Jacobus de Voragine, during the thirtieth year of the reign of Theodosius—that very Christian emperor was aggrieved to see that a heresy was spreading that denied the resurrection of the dead. God then performed the following miracle. Guided by a young man sent by God, Theodosius went to the place where the Seven Sleepers had been enclosed and asked God to resuscitate them. Since they were still alive, God permitted them to die, but then did indeed resuscitate them. Always a skeptic, Jacobus de Voragine points out that the miracle of the Seven Sleepers must have taken place in the year 448, and that the Sleepers therefore had not slept 372 years but only 196. Once again, we see how, in his treatment of time, Jacobus de Voragine combines respect for miracles with source criticism, particularly of oral sources.[18]

## Saint Maurice and His Companions

Maurice, whose feast day is September 22, is a military saint and the only Christian saint who is black. In the etymological introduction to his chapter on Maurice, Jacobus de Voragine recalls that, according to Isidore of Seville, the probable origin of his name was the Greek word *mauron*, which means "black." Maurice is based on a legendary personality of pagan antiquity, the chief of the Theban legion, a famous military troop that appears in Greek history but was transported by Christianity to Egypt and to the city of Thebes, on the Nile. Jacobus connects the historical life of Maurice and his companions with Christianity's determination to conquer all the lands within reach, beginning with those close to the Mediterranean. Thus he has Saint Maurice and his companions living under the reign of two great persecutors of Christians, the emperors Diocletian and Maximian, the beginning of whose joint reign he sets at 287 (the actual date was 285).

Here Jacobus de Voragine follows his predecessor, the Dominican Jean de Mailly, who in turn took inspiration from the oldest source that mentions the Theban legion, Saint Eucher of Lyon, bishop of Valais in the fifth century, who originated a pilgrimage to the church of Agaune in that region. Always obsessed by numerical symbolism, especially when applied to certain portions of time, Jacobus presents the Theban legion as a corps of 6,666 soldiers under the command of Maurice, which the emperor is reported to have sent to combat Christians. As the story goes, the soldiers refused to do so, proclaiming themselves Christians, and their refusal brought about their martyrdom, which Jacobus dates around the year 287. Reflecting the interest that he always shows for the translation of relics, a topic that combines space and time in the making of a Christian domain, Jacobus de Voragine indicates that in the latter half of the tenth century certain monks obtained authorization from the pope, then from the abbot of the monastery of Agaune, to move the body of Saint Maurice and the head of one of his companions, Saint Innocent, to the church of Saint-Germain d'Auxerre. Curiously, although the tradition had been established by the twelfth century, Jacobus de Voragine does not say that within Christianity Maurice was considered a black man. When he follows his usual procedure of investigating the meaning of the saint's name, he cites the Greek for the word for "black" but does not mention the color of the saint's skin, speaking only of his self-image ("he was black in his contempt of self").[19] Thus it seems that the color of Maurice's skin did not cross south of the Alps during the latter half of the thirteenth century. This may be a sign that the city of Genoa's great opening to the world had its limits.

## Saints Dionysius, Rusticus, and Eleutherius

Saint Dionysius (Saint Denis) interests us because he is the result of the fusion of three different saints, whom Jacobus de Voragine treats as one and whom he considers to be the most important of the three primitive saints of that name. Christianity in fact venerated an orator of ancient Greece, Dionysius the Areopagite, supposedly converted by Saint Paul. Another Denis, the first bishop of Paris, is reported to have been martyred in the second or third century; and yet another Denis was the author of mystical theological texts of Neoplatonic inspiration that were supposedly introduced into the West in the ninth century and had great influence in the Middle Ages. Contemporary history attributes these texts to one Pseudo-Dionysios the Areopagite. What is certain, as is well explained in the commentary to the French edition of the *Légende dorée*,[20] is that the merging of these three saints was the work of the Abbey of Saint-Denis, near Paris, which was founded in the third century and became the royal abbey under the Merovingians and the Carolingians. The critical event was the gift by the Byzantine emperor Michael to the Carolingian emperor Louis the Pious of a group of texts attributed to a Greek Saint Denis. In 827 that manuscript was transferred to the abbey of Saint-Denis and translated into Latin by Abbot Hilduin, who composed a life of a combined Saint Denis for the occasion that was henceforth the source for the hagiography of the saint of that name. Thus Jacobus de Voragine connects Saint Denis with Saint Dionysios the Areopagite of Greek antiquity and presents him as a great philosopher whose writings were translated into Latin in the ninth century by Anastasius, the librarian of the apostolic see, and who in fact revised Hilduin's translation. Jacobus de Voragine also picks up the tradition of the conversion of Denis by Saint Paul, but he makes that event depend on an unusual temporal sign that enriches his system for marking time. He reports that the conversion of Saint Denis took place on the day of a solar eclipse that had been predicted and explained by Saint Paul, which attracted Denis to the religion that had inspired the apostle's preaching. This chapter makes an explicit point of the fact that Denis, citing Saint Paul, said that attention should be paid to the days and the years of eclipses as signs of divine power. Jacobus de Voragine then introduces another significant division of time: the formative period of a convert who becomes a bishop. He notes that Saint Paul instructed Denis for three years before the latter was ordained as bishop of Athens. Jacobus, who was well aware of the Saint Denis's popularity in France, a land in which he took a special interest, has Dionysius go from Athens to Paris. While he was preaching in Paris, he was captured by a pagan prefect sent by Rome, and he found martyrdom on one of the hills overlooking Paris, the Mont des Martyrs (later Montmartre). His body was placed with those of two other recent martyrs, Rusticus and Eleutherius, who had become his companions. The prefect ordered that their bodies be thrown into the Seine to prevent their place of martyrdom becoming a pilgrimage site, but a noble lady who was a secret Christian had them interred on her property on Montmartre, where she buried the body of Denis holding his severed head between his hands. This image became the basis for later representations of the saint that show him carrying his head. According to Jacobus de Voragine, his martyrdom took place under the emperor Domitian, in the year 96, when Saint Denis was ninety years old. In order accommodate what various sources say about Saint Dionysius/Denis, Jacobus combines their information in his single life of a half-Athenian, half-Parisian Denis. Thus he recalls that around 815 the emperor Louis, the son of Charlemagne, received books on hierarchy that Denis had written in Greece and had them translated. This act produced a still on-going series of healings in the church of Saint Denis near Paris.[21] Finally, Jacobus de Voragine notes that, according to one chronicle, written about the year 644,[22] King Dagobert had "held Saint Diony-sius in fervent veneration," and at his death a holy man had a vision of the king being snatched by Saint Denis from the clutch of "wicked angels" who were bearing him off to hell.[23]

## The Eleven Thousand Virgins

The feast day of this group of saints, which enjoyed great popularity in the Middle Ages and which has an extremely complicated origin in the sources, seems to inspire Jacobus de Voragine to praise virginity in general and to describe the geography and the travel routes of the Christian world, given that the story of the Eleven Thousand Virgins takes place between England, Rome, and the Rhine region. From a temporal perspective, our Genoese Dominican concentrates on a spectacular and dramatic episode that took place, he tells us, during one of the most horrible periods of the Middle Ages, the invasion of the Huns. The story begins with Ursula, the daughter of a king of Brittany who was engaged, against her will, to the son of the king of England and who, wishing to avoid marriage and conserve her virginity, gathers together virgins from many kingdoms and sets off with them on a pilgrimage to Rome. This attention-getting troupe of young girls is joined by many young men and several bishops, eventually including Ursula's former fiancé who, having converted to Christianity, is eager to experience with them the martyrdom that an angel had announced to Pope Cyriacus. Here again Jacobus de Voragine, ever skeptical concerning his sources, rejects the year 238 for their martyrdom, preferring the date of 452 that had gradually won favor after the tenth century and was confirmed in the twelfth century with the discovery in 1106 of an ossuary in the old ceme-tery of Saint Ursula's church in Cologne and further supported by the praise that the visionary Elizabeth of Schönau bestows on Saint Ursula and her companions in her 1152 *Revelations*. Those archaeo-logical discoveries and texts fed a thriving commerce in relics, which Pope Boniface IX finally halted in 1381.

Having rejected 238 as a date, Jacobus de Voragine can now turn to sources that place the martyrdom by the Huns of Saint Ursula and the Eleven Thousand Virgins in Cologne in 452. The emperor Marcian had turned against them the murderous fury of the barbarians who had invaded Christiandom and who, as history records, were not stopped by the Romans until the battle of Catalaunum (Châlons-en-Champagne), not far from Troyes. That historical event took place in 451, so the discrepancy often found between Jacobus's date and the true date is not great, and Marcian was indeed Roman emperor at the time. It is clear that Jacobus de Voragine had three objectives in mind in this chapter: evoking a martyrdom that made a particularly great impression on the men and women of the Middle Ages; praising the city of Cologne as a seat of relics (in the twelfth century the relics of the Three Kings would be moved there); and integrating into his research on time the terrible moments endured throughout history by Christian humanity because of its sins, in the case of Saint Ursula and the Eleven Thousand Virgins bringing together the Roman pagans and the most frightening of barbarian pagans. Jacobus Voragine wanted to encourage the celebration of the feasts that mark the time of humanity, but he included painful eras and events in the time of pilgrimages because, although the incarnation of Jesus made the time of reconciliation possible, during the time of pilgrimage God worked both to reward devotion and virtues and to repress the vices that were redeemed but not totally effaced by the incarnation of Jesus.

## The Four Crowned Martyrs

The Four Crowned Martyrs, whose feast day is celebrated on November 8, present, as the commentary to the French translation of the *Golden Legend* so well puts it, "the curious case of a superposition under one collective name of two celebrations, held at the basilica not far from the Lateran that was dedicated to the Quattro Coronati in the fourth century,"[24] and became, in the twelfth century, an imposing fortified church magnificently decorated with frescoes. This rather astonishing case of a redoubling of time marked by replacing one series of saints with another has, as Jacobus de Voragine tells us, a strange explanation. The emperor Diocletian had ordered the killing of the men who are called the Four Crowned Saints and whose names—Severus, Severianus, Carpophorus, and Victorinus— were discovered several years after their martyrdom. At the time, given that their existence was known but not their names, the Church decided to honor them under the name of other martyrs who had suffered two years earlier. In fact, the latter numbered not four, but five. Around the year 287, they had been tortured, then placed alive in lead coffins and thrown into the sea. The Church thus deliberately mingled four unknown martyrs and five known ones. Pope Melchiades (310–314), ignoring the fact that there were five of them, had them called the "Four Crowned," the collective name that has remained theirs, even after the discovery of their real names. Jacobus de Voragine surely chose this exceptional and curious case to show that anomalies are possible when saints are used as markers of time.

## Saint John the Baptist

Saint John the Baptist is the subject of two chapters in the *Golden Legend*, as Jacobus de Voragine follows the Roman calendar that places the feast of Saint John the Baptist on June 24 and that of his beheading, as we have seen, on August 24. Alain Boureau points out that only John the Baptist, the precursor of Christ, is celebrated, as are Jesus and Mary, on the day of his birth rather than on that of his death, because the Church considers that all three were unique in having had an immaculate birth.[25] They are all the more exceptional because, since almost all the early saints were martyrs, it was the day of their martyrdom—that is, of their death—that was celebrated. In fact, as Jean-Claude Schmitt has shown, it was not customary to recognize birth anniversaries (the *Golden Legend* mentions only that of Herod) until the late fifteenth and early sixteenth centuries.[26]

In the chapter devoted to the birth of Saint John the Baptist, Jacobus de Voragine presents, among John's many titles, that of "forerunner of the King."[27] Thus with this exceptional saint, Jacobus finds an opportunity to show that time can define not only a "before" and an "after," but can also provide a marvelous annunciation of great events to come, the most typical case being that of the annunciation to Mary. The birth of John the Baptist, Jacobus de Voragine notes, was announced by the archangel Gabriel, and the *Golden Legend* takes pains to relate in great detail the various temporal stages that marked the parallel pregnancies of Saint Elizabeth and the Virgin Mary, who would give birth, respectively, to Saint John and Christ. He notes that Zachariah filled the office of high priest to which King David had appointed him for seven days and then returned home, where, despite their advanced age, he and his wife Elizabeth conceived a child. Mary, who was already carrying Jesus, went to aid her cousin Elizabeth by living with her for three months. As for John, Elizabeth's son, he was the first to announce that the child born of Mary was the Son of God. Jacobus de Voragine, who inherited the fundamental concept of prophecy from the Old Testament, thus shows that a prophecy can interject the miraculous announcement of a future event into time. He also insists that the chronological order of the respective feast days of Saint John the Evangelist and Saint John the Baptist does not indicate anything about their relative importance. Feast days are a reference to the day of a saint's birth or, more often, of their death, and we cannot draw from them any other conclusions about these two saints, who were equal in time. Only the date of the Nativity of Christ takes precedence over other dates, and Jacobus de Voragine, who restores time to its place in nature much more than has been thought, notes that it is a sign of the preeminence of the nativity of Jesus over that of John that whereas the days are beginning to get shorter on the day of John's birth, they begin to lengthen on the day of Christ's birth.

In the chapter on the Beheading of Saint John the Baptist, Jacobus de Voragine states that the feast day was instituted because it refers to four exceptional events that occurred at and after his behead-ing. Jacobus de Voragine disagrees with the dating of this feast to the birthday of King Herod because, according to him, it took place in the year preceding Christ's passion, and "the lesser event should yield to the greater."[28] Three other events that occurred after John's death make him a super-martyr and a super-saint. First, after his beheading his body was burned as if in "a second martyrdom." Here Jacobus takes the opportunity to note that relics from this decapi-tated and burned body were taken to Genoa, Jacobus's own beloved city, and that during their voyage the sea, always a powerful source of fear for the men and women of the Middle Ages, remained excep-tionally calm. Next, although the remains of John's body had been brought to Genoa, his head had disappeared, and it was on his feast day during the reign of the emperor Marcian (who came to power in 452), that it was miraculously found and carried to Constantinople. Finally, it was also on his feast day that "the finger with which he pointed to the Lord" and that "could not, we are told, be burned" was recovered and taken away by Saint Thecla. She deposited the finger, miraculously intact, in a church in Maurienne. Through his use of the history of the feast of the Beheading of Saint John the Baptist and of the posthumous fate of his decapitated head, Jacobus de Voragine calls attention to two dogmas that he wants to promote. The first is that feast days have a unique ability to concentrate in one particular day of the year a series of marvelous or miraculous events that took place over a period of time, and, second, that the saints not only leave their mark on time by their feast days, but also leave an imprint on the geography of the places in which their relics were found and are conserved.

## Saint Peter, Apostle

Jacobus de Voragine writes at some length on the name "Peter" be-cause it was given to the apostle by Christ. One of Saint Peter's earli-est miracles made use of the auspicious or inauspicious quality of certain numbers. Peter sent two of his disciples off to preach, and one of them died after twenty days, an inauspicious number. But Peter resuscitated him after he had lain dead for forty days, an auspicious number. Jacobus de Voragine stresses Peter's close ties to Rome during his earthly life. He lived in that city for a long and happy period of twenty-five years during the reign of the emperor Claudius, and it was in the thirty-sixth year after the Passion of the Lord that Peter is supposed to have been crucified by Nero. Jacobus de Voragine ends this long chapter by describing, in abundant detail, the reign of the emperor Nero as an example of a time of a typically atrocious period of imperial rule. Among the emperor's monstrous acts he mentions that Nero caused Rome to burn for seven days and seven nights. Jacobus de Voragine, who is here, as always, more critical of his sources than has been generally admitted, is skeptical of the tradition that Peter and Paul were martyred in Rome on the same day, but when Saint Jerome, one of his favorite sources of inspiration, confirms the fact, he accepts it. He transforms a difference in days into a difference in location, however: the two apostles went to their martyrdom on the same day, but not in the same place. Christ had demonstrated his preference for Peter by placing him at the head of his future Church, and so Jacobus, following the opinion of Gregory the Great, states that this difference in rank dictates that Peter's feast day be celebrated a day before Paul's. As he does only on very rare occasions, our Dominican diverges from Roman Church tradition, which, in his day and still today, celebrates Peter and Paul on the same day, June 29.

## Saint Paul, Apostle

As we have just seen, Jacobus de Voragine had already devoted a chapter to Paul—or, to be exact, to the conversion of Saint Paul. The church had dedicated a feast day (January 25) to this event, which it considered one of the great events in the early history of Christianity. In the Middle Ages, however, the conversion of Saint Paul was usually celebrated, along with the saint himself, on June 29. In the present chapter Jacobus de Voragine seems to want to restore to Paul an importance that had been denied him in comparison with Peter, but he bases that importance on aspects in which temporality does not play the most important role. It is not time but space that Paul touched with sacrality by his many voyages on all continents. He also distinguished himself by two quite different manifestations that do bear on time. For one thing, he more than any other saint benefitted from those exceptional moments that are direct conversations with God, supreme moments that went far beyond anything experienced by any other prophet or apostle. For another, Saint Paul stands out as the saint who displayed the greatest number of fits of anger and moments of concentrated fury. Jacobus takes advantage of this behavior attributed to Saint Paul to praise the benefits of saintly anger. There are times when one is confronted by persons or events that are intolerable and when the best possible reaction is anger.

## Saint Christopher

The time of pilgrimage leads quite naturally to the chapter that Jacobus de Voragine devotes to this extraordinary saint of the Middle Ages, a saint whose reputation Jacobus himself did much to enhance. Veneration of Saint Christopher was addressed to two marvelous men combined in one. The first was a marvel of nature on account of his physique: he was a giant. The second was the man privileged to carry Christ on his shoulders, and although the Christ he carried was but a child, the power of that infant God made him the heaviest weight that a man has ever had to bear. Christopher, too, is more a saint of space than of time: he helped ferry people across rivers and carried the weak over long voyages. As for his relationship with time, Jacobus de Voragine stresses that, even outside the conversion experience, a human being, no matter how singular he may be (for example, by his height), can lead an ordinary life for a long time and then, from one day to the next, be completely changed by some event. For Christopher, this transformative event was Jesus's request that Christopher take him on his shoulders and ferry him over a river. Up to that point, Christopher was a man searching for God in his thoughts but, except for a meeting with a hermit, was in other respects leading a totally ordinary life. Jacobus de Voragine expresses the banality of such an eventless time. Time simply passes. And then, unexpectedly, the event arrives and the transformation is immediate. "The next morning he rose . . ."[29]

## Saint Dominic

The time of pilgrimage now brings us to a chapter on a saint who occupied a place of particular importance for Jacobus de Voragine. This was Saint Dominic, one of the few saints of recent times who is included in his book, for he died in 1222, not long before the probable date of Jacobus's birth. Dominic was the founder of the Dominican Order of Preachers to which Jacobus belonged. Given their proximity in time, Jacobus's chapter on Saint Dominic is one of those that most resemble an ordinary historical narration. To be sure, the Dominican Order lagged behind the Franciscan Order, which is well known to have engaged Saint Bonaventure to write a life of Saint Francis of Assisi that was intended to replace all of it predecessors, which were burned. The masters general of the Order of Preachers had made suggestions, but they never officially sanctioned the most highly respected life of Saint Dominic, the one written in 1254 by Humbert of Romans, the fifth master general of the Order, which, though clearly a eulogy, was in fact fairly objective. Jacobus de Voragine went beyond that primary source. He consulted and borrowed from the work of Saint Dominic's first biographer, Constantine of Orvieto. On instructions from the master general of the Order, he even used certain unpublished items that his fellow Dominican Gérard de Frachet had inserted into his *Vitae fratrum*, a work that was not completed until around 1260, just before Jacobus de Voragine began writing his *Golden Legend*. Although Jacobus does indeed relate the events of the Spanish saint's life in chronological order, he furnishes few dates. He states that before the foundation of the Order Dominic spent ten years or so in Toulouse (in fact, from 1207 to 1215) and that he obtained confirmation of his Order from Pope Honorius III in 1216. He calls the span of Dominic's life an "earthly pilgrimage," just as the time after the incarnation of Christ is a time of pilgrimage, and he indicates that Dominic's pilgrimage came to an end in 1221, a date that happens to be accurate even though in Jacobus's time the year did not begin on the same date as it does today.

## Saint Bernard

In Saint Bernard of Clairvaux we have yet another "modern" saint— or, more precisely, a saint of the twelfth century—who belongs to the time of pilgrimage. Bernard was famous in his own day, and although historians tend to contrast the intellectualism and urban focus of the Dominicans to the mysticism and feudal nature of the Cistercian Order to which he belonged, Jacobus de Voragine nonetheless greatly admired this saint, who was one of his principal sources.

Saint Bernard died in 1153. He was canonized in 1174. His feast day was celebrated on the day of his death, August 20. Jacobus de Voragine relies on the earliest life of Saint Bernard, written by his disciple Guillaume de Saint-Thierry, and also on the many texts written in Bernard's honor after his canonization. Thanks to the fact that Bernard was a near contemporary who had close connections with his first biographer, Jacobus's summary of his life is more accurate than some of his lives of earlier (not to mention imaginary) saints. However, as was true of Saint Dominic, whom we have just met, and of some of the modern saints to be discussed below, Jacobus de Voragine treats the lives of modern saints no differently than he does those of earlier times. He is equally attentive to the periods of the saint's terrestrial life and to events that affected his or her behavior; in particular, he takes note of progress toward sainthood whether it results from some sudden event that brings on immediate conversion or is more gradual. There is thus a time of life that is comparable for all men and all women but that, for the saints, has the particular quality of making one day, one year, or one period of life sacred. Saint Bernard's relationship with time was clear even in his childhood. One Christmas Eve, while he was still a young boy, he was waiting for the office of matins in the church of his family's castle, and he asked at what hour of the night Christ was born. Then and there the Infant Jesus appeared to him.[30] That night and that vision marked him for life. One might think that this episode was one of the reasons for Jacobus de Voragine's special devotion to Saint Bernard because, as we have seen, the Nativity of Jesus was the day when the event central to his conception of sacred time took place: the time of the reconciliation of man with God, a reconciliation that original sin had prematurely postponed.

Jacobus de Voragine probably did not know the exact year of Saint Bernard's birth, because birth dates, even those of great persons, were only very rarely recorded before the fifteenth century. On the other hand, he indicates that Bernard entered into the Cistercian Order in 1112, the fifteenth anniversary of the founding of that Order, adding that he was twenty-two years old.[31] Jacobus de Voragine gives few dates for the rest of Saint Bernard's life. He does note, however, that the abbot of Cîteaux appointed Bernard abbot of the house of Clairvaux, which he had founded, and Bernard and other monks lived there for a long time. But, although Jacobus stresses the length of time that Bernard spent as the head of the abbey of Clairvaux, he adds that Saint Bernard "denied himself sleep to an extent beyond human endurance," and that he complained that time spent sleeping was time lost. Here our Dominican sacralizes the balance between the length of time spent awake and the time spent sleeping, considering, in his own system of the valorization of time, that time awake was superior to nighttime. But at times Jacobus seems to grant a corrective to that basic inequality, for in several places in the *Golden Legend* he notes that during the night a saint is not merely a sleeper, but is often favored by dreams and visions. A time of unconsciousness comparable to that of death, night is also the highly sacralized time of apparitions. Because he wanted his listeners and readers to be attentive to the importance of the various moments of the day and to man's daytime occupations, Jacobus de Voragine stresses that Bernard found time for meditation and prayer "in the woods and the fields," adding that he "had no teachers except the oaks and the beeches." It is as if Jacobus were distinguishing between the time of solitude and nature and the time of the town and favoring the former over the latter. Given that these statements come from a Dominican who was Genoese to his core, one might wonder if they hint at an urban man's secret admiration for rural man. Was Jacobus simply noting a point of continuity between a religious order devoted to solitude—the Cistercian Order—and the new and essentially urban Dominican Order? Or did he guard, in the bottom of his heart, a nostalgia for the monastic spirituality of a still-recent past? It is hard to say. But it is clear that in his effort to introduce into the *Golden Legend* all possible forms and spans of time, Jacobus de Voragine, a city man if there ever was one, did not forget that there is a time of nature and of solitude.

Some aspects of Jacobus's life of Saint Bernard show that, although he wanted his *Golden Legend* to be above all a *summa* on time, he also intended to include in it, in the encyclopedic spirit of his age, all that characterizes the human condition, including daily activities, a subject of polemics in the twelfth and thirteenth centuries. Speaking of Saint Bernard's clothing, he seizes the opportunity to point out that poverty, the ideal of his own Dominican Order, does not also imply slovenliness, which is condemnable. Jacobus de Voragine had probably heard of the debates among university figures of his own era on the topic of whether Jesus had ever laughed, even once in his life, and he notes that Saint Bernard never laughed, but that he often had to control himself to keep from laughing.[32] For Jacobus, the half-spiritual, half-bodily phenomenon that is laughter does not seem to have been a problem, as there is laughter everywhere in the *Golden Legend*. We almost get the impression that he subscribed to Aristotle's dictum that laughter is the proper of mankind.[33]

After recounting the life of Saint Bernard, stressing above all his virtues and concentrating more on his miracles than on what might be termed his political activities—his work in opposition to heretics and in support of the crusades—Jacobus de Voragine correctly dates the saint's death to the year of our Lord 1153.

## Saint Augustine

Saint Augustine, as I have already noted, is for Jacobus de Voragine, as for many intellectuals and spiritual leaders of the Middle Ages, the great Christian doctor. In his etymological introduction our Dominican takes pains to associate his name with terms that cast a brilliant light on him. He compares Augustine to the emperor Augustus; to the sun; to the month of August, the most beautiful, most luminous, and warmest month of the year; and in this first paragraph he expresses his life-long interest in time by placing him, in this introductory paragraph, in "eternal life."[34] Since Jacobus was writing about a saint who had told the story of his own life in his *Confessions*, Augustine's biography is a long one. It is followed by mentions of several of Augustine's great admirers from the fifth to the thirteenth century; by an account of the translation of his relics (which, for Jacobus de Voragine affected in essential ways the space and the time rendered sacred by the remains of a saint); by the narration of thirteen miracles and —something quite out of the ordinary in the *Golden Legend*—he ends with a chronological list of a great many of the works of Saint Augustine.

Jacobus de Voragine notes an important step in Saint Augustine's progress toward Christianity. At the age of nineteen he was reading Cicero and he was disappointed to find no mention of the name of Jesus Christ. Cicero appealed to him very much, and his Christian mother had spoken to him about the exceptional person of Jesus, whom he therefore would have liked to encounter in Cicero's writings. There is in this an early indication of one aspect of Augustine's future greatness, the union in him of Christianity with what was best of ancient pagan culture. Next Jacobus tells of the trip that Augustine took to Rome after a number of years spent in Carthage. It was an event that both enriched Augustine's cultural formation and brought him closer to Christianity. Finally, when Augustine was thirty, the crucial moment arrived. Following the example of his mother and the preaching of Saint Ambrose, Augustine received baptism, and since up to now he had led a pagan existence and had a son, the child was baptized with his father.

For Jacobus de Voragine, the time of conversion was a moment of critical importance in a life. It might be a true conversion, a turning from paganism or unbelief to Christianity, or it might consist in the inner conversion that occurs when a tepid Christian is seized by a renewed and ardent faith. Conversion, then, can bring various kinds of time into play. It can be instantaneous, produced by an apparition or a miracle. But Jacobus is also interested in gradual conversions like that of Augustine. He takes a particular interest in the rhythm with which human phenomena are inscribed in time. Thus he cites a famous passage in the *Confessions* in which Augustine tells of the day during the long period of his on-going conversion when he spent many hours under a fig tree in his garden, crying out inwardly, "How long, how long will it be 'Tomorrow, tomorrow! Not right now, hold on a little while'?"[35] Jacobus de Voragine has found here in Saint Augustine's *Confessions* a particularly moving and anguished form of time: a time of indecision and waiting. He does not furnish many dates in this life, long and detailed though it is. For example, he does not name the year in which Augustine became bishop of Hippo in North Africa. But since the time of childhood especially interested him—and I shall return to the topic—he notes the sixteen-year-old Augustine's remorse at having stolen some pears from a tree near his own vineyard. Finally, after describing his constant struggles against the heretics of his age, Jacobus lingers over two important moments of Augustine's life. First, Jacobus often notes in his sanctorale that

Augustine reacted to approaching death citing the attitude of three earlier bishops, Ambrose, an unnamed bishop, and Cyprian, when faced with the same situation. There is in fact toward the end of the life of many men a time of preparation for death, and in this connection as well, the saints—and saintly bishops even more—stand as examples. Second, Jacobus de Voragine emphasizes that Augustine lived during the tragic period long known as the "barbarian invasions," and that this tragedy had a great influence on him. It was after the Goths took Rome (Jacobus does not give the date, but it was 410) that Augustine, reflecting on that world-changing event, wrote his greatest book, *The City of God*. Jacobus places Augustine's death in the 440s (in fact, he died in 430), just as the Vandals invaded the province he served as bishop, pillaging and massacring as they went.

Next Jacobus de Voragine asserts that Augustine "incomparably surpassed all the doctors of the Church," both by his "native gifts" and his "acquired knowledge."[36] He offers as one proof, among others, that Augustine wrote so many works that no one, even working day and night, could copy them all or even read them. This remark would be a platitude if it did not point out that men, especially men of letters, spend considerable time in their lives dictating, writing, copying and reading books, which makes it natural that Jacobus should end his long chapter on Saint Augustine with a list of his literary works. Before he does so, however, Jacobus speaks of an event that is for him highly significant: the translation of Augustine's relics. This was not done in a day but took place in stages, and the chapter thus shows us how Jacobus de Voragine conceived of time as marked by the translation of relics (as was space, as we have seen) because in the case of Saint Augustine's relics it becomes a time that moves forward in a number of stages. Christians transferred the body of Saint Augustine to Sardinia, out of the reach of the Vandals in Africa. Then, according to Jacobus, when Sardinia was invaded by the Saracens, the king of the Lombards had the saint's remains taken to his own capital, Pavia. Jacobus shows a particular interest in this long translation because one stop along the way —Rome—was especially important to him. This entire story in Jacobus's *Golden Legend* seems to me to be a masterwork of narrative art. The original text is in Latin, but linguists consider it to be of exceptional quality for its time, the latter half of the thirteenth century.

For that reason I will offer the reader almost all of the narration of this extraordinary time that saw the extraordinary translation of the relics of an extraordinary saint:

After his death, when the barbarians overran that region and profaned the churches, the faithful took Augustine's body and transported it to Sardinia. About AD 718, 280 years after the saint's death, Liutprand, the deeply religious king of the Lombards, heard that the Saracens were depopulating Sardinia, and sent a formal delegation there to take the holy doctor's relics to Pavia. Having paid a high price, they obtained the saint's body and brought it as far as Genoa. When the devout king learned of this, he went with great joy to that city and reverently met and accepted the body. However, when they wanted to carry it farther, they could not move it from the place until the king had made a vow that if Augustine allowed him to go on from there, he would build a church at that place in his honor. Once the vow was made, the body was carried away without difficulty, and Liutprand fulfilled his vow and had a church constructed as promised. The same miracle occurred a day later in a country villa called Cassella in the diocese of Tortona, and the king built a church there in honor of Saint Augustine. In addition he granted the villa itself and all its appendages to be owned in perpetuity by those who would serve that church. By this time the king saw that it pleased the saint to have a church built in his name wherever his body had rested. Liutprand feared that Augustine might choose for his final resting place a location other than the one the king wanted, so he arranged for the erection of a church everyplace where he and the relic were given hospitality overnight. So the sacred body was finally brought into Pavia, welcomed with much jubilation, and enshrined with honors in the church of Saint Peter, which is called Golden Heaven.[37]

## Saint Michael, Archangel

Saint Michael presents an exceptional case in the *Golden Legend* because, even though he has certainly played the role of a saint in Christian devotion, he was in fact an archangel. As Alain Boureau notes,[38] Saint Michael is the only one of the three archangels mentioned in the Old Testament (the two others being Gabriel and Raphael) to whom Jacobus de Voragine devotes a chapter. The principal reason for this, I believe, is that Michael plays a particularly important role in the sacralization of time, which, I am attempting to show, is the underlying theme of the *Golden Legend*. Unlike Alain Boureau, however, I do not think that the presence of Saint Michael in this *summa* is connected with the emergence, at the beginning of the scholastic period, of the notion of the *aevum*, a time particular to the angels and distinct from terrestrial temporality. Although Saint Michael appears at the beginning of creation as one of the great troupe of the angels, he is nonetheless linked to human temporality in a special and essential way. He represents, in fact, the third element of sacred time that Jacobus sees as drawing toward eternity, the other two kinds of time given to humanity by God being the liturgical time of the temporale and the linear time of the sanctorale. It is Saint Michael who, on the Day of Judgment, will recall to the resuscitated dead what Jesus gave to them by his incarnation and who will display before them the cross, the nails, the lance, and the crown of thorns. Although Jacobus de Voragine (unlike many of his contemporaries) was not obsessed by millenarianism or by the vision of the Last Times, he was aware that the time of humanity is bound toward an end, and he saw in Saint Michael as a good spokesman for the importance of that eschatological time. While waiting for Judgment

Day to reveal his role as the herald of humanity's end time, Michael is credited with playing a critical and highly original role in the theology of temporality developed in the *Golden Legend*. In fact, Saint Michael has manifested himself within human history by means of an apparition, a rare but essential kind of temporality, charged with the supernatural, that lasts for only a flash of time.

Saint Michael's apparitions have left their mark on the chronology of terrestrial time or, to put it more simply, on history. Jacobus de Voragine declares that there have been several apparitions of Saint Michael and, in fact, he cites five of them. The first took place, he tells us, in the year 390 at Mount Gargano in Apulia. The second occurred about AD 710 on the coast of Normandy and was memorialized by the building, on a rock, of an extraordinary church, the abbey of Mont-Saint-Michel. The third apparition took place in Rome in the time of Pope Gregory, who reigned from 590 to 604, and it led to the transformation of the former pagan tomb of the emperor Hadrian on the banks of the Tiber into a Christian palace-church known as the Castel Sant'Angelo. The fourth apparition refers to the many visions of choirs of angels. The fifth apparition, cited by Cassiodorus in his *Tripartite History* (sixth century), took place in the Byzantine Christian world, near Constantinople.

After defining Saint Michael by his apparitions, Jacobus de Voragine turns in his *Golden Legend* to Michael's association with the notion of Victory, a privileged moment when good triumphs over evil. One of Saint Michael's most celebrated victories was of course his defeat of the dragon, but rather than dwelling on this legendary tale of the princess delivered from the monster who was holding her captive, Jacobus portrays Michael as the standard-bearer of the divine army that defeated the dragon (who represents Lucifer), a victory that drove Lucifer from heaven and into the "dark air" that the author situates not in a subterranean Hell, but in the space between heaven and earth.[39] But beyond these specific and highly important victories, Saint Michael provides Jacobus de Voragine with an opportunity to recall that the angels win victories over demons every day. Thus the evocation of Saint Michael provides an occasion to stress that, within the time of humanity that unfolds daily, there is something like a time of the victory won on a daily basis by those divine creatures who are the angels and demons, some of whom have remained good while others have fallen into evil. The *Golden Legend* is full of them, for, even aside from apparitions, all men are constantly within the reach of these beings, ready to be helped or attacked. This chapter dedicated to Saint Michael thus gives witness to the belief, which was very important in the thirteenth century, in guardian angels who assist every human being individually, and who, although they will live into eternity, live also within the terrestrial time of each person whom they protect. Finally, Jacobus de Voragine recalls that Saint Michael's greatest victory will be over the Antichrist, at the hour when he kills him. Saint Michael is thus the principal actor in the great event that will announce the end of time on earth.

## Saint Jerome

Jerome was, along with Ambrose and Augustine, the Father of the Church who exerted the greatest influence over Jacobus de Voragine. In spite of this, the chapter that Jacobus dedicates to him is fairly short. He does not give Jerome's birth date, but he indicates that when still a youth, he left his native Dalmatia for Rome to follow the teaching of the famous grammarian Donatus, and most readers of the *Golden Legend* could be counted on to know that Donatus had lived in the fourth century in a Roman empire on its way to becoming Christian after the conversion of Constantine. It is known that Jerome, who was born around 345 in Dalmatia, went to Rome at the age of twelve and received Christian baptism around 366. Chronological details concerning Jerome appear only later in Jacobus's summary of his life. Jerome was thirty-nine when he was ordained a cardinal priest in the church of Rome, and he was designated to succeed Pope Liberius, whom we know died in 366. Jacobus de Voragine describes Jerome's flight from Rome in an anecdote worthy of a vaudeville act. The victim of a ruse on the part of his enemies, he dons women's clothes and is forced out of Rome under a hail of insults and mockery. After a fairly long stay in Constantinople, he took refuge in the the desert of the Holy Land where, like many who were known as hermits, he was in fact continually surrounded by disciples and visitors. Jacobus de Voragine records two epochs of Jerome's life when his comportment won him a saint's halo: the first being a period of four years of penance in the desert; the second (a period of time particularly important for eminent Christians), the years that he dedicated to pious labors, which meant in Jerome's case the time that he spent translating the Bible from Greek into Latin, which, according to Jacobus, took him fifty-five years and six months. Our Dominican stresses the immensity and the depth of Saint Jerome's learning and the importance of the library that he gathered together in Bethlehem, not far from his desert wilderness, and also his contribution to the organization of the ecclesiastic liturgy, in particular the order of readings. Jerome is without doubt the model of the Christian scholar and man of letters who knew Latin, Greek, and Hebrew. In the thirteenth century he had a special appeal for the Dominicans, who wanted to preserve and advance knowledge as much as possible so as to fulfill their vocation as preachers and teachers. Although Jacobus de Voragine does mention the episode, become legend, of Jerome taming a lion who then became his companion and his symbol, he also attributes to Jerome a gift that relates to his own reflections on time. Jerome, Jacobus tells us, knew the future. This is perhaps not stated here with the same force and clarity as in other chapters of the *Golden Legend*, but it is apparent that for Jacobus de Voragine the saints are not only markers of time but that they, during their lifetimes, know what the future will bring. Their role in the unfolding and use of time was thus essential. We see from this that, over and above their exemplary natures, saints played and still play a role within Christianity that is different from that of holy persons in all other religions.

Toward the end of his chapter on Saint Jerome, Jacobus de Voragine mentions two things that enhance Jerome's importance for him. First, he emphasizes that his great master Saint Augustine had a profound respect for Jerome, which he expressed in the letters that he wrote to him. Second, he notes that Saint Jerome died at a very advanced age, which is the sign of a particular divine protection and communicates that terrestrial time, when it is long enough, can be a source of benefits for a human being and serve as an example. Jacobus states that Saint Jerome was buried in a tomb that he had built for himself "at the mouth of the cave where the Lord had lain" at the end of his short earthly life, and that Jerome was ninety-eight years and six months old when he died about AD 398.[40]

## Saint Francis

Francis is, along with Saint Dominic, Saint Peter Martyr, and Saint Elizabeth of Hungary, one of four thirteenth-century saints who figure in the *Golden Legend*. The fairly short chapter that Jacobus devotes to him clearly manifests his desire, as a Dominican, to render homage to the founder of the other great mendicant order of the thirteenth century. He not only avoids any suggestion of a ranking of the two saints, but recalls the friendship that is supposed to have existed between the two and to have been manifested in a meeting mentioned in other thirteenth-century texts and in iconography, although it most probably never occurred. Jacobus de Voragine offers a brief summary of the life of Saint Francis, which was well known at the time. He recalls that Francis's life was typical of conversions to Christianity in that he went from leading a life that was, if not actually dissolute, at least empty of piety, to a life that is a model of profound spiritual engagement. Jacobus estimates that what he calls Francis's "vain and frivolous life"[41] lasted for twenty years. He recalls that such conversions, even when they are sudden, have often been caused by a series of shocks closely spaced in time. This observation permits me to introduce the notion of quasi-miraculous events in the *Golden Legend*. In the case of Saint Francis, these were an ill-ness; a brief imprisonment by the Perugians, enemies of the people of Assisi; and the miraculous voice of Jesus speaking to him from an image in the church of Saint Damian. Jacobus gives no dates in his biographical summary of Francis's life, probably because he assumed that most of the listeners and readers of his *Golden Legend* knew them already; perhaps also because he judged that exact dates, products of the chronological efforts dear to a historian like Jacobus de Voragine, were more critical for the distant past than for recent events.

The chapter on Saint Francis is not without its reflections on time, however. Saints are known by miracles, for it is miracles that distinguish their lives from their posthumous acts. In the early years of Christianity, popular piety had attributed to the saints the widely recognized and highly prized gift of performing miracles during their lifetimes. As the Holy See solidified its hold over the Church and the faithful, it began to count as true miracles only those that a saint had accomplished after death, going so far as to draw up for-mal rules on the topic in the early thirteenth century. Indeed, tak-ing posthumous miracles into consideration provided an objective basis for recognizing saintliness, a judgment now reserved to the pro-cess of canonization; and it also made it easier to distinguish true saints from impostors who simulated miracles. By the difference be-tween the acts of his lifetime and his posthumous actions, the saint showed himself to indeed be a great marker of time.

## Saint Martin, Bishop

In the florilegium of saints that I have gathered together to sup-port my hypothesis that the *Golden Legend* is above all a *summa* on time, the last male saint is Saint Martin. He was, to begin with, more popular than any other saint of the Middle Ages, as witnessed by the fact that "Martin" is the most common given name in all lands and all languages of medieval Christianity. Among the saints of the early Middle Ages, he is also the one for whom we possess the most reliable biographic information, in the form of a biography reacted by Sulpicius Severus, his disciple, who knew him well. This document permits a close study of the way Jacobus de Voragine uses an authentic and dependable source. Alain Boureau and his editorial team remind us also that Saint Martin's feast day, celebrated on November 11, was one of the central events of the year in the medieval West, an allusion in particular to the "summer of Saint Martin."[42] They add that although Jacobus does not dwell on this point, Martin is one of the few saints who have contributed two feasts to the calendar: that of his death (November 11) and that of the translation of his relics (July 4). With the support of a guide as reliable as Sulpicius Severus, Jacobus de Voragine is able to recall that Martin was born in Pannonia (now Hungary) but was raised in Italy, in Pavia, and that against his inclinations he became a soldier in the pagan Roman army of the emperors Constantine and Julian, even though he had felt the attraction of Christianity from the age of twelve and had attempted to resist enlistment, which took place in 331, when he was fifteen. He served in the pagan Roman army for two years, but in 333 he managed to leave it for good and placed himself under the protection of Saint Hilary, the bishop of Poitiers. Baptized at the age of eighteen, he retired to a monastery, but the Christians of Tours removed him from there and made him their bishop.

Martin is one of the saints to whom Jacobus de Voragine grants the most importance, because he views him as equal to the apostles and because he possesses Sulpicius Severus's precise, detailed, and trustworthy biography. Jacobus thus found himself working under the conditions he most appreciated—those of actual history. For, although the basic function of saints may be to work miracles by the will of God and to stand as examples of Christian virtue, in my opinion their principal role in the *Golden Legend* was, as I have indicated before, the enchanting of human time by their marvelous lives. Where the life of an ordinary man is only a segment of chronology, the life of a saint is a segment of sacred time. Following Sulpicius Severus, Jacobus de Voragine thus relates many miracles done by

Saint Martin, some of which are simply remarkable gestures of piety, like the famous story of Martin cutting in two the cloak he was wearing and giving half of it to an "almost naked" poor man. Although Jacobus always cleaved to Church doctrine and was respectful of the primacy of Rome (when it seems to him to serve his own appointed task), he broached the boundaries that the papacy attempted to set, especially beginning in the late twelfth century, when it came to questions of sainthood. He recorded the miracles worked by Saint Martin during his lifetime as well as those he performed after his death. Saint Martin also provides Jacobus with an opportunity to introduce into the time of all creation the sacralization of the duration of human life that is, in my opinion, the underlying objective of the *Golden Legend*. Some commentators—including some contemporary historians—have thought it necessary to point out that although Jacobus de Voragine took a profound interest in man, he was relatively indifferent to nature, except for the importance that he grants to the rhythm of the seasons, which are for him major divisions of the temporality that God has given to humanity. I hold this view to be erroneous. The chapter on Saint Martin is a good example of the almost "ecological" interest that Martin has in nature. Among his core virtues, Jacobus mentions Martin's ability to make himself obeyed by what he calls "inanimate, vegetable, and nonrational beings."[43] Such creatures of God may have been deprived of reason, but they were not without life. In a manner completely different from Saint Francis of Assisi with his love for all living creatures, and with a much more intellectual focus reflecting the encyclopedic spirit of the thirteenth century, Jacobus de Voragine introduces into the enchanted and sacralized time that he is striving to reveal the time of these beings without reason but not without life, and he does so by means of the saints who include them in their apostolate on an equal basis with men. Fire and water, Jacobus tells us, obeyed Saint Martin. In another miraculous episode, he makes a pine tree obey him. He stops dogs who are chasing a little rabbit, turns back a snake swimming across a river, and even stops the annoying barking of a dog.

In sum, certain exceptional gifts make the saints stand out within human temporality. They can foresee the day of their death, and their miraculous foreknowledge of the particular day that will mark the end of the trace that they leave in human time enables them to choose the place where they want to go to die, thus once again bringing about those unities of time and space that, as we have seen, are strongly evidenced in the lives of the saints and, even more, in the stories of their relics. Thus Saint Martin chooses the diocese of Candes as his place of death and Jacobus de Voragine, true to his habit of noting the age and the date of the terrestrial death of his saints, notes that Martin "yielded his spirit to God," "in the eighty-first year of his life"[44] and in the reign of Arcadius and Honorius, which, according to Jacobus, began around the year 398. Saint Martin did indeed die at the age of eighty-one; the exact date of the beginning of the reign of Arcadius and Honorius is 395, a date close to the one that Jacobus gives.

Through the day of his death, and then posthumously, Saint Martin again illustrates the importance of a saint's terrestrial life and of the quality of that life for human temporality. A first miraculous effect on time of the day of Martin's death came when the archdeacon of the bishop of Cologne heard angels and demons quarreling in heaven over a human soul. The angels won, and their elect spirit was Saint Martin, about whose day and hour of death the archdeacon had learned in a vision.

We know, however, that the miraculous actions worked by the saints on time are not limited to the duration of their lives and the hour of their death. Their relics remain charged with sacrality, and any translation of those relics puts its commemorative mark on time. Jacobus de Voragine notes that sixty-four years after Martin's death his body was transported to a church in Tours that had been magnificently enlarged. The saint had long opposed that translation by making his sarcophagus insurmountably heavy until the moment when, ceding to the prayers of the men who were attempting to move it, Martin himself came from heaven to help move his relics "with ease and speed."[45] In St. Martin's case, this critical moment in the sacralization of time that is the day of the translation of the relics of a saint was so important that it was long celebrated by the Church on July 4.

## Saint Elizabeth of Hungary

Saint Elizabeth occupies a special place in the *Golden Legend*. Her presence within the sanctorale has astonished a number of commentators.[46] If Jacobus de Voragine wanted to honor a female saint of his own times, why did he not choose Saint Clare rather than Elizabeth of Hungary, who was much less widely venerated? Jacobus, who probably traveled to Budapest as part of his pastoral duties, may have heard tell of this extraordinary woman who had died not long before: born in 1207, she died young in 1231 and was canonized by Pope Gregory IX in 1235. Jacobus may have been struck by her exceptional character and seduced by the idea of featuring in his sanctorale a person who, from the social, personal, and geographical points of view, remarkably enlarged the world of saints. To begin with, Saint Elizabeth was the daughter of a king, Andrew II of Hungary. Despite her strong desire to remain a virgin, she was forced, for political reasons, to marry the eldest son of the landgrave of Thuringia and she bore him three children. Widowed quite young, she retired, not to a convent but to a modest hut, and later to a hospital for the poor. Although strongly influenced by Franciscan spirituality, she did not enter an order, and Jacobus de Voragine may have chosen her to represent those thirteenth-century women who lived lives poised somewhere between the lay state and the convent, manifesting a new type of piety that was all the more remarkable in Elizabeth because she was the daughter of a king, the widow of a prince and because, despite her attraction to virginity, a common characteristic of female saints, she had given birth to several children. She represents a truly exceptional case, but at the same time, she bears witness to a female spirituality, the fullest example of which was that of the Beguines. Jacobus de Voragine recognized the interest of such a case of extreme female sanctity, one that was exceptional in terms of time as well. He notes that when Elizabeth was only five years old she was spending long hours in church in prayer—much longer than was normal even for adult women. We can follow this remarkable trait in her as, in Jacobus's words, "Elizabeth grew in age and even more in the intensity of her devotion."[47]

Here, then, is an example of a temporality that embraces both the natural time of growth of the human body and the spiritual time of progress toward sainthood. Saint Elizabeth, both as a child and as an adolescent, insisted on dressing to accentuate the time to be given to devotion in her daily life, rejecting all dictates of custom regarding clothing. On feast days she refused to allow decorative sleeves to be stitched onto her dress until after the celebration of Mass. "She forbade herself the wearing of gloves before noon on Sunday."[48] Forced to marry and feeling obligated to bear children by her married state, she wore neither jewelry nor a beautiful gown when she went to be churched after childbirth. Similarly, she showed little regard for the difference between daytime activities and nightly rest, which was normally a time exempt from acts of devotion. She spent sleepless nights in order to give herself to prayer and to petition the Heavenly Father in secret.

Jacobus de Voragine also celebrated the things that made a saint like Elizabeth an exception in the use of human time. Saints, male and female, experience special moments unknown to the simple faithful: on the one hand, there are the apparitions, ecstasies, the hearing of divine voices, etc.; and then on the other, the daily efforts to perform acts of devotion or charity. She lived in a castle perched on a hilltop, but Saint Elizabeth of Hungary found the strength to descend the hill and climb back up it every day to bring aid to the poor. Jacobus also stresses the fact that one day in church during Lent she experienced an extraordinary ecstasy, and when she had recovered herself and returned home, she was so filled with happiness "that she burst out laughing" (Risus mirabilis). We see here the laughter, long repressed by the theoretical and practical rigors of monastic spirituality, that was liberated at last in the thirteenth century, in the mendicant orders and among most of the Scholastics. Universities of the age still posed the classic question: "Did Jesus laugh, even once in his lifetime?" Jacobus de Voragine is the echo of his century here: during the thirteenth century, saints, male and female, laughed—loudly or not, often or seldom, but in free fidelity to God. A mother despite herself, Saint Elizabeth felt, in this circumstance, the sacred nature of the moment, not unlike the moment when a newborn child enters into human temporality. In the same vein, she once held at the baptismal fount the baby daughter that a poor women had just given birth to and she gave the baby her own name.

As we have just seen with Saint Martin, so too Saint Elizabeth received from God the news of her approaching death, which she then shared with those around her. Faithful to his desire to insert that intense and sacred moment into ordinary chronology, Jacobus de Voragine states that she died in 1231, a fact that was not difficult to ascertain with exactitude for so a near contemporary, but one that he always sought to note when it came to those markers of time who are the saints. He also notes that the moment of a saint's death is generally the occasion for some marvelous manifestation. This was the case at Elizabeth's death, for soon after she died "flocks of small birds that had never been seen there before clustered on the roof of the church,"[49] singing in sweet harmony. And Jacobus de Voragine, who always surrounds mortal men and women with eternal beings— angels who come to their aid and demons who come to tempt them—suggests that the birds celebrating this marvelous moment of human time were in reality angels.

Jacobus is also attentive to what was known as the "ages of life," another aspect of human temporality. Perhaps because Saint Elizabeth died young, displayed her own sainthood at an early age, and was the mother of three children, he presents her as a saint with a particular interest in children. Among the miracles that he cites is the saint's resurrection of a four-year-old child who had fallen into a well and the healing of a five-year-old, born blind, who recovered his sight when his mother took him to Elizabeth's tomb.

Finally, we find also in the life of Saint Elizabeth an example of the dual temporality that a miracle can embody. Many miracles are immediate, but some require a period of waiting and redoubled prayer and patience. This was the case of a certain Dietrich of the diocese of Mainz, whose legs were paralyzed up to his knees, and who came to pray to Saint Elizabeth after spending eight days traveling to her tomb. He waited there for four weeks, but gave up in desperation and returned home. That night he woke up and discovered that he could walk again. The saint had cured him.

## Saint Catherine

Jacobus de Voragine, in his eagerness to make the *Golden Legend* a *summa* on time, took a special interest in Saint Catherine because she had been extremely popular since antiquity and because Alexandria, a great center of religion and culture, was in a constant state of evolution during the medieval period. His chapter on Catherine accentuates certain essential moments of her life. He places her birth in the reign of the emperor Maxentius (306–312) and dates her martyrdom to 310. She affirmed her Christian faith at the age of eighteen, which means that she had time to profit from the great source of erudition that was Alexandria to acquire a store of knowledge that made her a female link in the chain of scientific advancement that is one aspect of humanity's progress through time.

In treating the martyrdom of Saint Catherine, Jacobus de Voragine returns to certain temporal elements that he liked to introduce into what might be called the time of martyrdom. First imprisoned, she was then left without food for twelve days. After that, in preparation for her martyrdom, the future saint was told of the "exquisite torture" being readied for her.[50] She was made to watch for three days as a machine was constructed, with "four wheels studded with iron saws and sharp-pointed nails." In point of fact she was killed by decapitation, so her torture was over in one day. Faithful to the abundant tradition concerning the life and the cult of Saint Catherine (there was even an Arabic version of her passion), Jacobus de Voragine states that immediately after her execution she was carried by angels to Mount Sinai and buried there, on the spot where a superb monastery was later built. He also notes that "a certain monk from Rouen" stayed at that monastery honoring Saint Catherine for seven years, and as a reward he received a fragment of her body (a finger) to take back to his monastery in Normandy. It is in fact known that a monk from the Benedictine abbey of La Trinité-au-Mont in Rouen returned from Mount Sinai in 1028 with relics that he asserted came from the ones conserved in that place. This example confirms the observation that Jacobus de Voragine, in his desire to sacralize and to "enchant" human life, used relics and their translation to link time and space in the history of humanity.

Finally, in the last lines of this chapter, our Dominican furnishes one of the best examples of the critical spirit that is too often denied him: he mentions the doubts that some had raised as to whether Catherine's martyrdom took place under Maxentius (306–312) or under Maximinus.[51]

## All Saints and the Commemoration of All Souls[52]

Following the Roman calendar, which he does not cite here but which is his guiding thread, Jacobus de Voragine arrives at two days of joint celebration that were already establised in the thirteenth century (on November 1 and 2). The first of these is All Saints Day. Within the sanctorale that is for Jacobus de Voragine one of the three ways of organizing the time of humanity, this is clearly quite a special time as it commemorates not one saint, but all of the saints.

Jacobus de Voragine venerates this day all the more because it enables him, better than the Church or anyone else could, to show all the saints participating in the time of humanity, and not just those included in his sanctorale, which was, as we know, limited to 153 saints. He cites four reasons for the institution of this feast. The first reflects his desire to eliminate everything from the time of a humanity that had become Christian anything that might recall pagan religion. Thus he begins by stressing that All Saints celebrates the day on which the Church replaced the pagan feast of all the gods by transforming the illustrious Roman building consecrated to them (which bore the Greek name of Pantheon) by dedicating the building, now a church, to all martyrs. Here Jacobus de Voragine, obviously unable to find a common date for the death or the celebration of a multiplicity of saints, has to be content with turning the feast of all the gods into a Christian feast of all the saints. And since a historical event is concerned, he recalls that the transformation of the Pantheon into a church of all the saints, which led to the creation of the feast of All Saints, was the work of Pope Boniface IV and took place around 605 (actually, 609). Jacobus was well aware that Boniface IV instituted this feast on May 13, and not November 1, but the May date was not long respected by the Church, since in the ninth century Pope Gregory IV transferred the feast of All Saints to November 1, where it remains to this day. Always ready to link religious time with the time of nature, which is also a creation of God, Jacobus stresses that the transfer to November 1 was a result of the Church's desire to set this great feast at a time of the year in which "supplies were ample after the harvest and the vintage was finished."[53]

Next, in total fidelity to tradition, Jacobus de Voragine indicates that one of the major reasons for the institution of this feast day had been the desire to remedy both the omission of certain saints and the human impossibility of finding within the year as many days as would be required to devote one day to each, since their number surpassed that of the days in the year. This provides him with an opportunity to stress, this time in connection with the temporale and with the liturgical time that combines with the sanctorale or the time of the saints, in what he calls the "brevity of time."[54] Given that the time of humanity, considered in its totality as the *Golden Legend* strives to do, is an open time, and because we do not know when God will decide to end the fourth and last time, that of pilgrimage, the time of each human being is brief, and the time that God has given to humanity as a whole is very probably also a brief moment in the midst of eternity.

Jacobus de Voragine, as we have seen him do so often, ends this chapter on All Saints Day with an *exemplum*. A year after the pope's institution of this feast day, the warden of the church of Saint Peter's in Rome is reported to have had a vision of the celestial court, before which all the saints had come to thank God "for the honor done them by mortals on this day, and to pray for the whole world."[55] Rarely has there been such a forceful expression of the connection between men and saints, and the author of the *Golden Legend* takes advantage of the feast of All Saints to show, in the unitary spirit that is typical of him, the strength of the ties that bind saints and men and, since it is known that the saints are the principal intermediaries between man and God, also to show the strong bonds that unite both saints and men with God.

Situating the feast of All Saints within time and exploring the role of the saints in relation to God and their ties with men was not enough for Jacobus de Voragine, however. He went further, reinforcing his desire for globalization by explicitly connecting the November 1 feast of All Saints with the commemoration of All Souls that follows it on November 2. Indeed, in the vision of the warden of Saint Peter's, the angel who leads him to the celestial court and to the manifestation of all the saints also takes him to a place peopled by men who, dead in the earthly sense but intended for heaven, are waiting for other intercessors. This place was Purgatory, and it held the special category of the dead known as souls in purgatory. This quite naturally leads Jacobus de Voragine to dedicate his next chapter to the following day of the sanctorale, the Commemoration of All Souls. This date commemorates all the faithful dead, among whom the saints function as models. The saints provide the second systematic construction after the temporale, on which eschatological time is structured, whereas eschatological time escapes chronology because, following God's will, it moves toward the Last Days and eternity.

In Jacobus de Voragine's treatment of the November 2 feast he gives a remarkable historical and theological summary of the relations between the living and the dead and between the dead and God. He shows—and this is in total conformity with history—that the Christian Church, beginning in the tenth and eleventh centuries, had displayed a growing interest in the fate of the dead, which peaked in the installation of the commemoration of All Souls on November 2 and in the institution of Purgatory, a third place in an as-yet ill-defined Beyond. He also emphasizes—again, in conformity with history—the significant role that the Cluniac Order played in the emergence, in Christian liturgy and devotions, of prayers for the dead. He recalls that as Saint Odilo, the abbot of Cluny from 994 to 1049, was making his way back from the Holy Land, from his boat off the Sicilian coast he heard coming from the crater of Mount Etna the howls of demons complaining that prayers and alms were snatching the souls of the dead from their clutches. Odilo concluded that even more prayers for the faithful dead were needed. He also planted in the imaginations of men of the Middle Ages the notion that there was a place or places in which the dead were not subjected to the demons' torments for all eternity, as they were in Hell. This was the concept that led, during the latter half of the twelfth century, to the definition of Purgatory as a third and temporary place in the Beyond.[56]

Jacobus de Voragine devotes considerable space to the subject, but I hope that my readers will forgive me if I do not go into detail on his discussion of Purgatory and its inhabitants. He shows that the mendicant orders, both in their preaching and in their pastoral care, played an important role in the spread of that belief and in the development of the cult of the souls in Purgatory, a cult that was not always welcomed by the Church throughout Christendom and which, for all practical purposes, disappeared from Christian devotions in the twentieth century with the Second Vatican Council. That Council, despite the fact that to a great extent it broadened spiritual horizons, neglected certain historical moments in Christianity. And among the most important, the most interesting, and the most "progressive" of these, I would include the rise of Purgatory as a specific place in the Beyond. Jacobus de Voragine's reflections on Purgatory reveal an important element of his perception of human time, which is the way humans, living or dead, perceive the slowness, the acceleration, or the velocity of time. Indeed, the prayers of the living on behalf of the dead can, as Jacobus himself puts it, permit the souls in Purgatory to be "freed more quickly."[57]

Jacobus de Voragine next describes how the Church instituted a particular temporality so as to come to the aid of the faithful dead. He writes: "The Church has usually observed three orders of numbers of days; namely, the seventh, the thirtieth, and the anniversary. . . . The seventh day is observed . . . so that all the sins may be remitted which [the departed] committed in life, life being lived seven days at a time. . . . The anniversary is observed so that from the years of calamity [the departed] may come to the years of eternity."[58]

Jacobus de Voragine returns to the time of Purgatory at the end of this chapter on the commemoration of All Souls (November 2) to relate a legend that dates to the time of Charlemagne. Eight days after a knight was killed in the war against the Moors he appeared to one of his cousins and reprimanded the man for not having given to the poor the money that had been realized from selling his horse, as the knight had requested. This act would have freed him from Purgatory, where he would now have to remain until other prayers liberated him. Thus Purgatory makes it possible for time to become the stakes in a combat between the anguish of dead individuals and the fidelity to them of certain living individuals. Jacobus de Voragine understood that Purgatory introduced new possibilities into the treatment of human time.

# Saint Pelagius, Pope:
# The History of the Lombards

The time has come to discuss the two final chapters of the *Golden Legend*, which have often bewildered commentators. The next-to-last chapter is placed under the patronage of Saint Pelagius, pope. As it happens, however, only its first two paragraphs are devoted to this saint, after which the text takes on a non-hagiographic nature (to which I shall return in a moment). In fact, Pelagius himself has puzzled scholars, and at times doubt has been cast on both his saintliness and his very existence.

On the question of his existence there is little reason for doubt: Pelagius I was indeed pope from 555 to 561, and Jacobus de Voragine takes care to distinguish him from the better-known Pope Pelagius II, who succeeded Gregory the Great. Moreover, Jacobus situates him chronologically in relation to an event of great importance for Italy and for the papacy—the conquest of Northern and Central Italy by the Germanic Longobards, or Lombards, which did indeed take place from 568 to 572. Much more is known about their invasion than most commentators will allow.[59] As for Pelagius's sanctity, Claire Sotinel writes that the inscription on his tomb in Saint Peter's says that he had been beatified, which means that the title of "saint" is simply an exaggeration of historical reality.

This chapter on Pelagius I is interesting primarily because the greater part of it contains an abridged general history of the period from the sixth to the thirteenth century. The presence of this section in this next-to-last chapter of the *Golden Legend* has been attributed either to the author's desire to connect it with a much more important work or to scribal error. It seems to me that, quite to the contrary, this chapter, placed where it is, enters perfectly into Jacobus de Voragine's plan for the *Golden Legend* to function as a *summa* on time. Although he does not mention it explicitly, Jacobus makes use of a kind of utilitarian time—calendar time or, more precisely, the time of the Roman calendar proposed by the Church. Indeed, all the feast days to which Jacobus de Voragine devotes chapters in the *Golden Legend* follow the order of that calendar, thus offering a succession of reference points. Aside from the utilitarian time of the calendar and the sacred time defined by the four times of deviation, renewal, reconciliation, and pilgrimage, Jacobus de Voragine considers that there exists a third way to present the time of humanity, which is what we call "history." He used that very method to highlight the importance of historical time when he wrote a chronicle of Genoa that met with considerable success and that remains, in the eyes of the medievalists who have studied it, one of the best chronicles written in the Middle Ages.[60] The chapter on Saint Pelagius is thus an opportunity for Jacobus to enrich his *summa* on time in a way that he finds particularly interesting, which is by presenting a sample of one way to treat historical time. Despite his use of some techniques that are strictly his own, Jacobus de Voragine essentially follows chronological order by examining and summarizing the thought of three authors: Paul the Deacon, the author of an eighth-century *Chronicle of the Lombards*; Sigebert of Gembloux, who wrote a *Chronicon* of the years from 381 to 1110; and a near contemporary, the Dominican Vincent of Beauvais, who died in 1264 and was the author of a vast encyclopedia and a *Speculum historiale*.

I shall not attempt to use this chapter on Saint Pelagius and the Lombards to define Jacobus de Voragine as a historian. I wish only to show how this text fits into his project of a *summa* on time. Jacobus de Voragine names great figures and accords them importance as makers of historical time. He does not disdain collective traits, however, thus showing that he was a historian who was sympathetic, when the need arose, to ethnological observations. In his care—which is evident throughout the *Golden Legend*—to enliven his historical narratives with *exempla*, anecdotes, and picturesque details, he notes, for example, that "it was the custom of the men of this tribe to wear very long beards," which was why they were called "Longobards." He then goes on to tell an amusing anecdote about the connection between the Lombards' long beards and spying. The passage ends with a play on words. When a seer, a man "who had the spirit of prophecy" opened his window, he cried, "Who are all these Longobards (long-beards)?"[61] His wife added that those whom he called by that name would be victorious. Jacobus de Voragine accorded great importance to all that concerned the Church and religion, which is hardly surprising. What is more unusual is that within historical evolution he leaves significant room for developments in liturgics. Thus, after recalling the time of the conversion of the Lombards to Christianity, he stresses the fact that in the time of Charlemagne, the Ambrosian office had largely been abandoned and replaced by the Gregorian office. He also pays close attention to the evolution of Gregorian chant and to everything that made the offices, the Mass in particular, more beautiful. Among the important figures in this history, Charlemagne occupies a special place and, quite exceptionally, Jacobus gives a highly vivid description of the emperor's physical aspect and habitual behavior. Among the conversions to Christianity that interest him all the more because they transformed Europe into a Christian zone, he cites first the conversion of the Frisians, then that of the Bulgars, and finally that of the Hungarians, stressing in the latter case the importance of the piety of King Stephen, who became Saint Stephen. Within this "European" perspective, Jacobus notes that around the year 644, under the reign of Dagobert, the king of the Franks, closer ties were established between the Frankish monarchy and the abbey of Saint-Denis. He also shows an interest in the spread of Christianity in England and the role that a monk, the Venerable Bede, to whom he pays great homage, played in it around the year 687. He mentions the translation of the relics of Saint Benedict to the monastery of Fleury-sur-Loire, in Gaul. He calls attention to the fact that in the ninth century newly elected popes developed the habit of taking a new and more dignified name. Like all medieval chroniclers, he takes an interest in natural catastrophes, which were often taken to be marvels. Thus he notes that in the ninth century, in Italy, near Brescia, "blood rained from heaven for three days and three nights," and that at the same time "hordes of locusts appeared in Gaul."[62] Among the translations of relics that left their mark on historical time, he accords special importance to the translation of Saint Nicholas's relics from the East to Bari, which leads him to note the creation, in thirteenth-century monastic history, of the Dominican and Franciscan Orders, to remark that they were preceded by the foundation of the Cistercian Order by the abbot Robert of Molesmes. He also notes the growing authority of the Cistercians in comparison with the Cluniacs who had preceded them. Although he does not speak of the community of Saint-Victor in general, he renders lengthy homage to Hugh of Saint-Victor.

The most astonishing aspect of this passage on the history of Christianity considered as universal history is Jacobus's introduction of a long digression on Muhammad and the Muslims, elaborated on the basis of a great many Christian sources, first among them being a translation of the Koran into Latin that was carried out in the twelfth century on the order of Peter the Venerable, the abbot of Cluny. To be sure, Jacobus de Voragine treats Muhammad in particular and Muslims in general as deviants, who had been led into error, much like the Chrisitan heretics about whom he will speak later. But he nonetheless considers the coexistence, despite conflicts, of the three monotheistic religions, the Judaic, the Christian, and the Muslim, to be a historical fact worthy of note. He lingers over the rites of the Muslims, returning to the "ethnological" attitude that he had adopted in regard to the Lombards. Always attentive to connections between space and time, he notes that in the three religions worshipers turn in different directions when they pray. Jews turn to the west and Christians to the east, while Muhammad specified that Muslims, whom our Dominican calls "Saracens" in accordance with medieval custom, must pray facing south. Jacobus is visibly intrigued by, and almost admiring of certain Muslim rites, the significance they accorded to bodily cleanliness, and the fast of Ramadan. He takes care to note both the similarities and the differences between the three monotheisms, especially between Christianity and Islam, as if that diversity, although regrettable, should be noted (if not respected) rather than combated. Here Jacobus de Voragine orients his study of time toward a search for common origins and points of divergence to be surmounted. In speaking of the Muslim conception of the Last Judgment, he places Islam not only on the road of historical time, but also of eschatological time.

Jacobus de Voragine takes this summary of universal history up to his own time, the thirteenth century. He recalls that there are still saintly persons, women among them, who contribute to the pursuit of an unfolding sacred time. Thus he inserts into this chapter a long reference to Saint Elizabeth of Hungary. Jacobus concludes, finally, with a brief presentation of the historical acts of the most recent emperors and popes. He speaks of the woes of Gregory IX and of his courage, and he notes that the most recent pope about whom he speaks, Innocent IV, was of Genoese origin, hence his compatriot, and that he ordered the convocation, in 1274, of the Ecumenical Council of Lyon, thus reconnecting with an act of the Church that affects all of Christianity. The final paragraph in this astonishing chapter affirms that after the deposition and the death in 1254 of the emperor Frederick II, at first a great supporter of the Church and of religion but later their great enemy, "the imperial throne is vacant to this day."[63] This moment was indeed what later historians called the great interregnum, which ended only when Rudolph of Habsburg was elected Holy Roman emperor in 1271 (but not crowned by the pope). Historical time thus contains surprises and questions about the future. It is an open time, an unfinished time, the very image of the sacred time of pilgrimage.

Stefano Mula gives an interpretation of the next-to-last chapter of the *Golden Legend*, "Saint Pelagius, Pope: The History of the Lombards," that is close to the one that I propose.[64] Mula contests—I think rightly—the suggestion that this chapter is not in its right place in Jacobus de Voragine's book, and that it is, moreover, of no interest. I think, to the contrary (as does Mula) that it conforms to Jacobus de Voragine's plan for the *Golden Legend*. The importance of this chapter can be measured also by the fact that in the Middle Ages the *Golden Legend* was sometimes called *The History of the Lombards* (*Historia Lombardica*). It was Jacobus's habit to use several sources, and Stefano Mula convincingly demonstrates that here his principal source was the most recent, Vincent of Beauvais. Mula also shows to perfection that as a compiler, Jacobus de Voragine deploys here the originality that was expected of compilers in the Middle Ages.

My own position in regard to two important propositions of Stefano Mula's is as follows: First, Mula stresses that this chapter is to be found only in what is known as the second and final version of the *Golden Legend*. As I explained at the beginning of this essay, Jacobus de Voragine worked constantly on the *Golden Legend* from the moment he began it (probably around 1262) until his death in 1298. But, in my opinion, his conception of the work did not change substantially between those two dates. To be sure, the second version, which probably dates from around 1290, contains several additions to the original text, but far from modifying the meaning of what he had written earlier, they reinforce the interpretation that I have proposed here. What is more, if I thought it possible to undertake this essay, it was because finally—after serious and comprehensive studies of most of the medieval manuscripts of the *Golden Legend*—an edition had been published that, unlike earlier attempts, is a convincing rendering of the "true" text. Even though that edition notes in certain places (among them, the chapter under consideration) that the text belongs to what is called the second version, the primary editor and his team merged—and rightly so, in my opinion— the two texts known as the first and second versions, following the best manuscripts. This edition, published in 2007, is Iacopo da Varagine, *Legenda aurea*, text and commentary established by Giovanni Paolo Maggioni, with a translation into Italian by Francesco Stella accompanying the Latin text.

According to Stefano Mula, Jacobus de Voragine used this chapter to complete the *Golden Legend* because he wished to offer a contrast between the divine time of salvation and the unstable history of mankind. My interpretation is not quite the same. I believe—as I have already indicated—that Jacobus de Voragine wanted to make of his work a *summa* on time and, more particularly, on sacred time. He situates this essential time between a utilitarian time—that of the Church calendar, which he follows without naming it—and historians' time, an example of which he gives in this chapter through his summary of the history of the Lombards, the masters of the region in which he himself lived, and through a universal history, derived from Vincent of Beauvais, that summarizes the principal moments of the history of terrestrial Christianity dominated by the pope and the emperor. To be sure, he places that history on a much lower plane than the sacralized history that he wants to showcase in the *Golden Legend*, but, to my mind, he relegates it to a position of lesser importance to indicate that the time of pilgrimage in which men have lived since the passion and the resurrection of Jesus is a troubled time. If, at the end of his chapter, Jacobus leaves that Christianity without an emperor, even though the great interregnum has ended, it would seem to me that it is not, as Stefano Mula suggests, because that history of men "gives but a poor impression of instability," but rather because he believes that it is an open history that does not follow the path to eschatological time but remains open to the unpredictable future of human life on earth.

## The Dedication of a Church

The one hundred and seventy-eighth and last chapter of the *Golden Legend* concerns the dedication of a Church.[65] All commentators are agreed that this feast is not scheduled on a particular calendar date because it has taken place and will continue to take place on a wide variety of days. Already in Jacobus de Voragine's day, its celebration had become quite rare, and the last instance occurred in 1961. Alain Boureau and his fellow editors seem to me to be close to the truth when they state that this chapter, which is conceived more to be read than listened to as predication and which contains very little narrative (only two *exempla*) "forms an ecclesiological epilogue that accentuates the permanent dimension of the Church as a consecrated and separate institution."[66]

All the same, my interpretation is slightly different. I have noted several times during the course of the present essay that for Jacobus de Voragine, the sacralization of time can only be accomplished by a complementary and sometimes synchronic sacralization of space. The place in which sacred time can best be revealed, spoken of, commented on, or thought of is the Church. It matters little if the Christianity of the latter half of the thirteenth century constructed few new churches. The past and future construction of any church is an anchor for sacred time within the life of humanity. Since this final chapter of the *Golden Legend* is dedicated to the territorialization of the space of sacred time, it brings little that is new to that time, though it does make it possible to gather it together and consider it as a terrestrial whole. My commentary will thus be relatively brief, especially because the chapter explicitly concerns time only in brief passages.

To be sure, Jacobus de Voragine considers the Church as comprised of two realities that convey two meanings. A church is a material reality, a building of a particular type, because it is sacred and has been consecrated. But the Church is also a spiritual edifice that gathers together all the clergy and all the faithful who pray inside it, listen to preachers, and receive the sacraments there. Within that edifice Jacobus de Voragine draws a distinction between the altar, which is essential, and the temple—that is, the rest of the church. The altar is not without connections to time. First, because it is made for offering the sacrament of the Lord in remembrance of an exceptional time, the passion of Jesus, and because it, and to a lesser degree the temple, is decorated with images that recall Christ's preaching. Those images serve as books for the laity, and although I have not discussed the illustrations in medieval manuscripts because they seem to me beyond the purview of the *Golden Legend* and to have no connection with Jacobus de Voragine,[67] it remains true that Jacobus was aware that Christianity employs images, uses them as a support, and is a religion of images. The sacred time of the *Golden Legend* is a profoundly imagistic time.

The second reason for the consecration of the altar is also connected with memories of exceptional historical moments. The Bible tells us that the Lord appears to Abraham and tells him to build an altar. Saint Paul, in I Timothy 2, indicates how the Lord's name is to be invoked at the consecration of the altar. Every consecrated host given to a Christian by a priest during communion recalls the message that God sent to men by the incarnation of Jesus. Jacobus de Voragine refers to a "modern" text, written in the twelfth century by Hugh of Saint-Victor, in connection with the idea of the incessantly renewed meaning of the host.

This final chapter of the *Golden Legend* provides Jacobus de Voragine with an opportunity to show that time must be the bearer of the marvelous. To be sure, there are marvels, miracles, apparitions, and astonishing visions that make up the essence of this marvelous, but every instant is capable of being enchanted. Jacobus de Voragine emphasizes that the third reason for the consecration of the altar of a church is to permit the marvel that is "the singing of the chant" to occur,[68] an observation that gives Jacobus another occasion to proclaim his love of chant and of music in general. The sacred time of the *Golden Legend* is a time transfigured by the chant and by various instruments, among which he mentions stringed instruments such as the psaltery or the zither, the voice, and music "made by blowing," as with the trumpet. Thus we have returned, at the end of this rereading of the *Golden Legend* in which I have attempted to grasp the author's profound thought and the broad intent that that underlies his project, to one of the literary characteristics that contributed the most to the success of the work in the Middle Ages (but also to its rejection in the sixteenth century and afterward): its affection for the marvel and the marvelous and the skill with which Jacobus evokes them. The time that Jacobus de Voragine was seeking—and that we, following his lead, have been humbly seeking as well—is a marvelous time. I have attempted elsewhere and on past occasions to define the nature and the place of the marvelous in the medieval imaginary.[69] There I not only sketched the history of *mirabilia* but also stressed the distinction, established in the early thirteenth century by Gervase of Tilbury in his *Otia imperialia* (Recreation for an Emperor), between the *miraculosus*, the miraculous accomplished by God himself through the saints; the *mirabilis*, which is a marvelous and striking natural phenomenon that seems extraordinary; and the *magicus*, which is magic, the work of Satan and his fiends. Men and women of the thirteenth century were fascinated by the marvelous. Jacobus de Voragine was simply using his talent and imagination to feed their hunger for marvels as they sought to find things on this earth that would evoke Paradise for them, awakening their admiration and hope. A society such as our own, which is hungry for science fiction, spiritualism, serial crimes, and illusions of all sorts, is in a poor position to mock a society whose phantasms were often of a higher quality.

One of the reasons for consecrating a church does have a fundamental connection with time, to be specific, with liturgical and cyclical time. Here Jacobus de Voragine shows his debt to monastic practices, for what he cites, praises, and recommends is the seven canonical hours—Matins, Prime, Terce, and so on. He reminds us that the passion of Christ occupied the chronological span of an entire day. At Prime, "the first hour of the day," Christ might have awakened and gone to the Temple with the people to say Matins, but he was taken before Pilate. "At the third hour Christ was crucified by the tongues of the Jews and was scourged at the pillar by Pilate," and the Holy Spirit was sent to him. "At the sixth hour Christ was nailed to the cross and darkness came over the whole earth." "It was at the ninth hour that Christ gave up his spirit and the soldier opened his side," after which "Christ ascended into heaven."[70] Note that this abbreviated account does not specify the time of Christ's death and places his ascent into heaven immediately after his death. I see here one of the rare instances of Jacobus de Voragine's mistreatment of time and history, where the narrator of the marvelous gains an upper hand over the chronicler of time.

One form of time that occupies an important place in the *Golden Legend* is the time of gestures, which, taken together, form a ceremony that has a duration. Jacobus de Voragine goes into minute detail about the gestures required for the dedication of a church, both inside and outside, but he gives no indication of their duration. It seems as if a church is a place in which a sacred time is constantly alive and always prevails. Thus it is hardly surprising that chronological time returns when Jacobus de Vorgine speaks of profanations of churches. He cites three historical occasions when the house of God was profaned by three men: Jeroboam, Nabuzardan, and Antiochus. For Jacobus, these biblical episodes correspond to terrestrial sins repeatedly committed over time that prolong the misdeeds of the three profaners of the past—sins such as the avarice of clerics, the pleasures of the flesh and the gluttony of cooks, and the pride and ambition of clerics.

Fortunately, just as Christ's incarnation put an end to the time of deviation and the time of reconciliation began, these three profaners of the temple were replaced by three builders of the temple: Moses, Solomon, and Judas Maccabeus. Jacobus de Voragine at last ends the *Golden Legend* by citing Saint Bernard's invitation to man to bear the cross of Christ patiently. The person who is so disposed, Jacobus assures us, "will truly be a temple dedicated to God's honor,"[71] and in this way the saintly man who is absorbed into the Church is consecrated for all eternity.

# Conclusion

The new interpretation of the *Golden Legend* that I propose has drawn on remarkable works by a variety of authors. The list is headed by Giovanni Paolo Maggioni, Alain Boureau, and Barbara Fleith. To my eyes, the *Golden Legend* constitutes an attempt to write a *summa* on time that is based on the calendar time of daily life, which Jacobus de Voragine follows from Advent through to the end of the year, completing it with a historical sketch that relates to Pope Pelagius I and the sacred insertion of time within space that occurs when a church is dedicated.

Jacobus de Voragine, perhaps with the aid of a team of helpers, made use of a prodigious fund of erudition in the realization of his ambitious objective. In order for anyone to succeed in this task, he would have to find himself—as Jacobus did—in exceptionally favorable conditions. Jacobus was born in Genoa, and aside from a few voyages, the better part of his life was spent either in that city itself or elsewhere in Northern Italy (at the time called Northern Lombardy) from the Alps to the Adriatic, a region of great economic and cultural effervescence. He lived during the second half of the thirteenth century, a period that harvested the fruits of the rich Gregorian reform, witnessed the renewal of both cities and countryside, benefitted both clerics and the laity, and was borne along by the encyclopedic spirit. Finally, Jacobus belonged to what was probably the most learned and the most cultivated religious order of the age, as well as the order most engaged in using predication and reading to spread among the greatest possible number of Christians a multi-faceted body of knowledge, along with a pious enjoyment of the marvelous tale and—to use a term whose meaning has changed since Jacobus's day but probably enjoyed its greatest popularity thanks to him—of legends.

The *Golden Legend* was also the work of the Middle Ages that best expressed, in all of its richness and complexity, the originality —an originality fashioned by the dominant ideology of Christianity and by the exceptional personality of one of the greatest minds of that critical period—of the most fundamental theme of life in the history of a human society, which is time.

# Afterword

Although I have done my utmost to consult as many works on Jacobus de Voragine and the *Golden Legend* as possible, this essay is based primarily on a direct reading of the text. My basic resource has been the two-volume Latin edition of Giovanni Paolo Maggioni: Jacopo da Varagine, *Legenda aurea*, text and commentary established by Giovanni Paolo Maggioni, with a translation into Italian by Francesco Stella accompanying the Latin text, 2 vols. (Tavernuzzo / Florence: SISMEL / Edizioni del Galuzzo, 1998; Milan: Biblioteca Ambrosiana, 2007).

For French translations and for commentary I have relied above all on the excellent translation prepared under the direction of Alain Boureau: Jacques de Voragine, *La Légende dorée*, text presented, with notes, by Alain Boureau et al., preface by Jacques Le Goff, Bibliothèque de la Pléiade (Paris: Gallimard, 2004).

I have also made use of two recent and remarkable Italian translations: *Legenda aurea*, trans. Alessandro and Lucetta Vitale Brovarone (Turin: Einaudi, 1995), and the Giovanni Paolo Maggioni and Franco Stella edition cited above.

The present English translation of Jacques Le Goff, *À la recherche du temps sacré: Jacques de Voragine et la Légende dorée* (Paris: Perrin, 2011), makes extensive use of Jacobus de Voragine, *The Golden Legend: Readings on the Saints*, trans. William Granger Ryan, introduction by Eamon Duffy (Princeton: Princeton University Press, 1993, 2012), for the spelling of names and places, for chapter titles, and for quotations.

# Notes

## Preface

1. Baudouin de Gaiffier, "*Légende dorée* ou légende de plomb?" *Analecta Bollandiana* 83 (1965): 350–54.

2. Alain Boureau, *La Légende dorée: Le système narratif de Jacques de Voragine († 1298)*, preface by Jacques Le Goff (Paris: Cerf, 1984, 2007); Jacques de Voragine, *La Légende dorée*, text presented, with notes, by Alain Boureau et al., preface by Jacques Le Goff, Bibliothèque de la Pléiade (Paris: Gallimard, 2004).

3. Quoted by Bernard Ribémont in his modern French edition of Bartholomaeus Anglicus, *Liber epilogorum: Le Livre des propriétés des choses, une encyclopédie au XIVe siècle*, trans. Jean Corbechon (Paris: Stock/Moyen Âge, 1999), 10. Ribémont pertinently adds, "For Isidore, then, the compiler is not simply a poly-reader copying authorized maxims as extracts. He is an alchemist, combining various substances, himself bringing elements, binders, catalysts, so as to produce what is in the end a new material."

4. See the excellent study of Guy Philippart, *Les Légendiers latins et autres manuscrits hagiographiques* (Turnhout: Brepols, 1977).

5. See *L'Enciclopedismo medievale*, ed. Michelangelo Picone (Ravenna: Longo, 1994), in particular, Jacques Le Goff, "Pourquoi le XIIIe siècle a-t-il été plus particulièrement un siècle d'encyclopédisme?" 23–40.

6. Jacobus de Voragine, *The Golden Legend: Readings on the Saints*, trans. William Granger Ryan, with an introduction by Eamon Duffy (Princeton: Princeton University Press, 2012), 3. Quotations from *The Golden Legend* will be taken from this edition.

# Chapter 1

1. For essential information in this biographical note I am following Carla Casa-grande's excellent entry, "Jacopo da Varazze" in the *Dizionario biografico degli Italiani* (Rome: Istituto della Enciclopedia Italiana, 1960–), vol. 65 (2004), 92–102. Casagrande stresses that all that she knows of Jacopo de Voragine's life, stripped of inventions and errors, she owes to Giovanni Monleone and his "Studio introduttivo" to Jacopus de Voragine, *Iacopo da Varagine e la sua Cronaca di Genova dalle origini al MCCXCVII* (Rome: Tipografia del Senato, 1941; Turin: Bottega d'Erasmo, 1969–1970).

2. In his highly successful, *Otia imperialia*, written in the early thirteenth century, Gervase of Tilbury made a precise distinction between the miraculous that can only be accomplished by God and the marvelous that, although exceptional and astonishing, obeys the laws of nature. Jacobus de Voragine does not echo that distinction, and I shall return to the topic of the marvelous in the *Golden Legend*. See Gervase of Tilbury, *Le Livre des merveilles*, French translation with commentary by Annie Duchesne, preface by Jacques Le Goff (Paris: Belles Lettres, 1992).

3. In her highly interesting study, *Jacopo da Varagine, tra santi e mercanti* (Milan: Camunia, 1988), Gabriella Airaldi discerns in Jacopo de Voragine the same interest in far-off lands that she attributes to the Genoese merchants of his age. I am less sure, for although he certainly showed an interest in the idea of reviving the crusades (Palestine was definitively lost to the Christians in 1293), I think that he was addressing humanity as a whole and all the faithful of European Christianity.

4. There is an extensive bibliography on Saint Dominic and the Dominicans in the thirteenth century. I shall cite only one work, Marie-Humbert Vicaire, O.P., *Dominique et ses prêcheurs* (Paris: Cerf, 1977).

5. The French translation of Jean de Mailly's legendary was published in 1947 by Antoine Dondaine, who was also the author of "Le Dominicain français Jean de Mailly et la *Légende dorée*," *Archives d'histoire dominicaine* (Paris: Cerf, 1946), 1: 53–102.

6. Jacques Le Goff, "Du ciel sur la terre: La mutation des valeurs du XIIe au XVIIIe siècle dans l'Occident chrétien." in Le Goff, *Héros du Moyen Âge, le saint et le roi* (Paris: Gallimard, 2004), 1263–87.

7. Alain Boureau, "Le Prêcheur et les marchands: Ordre divin et désordres du siècle dans la 'Chronique de Gênes' de Jacques de Voragine (1297)," *Médiévales* 4 (1983): 102–22.

# Chapter 2

1. Jacques de Voragine, *La Légende dorée*, ed. Alain Boureau et al., preface by Jacques Le Goff, Bibliothèque de la Pléiade (Paris: Gallimard, 2004), 1357. The quotations that follow are taken from Jacobus de Voragine, *The Golden Legend*, trans. William

Granger Ryan, introduction by Eamon Duffy (Princeton: Princeton University Press, 2012), 502, 503, 513, 237, 493.

2. See Edmund Colledge, "James of Voragine's *Legenda sancti Augustini* and its Sources," *Augustiniana* 35 (1985): 281–314.

3. Gaston Duchet-Suchaux and Michel Pastoureau, *La Bible et les saints, guide iconographique* (Paris: Flammarion, 1990), 51.

4. Uguccio died in 1210. Among other works, he left an etymological dictionary entitled *Liber derivationum* and an *Agiographia*, available in a modern edition as *De Dubio accentu: Agiographia; Expositio de symbolo apostolarum*, ed. Giuseppe Cremascoli (Spoleto: Centro italiano di studi sull'Alto Medioevo, 1978).

# Chapter 3

1. François Dolbeau, "Les Prologues de légendiers latins," in *Les Prologues médiévaux*, Actes du colloque international, Rome 1998, ed. Jacqueline Hamesse (Turnhout: Brepols, 2000), 345–94.

2. I should note that the terms "liturgy," "temporale" (the part of the breviary or missal that contains the daily offices), and "sanctorale" (the part of the same pertaining to saints' days) date from the eighteenth century, but I think that they can be applied to what is the prefiguration and perhaps one of the sources of and models for them, the *Golden Legend*.

3. Pierre-Marie Gy, "Histoire de la liturgie en Occident jusqu'au concile de Trente," in *L'Église en prière: Introduction à la liturgie*, ed. Aimé-Georges Martimort, new edition, (Paris, 1983), vol. 1, *Principes de la liturgie*, 57–73; in English translation as *The Church at Prayer: Introduction to the Liturgy*, trans. Robert Fisher et al., ed. Austin Flannery and Vincent Ryan (New York: Desclée, 1968).

4. William R. Bonniwell, O.P., *A History of the Dominican Liturgy, 1215–1945* (New York: Wagner, 1945).

5. Albert Houssiau, in *Rituels* (mélanges offerts au père Gy) (Paris: Cerf, 1990), 327–37.

6. Pierre-Marie Gy, *Guillaume Durand, évêque de Mende (vers 1230–1296), canoniste, liturgiste et homme politique* (Paris: CNRS, 1992).

7. Jaccopo de Voragine, *The Golden Legend: Readings on the Saints*, trans. William Granger Ryan, with an introduction by Eamon Duffy (Princeton: Princeton University Press, 2012), 4. For the quotations that follow, see ibid., 771–73.

8. Geneviève Brunel-Lobrichon was well aware of the extent to which the *Golden Legend* transcends the genre of the legendary. Stressing "the originality of the *Légende dorée* in relation to other legendaries," she recalls that the work also includes folklore narratives (about which I will have something to say later), which led to a renewal of interest in it in the nineteenth century, given that its influence can be discerned in the famous *Bibliothèque bleue*, thus assuring the *Golden Legend*

a place within the *longue durée* of popular literature. See *Dictionnaire des lettres françaises, Le Moyen Âge* (Paris: Fayard, 1964), "Légende dorée," 924–25.

9. In Jacopo da Voragine, *Legenda aurea*, critical edition by Giovanni Paolo Maggioni, 2nd ed. rev., 2 vols. (Tavernuzze/Florence: SISMEL/Edizioni del Galluzzo, 1998), the original Latin reads: *Universum tempus presentis uite in quatuor distinguitur.* Quoted here from *The Golden Legend*, trans. Ryan, 3; for the quotation that follows, see ibid., 3–4.

10. See Heinz Meyer and Rudolf Suntrup, *Lexicon der Mittelalterlichen Zahlenbedeutungen* (Munich: Fink, 1987). I thank Alain Guerreau for this reference.

# Chapter 4

1. Peter Brown, *The Cult of the Saints: Its Rise and Function in Latin Christianity* (Chicago: University of Chicago Press, 1981), in French translation as *Le Culte des saints, son essor et ses fonctions dans la chrétienté latine*, trans. Robert Lamont (Paris: Cerf, 1984; 2011). Peter Brown relies here on two anthropologists who have shown that Islamic sainthood is not only peripheral, but more or less metaphorical: Ernest Gellner, *Saints of the Atlas* (Chicago: University of Chicago Press, 1969) and Michael Gilsenan, *Saints and Sufi in Modern Egypt: An Essay in the Sociology of Religion* (Oxford: Clarendon Press, 1973).

2. The number 153, which, according to the Gospel, is the number of fish caught in this miraculous event, was recalled in various ways in the Middle Ages, not only in texts, but in church architecture and decoration. Alain Guerreau, whom I thank, points out that the ceiling of the Romanesque church of Zilis in the Grisons is decorated with 153 painted panels.

3. Aviad Kleinberg, *Histoire de saints: Leur rôle dans la formation de l'Occident* (Paris: Gallimard, 2005), in English translation by Jane Marie Todd as *Flesh Made Word: Saints' Stories and the Western Imagination* (Cambridge, MA: Belknap Press of Harvard University Press, 2008).

4. Alain Boureau also stresses the narrative merits of the *Golden Legend* in Boureau, *La Légende dorée: Le système narratif de Jacques de Voragine († 1298)* (Paris: Cerf, 1984). For others who have inspired the current essay, see the Bibliography, section 8 on Saints and Sanctity, especially Sofia Boesch Gajano and André Vauchez, as well as Peter Brown and Alain Boureau, of course.

5. Iacopo da Varagine, *Legenda aurea*, critical edition by Giovanni Paolo Maggioni, 2nd ed. rev., 2 vols. (Tavernuzze/Florence: SISMEL/Edizioni del Galluzzo, 1998), 2: 1684.

6. Jacques de Voragine, *La Légende dorée*, text presented, with notes, by Alain Boureau et al., preface by Jacques Le Goff, Bibliothèque de la Pléiade (Paris: Gallimard, 2004), 1437.

7. Augustin Hollaardt, "La Toussaint: Son histoire, sa liturgie," *Questions liturgiques* 80 (1999): 91–105.

8. M. Lambert and Jean-Luc Solère, "Guillaume d'Auxerre," in *Dictionnaire du Moyen Âge*, ed. Claude Gauvard, Alain de Libera, and Michel Zink (Paris: Presses Universitaires de France, 2002), 627.

9. Jacobus de Voragine, *The Golden Legend*, trans. William Granger Ryan, with an introduction by Eamon Duffy (Princeton: Princeton University Press, 2012), 664. For the quotation that follows, see ibid., 665.

10. Jean-Thiébaut Welter, *L'Exemplum dans la littérature religieuse et didactique du Moyen Âge* (Paris and Toulouse: Guitard, 1927); Frederic C. Tubach, *Index Exemplorum: A Handbook of Medieval Religious Tales* (Helsinki: Suomalaineh Tiedeakatemia, 1969); Claude Brémond, Jacque Le Goff, and Jean-Claude Schmitt, "L'exemplum," in *Typologie des sources du Moyan Âge occidental* (Turnhout: Brepols, 1982); Jean-Claude Schmitt, ed., *Prêcher d'exemples: Récits de prédicateurs du Moyen Âge* (Paris: Stock, 1985); Frederic C. Tubach, *Les Exempla médiévaux: Introduction de la recherche suivie de tables critiques de l'*Index exemplorum, ed. Jacques Berlioz and Marie Anne Polo de Beaulieu (Carcassonne: GARAE/Hesiode, 1992); André Vauchez, "Exempla," in *Dictionnaire encyclopédique du Moyen Âge*, ed. André Vauchez (Paris: Cerf, 1997), 1: 568–69.

11. See Jacques Le Goff, *La Naissance du Purgatoire* (Paris: Gallimard, 1981), in English translation by Arthur Goldhammer as *The Birth of Purgatory* (Chicago: University of Chicago Press, 1981). I am differing here from the interpretation given of this image of Purgatory by Alain Boureau et al. in Jacobus de Voragine, *La Légende dorée*, ed. Boureau et al., 1441, n. 61.

12. On the topic of the various saints named James, see Jacobus de Voragine, *La Légende dorée*, ed. Boureau et al., 1223–24. A comparison between the table of contents of that book and the present book will show which of the saints with the same name I have commented on and those whom I have left aside but who have a chapter dedicated to them in the *Golden Legend*.

## Chapter 5

1. Jacobus de Voragine, *The Golden Legend: Readings on the Saints*, trans. William Granger Ryan, with an introduction by Eamon Duffy (Princeton: Princeton University Press, 2012), 4.

2. This fact justifies, among other things, the current success of a history of passions that may considerably enrich our knowledge of the Middle Ages.

3. Piroska Nagy-Zombory, *Le Don des larmes au Moyen Âge* (Paris: Albin Michel, 2000).

4. *The Golden Legend*, trans. Ryan, 13.

5. In Jacques de Voragine, *La Légende dorée*, ed. Alain Boureau et al., preface by Jaques Le Goff, Bibliothèque de la Pléiade (Paris: Gallimard, 2004), Boureau et al. state that "la Margondie" has not been identified; *The Golden Legend*, trans. Ryan,

14, n. 3, gives "Murgundia, also called Ethiopia." For the quotations that follow, see *The Golden Legend*, trans. Ryan, 14.

6. Ibid., 18.
7. Ibid.
8. Ibid., 56.
9. Ibid., 22.
10. Ibid., 25.
11. In *La Légende dorée*, Alain Boureau et al. mention the crusades only four times in the 1057 pages of text in their edition.
12. *The Golden Legend*, trans. Ryan, 27.
13. For a judicious and well-documented treatment of this topic, see Jacques Rossiaud, *Amours vénales: La prostitution en Occident, XIIe–XVIe siècle* (Paris: Aubier, 2010).
14. *The Golden Legend*, trans. Ryan, 29, gives the "very day Maximian has died" and places Saint Lucy's death "about the year of the Lord 310."
15. Ibid., 29, 30.
16. Ibid., 31.
17. See Jacques Le Goff, "L'Occident médiéval et l'océan Indien: Un horizon onirique," in Le Goff, *Pour un autre Moyen Âge: Temps, travail et culture en Occident: 18 essais* (Paris: Gallimard, 1977), 280–306; in English translation by Arthur Goldhammer as "The Medieval West and the Indian Ocean: An Oneiric Horizon," in Le Goff, *Time, Work and Culture in the Middle Ages* (Chicago: University of Chicago Press, 1980), 189–200.
18. *The Golden Legend*, trans. Ryan, 35.
19. If I insist on the fact, despite these criticisms, that Jacobus de Voragine was interested in chronology, I am not asserting that he was an expert. This date seems to indicate that the distant past was fairly confused in his mind.
20. Richard Trexler, *The Journey of the Magi: Meanings in History of a Christian Story* (Princeton: Princeton University Press, 1997), in French translation as *Le Voyage des mages à travers l'histoire* (Paris: A. Colin, 2009).

# Chapter 6

1. Jacobus de Voragine, *The Golden Legend: Readings on the Saints*, trans. William Granger Ryan, with an introduction by Eamon Duffy (Princeton: Princeton University Pres, 2012), 3.
2. Ibid., 37.
3. For one particular but significant instance, see Nicolas Offenstadt, *Faire la paix au Moyen Âge: Discours et gestes de paix pendant la guerre de Cent Ans* (Paris: Odile Jacob, 2007).
4. There is no chapter in the *Golden Legend* dedicated to Saint Joseph. For Jacobus de Voragine, Joseph was not a saint but a normal historical personage, a descen-

dant of the House of David and thus particularly worthy of being the putative but humanly official father of Jesus. His cult later developed thanks to Saint Theresa of Avila in the sixteenth century, but he was canonized by Pope Pius IX only in 1870. Jacobus de Voragine mentions him several times in the *Golden Legend*, in particular on the occasion of the Nativity, then of the flight to Egypt, but he never grants him the title of "saint."

5. *The Golden Legend*, trans. Ryan, 38, 39.

6. Ibid., 42.

7. Ibid., 43.

8. Ibid.

9. Ibid., 44.

10. Ibid., 48. For the next paragraph, see ibid., 46, 48.

11. Ibid., 50

12. Ibid., 53.

13. Ibid., 59.

14. Ibid., 61.

15. Ibid., 62.

16. Ibid., 71.

17. For a full explanation of the great originality displayed by Jacobus de Voragine in his treatment of the circumcision of Christ, see Pascal Collomb, "Les éléments liturgiques de la *Légende dorée*: Tradition et innovations," in Barbara Fleith and Franco Morenzoni, *De la sainteté à l'hagiographie: Genèse et usage de la* Légende dorée (Geneva: Droz, 2001), 105ff.

18. *The Golden Legend*, trans. Ryan, 74.

19. Ibid., 77.

20. Ibid., 78.

21. On this topic, see the fine book by Richard Trexler, *The Journey of the Magi: Meanings in History of a Christian Story* (Princeton: Princeton University Press, 1997).

22. *The Golden Legend*, trans. Ryan, 79.

23. Ibid., 82.

24. Ibid., 84.

25. Jacques Le Goff, "Le désert-forêt dans l'Occident médiéval," *Traverses* 19 (1980): 22–33, reprinted in Le Goff, *Un autre Moyen Age* (Paris: Gallimard, 1999), 495–510.

26. Here and immediately below, *The Golden Legend*, trans. Ryan, 85.

27. Ibid., 93.

28. See Jacques de Voragine, *La Légende dorée*, text presented, with notes, by Alain Boureau et al., preface by Jacques Le Goff, Bibliothèque de la Pléiade (Paris: Gallimard, 2004), 1265 and 1266. The Saint John and Saint Paul who emerged from this faulty reading were connected, for they are supposed to have been both attached to Princess Constantia, the daughter of Emperor Constantine.

29. *The Golden Legend*, trans. Ryan, 338.

30. Ibid., 119, 120.
31. Here and immediately below, ibid., 350, 351.
32. Ibid., 113.
33. Ibid., 117.

## Chapter 7

1. Heinz Meyer and Rudolph Suntrup, *Lexicon der Mittelalterlichen Zahlenbedeutungen* (Munich: Fink, 1987). My thanks to Alain Guerreau for this reference.
2. Jacobus de Voragine, *The Golden Legend: Readings on the Saints*, trans. William Granger Ryan, with an introduction by Eamon Duffy (Princeton: Princeton University Press, 2012), 134.
3. Ibid., 137.
4. Ibid., 139.
5. Ibid., 203.
6. Ibid., 206. For what follows, see ibid., 206, 208.
7. Ibid., 213, 214.
8. I agree with Brother Antoine Lion, O.P., who thinks that for Jacobus de Voragine in the *Golden Legend*, time is founded uniquely on what he holds to be essential in the temporality of Christ incarnate: the Nativity, the Circumcision, Epiphany, the Passion, the Resurrection, and the Ascension.
9. *The Golden Legend*, trans. Ryan, 147, 148.
10. Thomas Aquinas, *Summa theologica*, prima pars, q. 92, art. 3 (a work written around 1268). This explanation can already be found in Hugh of Saint Victor and Peter Lombard.
11. *The Golden Legend*, trans. Ryan, 200.
12. Ibid., 194.
13. Jacques Le Goff, *La Naissance du Purgatoire* (Paris: Gallimard, 1981), in English translation by Arthur Goldhammer as *The Birth of Purgatory* (Chicago: University of Chicago Press, 1981).
14. *The Golden Legend*, trans. Ryan, 194.

## Chapter 8

1. Jacobus de Voragine, *The Golden Legend*, trans. William Granger Ryan, with an introduction by Eamon Duffy (Princeton: Princeton University Press, 2012), 3.
2. Ibid., 216.
3. Ibid.
4. Ibid., 291.
5. Ibid., 292.
6. Ibid., 293.

7.  Ibid.
8.  Ibid., 301, 302.
9.  Ibid., 277.
10. Ibid.
11. As is known, the manger and Christ's crib are a late invention, probably of the twelfth century. They were much publicized by Francis of Assisi after he had visited a crèche in Greccio, with the result that less than a century later Jacobus de Voragine holds them to be a real phenomenon contemporary to the nativity of Christ.
12. *The Golden Legend*, trans. Ryan, 283, 284.
13. Ibid., 285.
14. Ibid., 285–86.
15. Jacques de Voragine, *La Légende dorée*, text presented, with notes, by Alain Boureau et al., preface by Jacques Le Goff, Bibliothèque de la Pléiade (Paris: Gallimard, 2004), 1235, n. 11.
16. *The Golden Legend*, trans. Ryan, 288.
17. Ibid., 229 (with some variation). For what follows, see ibid., 229–30.
18. Ibid., 237.
19. Ibid., 242.
20. Ibid., 245.
21. Ibid., 247.
22. Ibid., 257.
23. See Jacques Le Goff, *Le Moyen Âge et l'Argent: Essai d'anthropologie historique* (Paris: Perrin, 2010).

## Chapter 9

1.  Jacobus de Voragine, *The Golden Legend: Readings on the Saints*, trans. William Granger Ryan, with an introduction by Eamon Duffy (Princeton: Princeton University Press, 2012), 535.
2.  Ibid., 539. For what follows, see ibid., 539–40.
3.  Ibid., 540. For what follows, see ibid., 540–44.
4.  The Assumption of the Blessed Virgin Mary occupies thirty pages in the critical edition by Giovanni Paolo Maggioni of *Iacopo da Varagine, Legenda aurea*, 2nd ed. rev., 2 vols. (Tavarnuzze/Florence: SISMEL/Edizioni del Galluzzo, 1998), 2: 866–99. In comparison, the chapter on the Nativity of Christ is thirteen pages long (1: 74–87).
5.  *The Golden Legend*, trans. Ryan, 463.
6.  Ibid., 464.
7.  I relied in part on this episode, which had a wide resonance in the Middle Ages, to advance the hypothesis that after the Gregorian reform—when the Marian cult, which was already lively in Byzantium, took an extraordinary upward turn in the West—one might consider that Mary in fact became something like a fourth person of the Trinity,

since she had realized the divine nature that was within her. See Jacques Le Goff, *Le Dieu du Moyen Âge*, interviews with Jean-Luc Pouthier (Paris: Bayard, 2003).

8. *The Golden Legend*, trans. Ryan, 473. For a somewhat different version of what follows, see ibid., 474.

9. In her fine book on the Virgin Mary, the great British historian Miri Rubin states that the Marian cult experienced a truly exceptional rise, which had already begun in the twelfth century, thanks to these pages in the *Golden Legend*. See Miri Rubin, *Mother of God: A History of the Virgin Mary* (London: Penguin Books, 2009), 203.

10. *The Golden Legend*, trans. Ryan, 554.

11. Ibid., 537.

12. Ibid., 558.

13. The Feast of the Finding of the Body of Saint Stephen was eliminated in 1961, on the eve of the Second Vatican Council.

14. Jean-Claude Schmitt, *L'Invention de l'anniversaire* (Paris: Arkhe, 2010).

15. See Jacques de Voragine, *La Légende dorée*, text presented, with notes, by Alain Boureau et al., preface by Jacques Le Goff, Bibliothèque de la Pléiade (Paris: Gallimard, 2004), 1279.

16. *The Golden Legend*, trans. Ryan, 365.

17. For a slightly different account of the Seven Sleepers, see ibid., 402–404.

18. The theme of the exceptional personage—king, saint, Sleeping Beauty—who sleeps for a long time before reawakening is almost universal. It is the subject of a verse of the Koran. On this topic see the famous works of Louis Massignon, whose articles have been gathered together in his *Opera minora: Textes recueillis, classés et présentés avec une bibliographie*, ed. Youakim Moubarac, 3 vols. (Paris: Presses Universitaires de France, 1969), vol. 3. See also Francis Jourdan, *La Tradition des Sept Dormants: Une rencontre entre chrétiens et musulmans* (Paris: Maisonneuve et Larose, 1983).

19. *The Golden Legend*, trans. Ryan, 574.

20. Jacques de Voragine, *La Légende dorée*, ed. Boureau et al., 1418–19.

21. I might recall that perhaps from the twelfth century (certainly from the thirteenth), the kings of France had cured people suffering from scrofula (the "king's itch") in the cloister of the abbey church of Saint-Denis.

22. Dagobert actually reigned from 629 to 639.

23. *The Golden Legend*, trans. Ryan, 627. In the twelfth century the famous philosopher Abelard expressed doubt about the assimilation of two or three historical persons named Denis into one saint, but his example was not followed. Jacobus de Voragine makes a discrete allusion to him here.

24. Jacques de Voragine, *La Légende dorée*, ed. Boureau et al., 1446.

25. Ibid., 1262.

26. Schmitt, *L'Invention de l'anniversaire*.

27. *The Golden Legend*, Ryan trans., 328, 520.

28. Ibid., 520. For what follows, see ibid., 521, 525.

29. Ibid., 398.

30. Ibid., 485.

31. Ibid., 486. Saint Bernard was in fact born in 1090, as we have learned from sources discovered by modern historians. For what follows, see ibid., 486, 483.

32. " . . . never laughed but that it seemed he was forcing himself to laugh rather than to suppress laughter," ibid., 487.

33. On laughter, see Jacques Le Goff, "Le rire dans la société médiévale," in Le Goff, *Un autre Moyen Âge* (Paris: Gallimard, 1999), 1341ff.

34. *The Golden Legend*, trans. Ryan, 503.

35. Ibid., 506.

36. Ibid., 513.

37. Ibid., 514.

38. Jacques de Voragine, *La Légende dorée*, ed. Boureau et al., 1399.

39. *The Golden Legend*, trans. Ryan, 591.

40. Ibid., 601. In reality Jerome died in the year 420.

41. Ibid., 606.

42. Jacques de Voragine, *La Légende dorée*, ed. Boureau et al., 1448–49.

43. *The Golden Legend*, trans. Ryan, 681.

44. Ibid., 684.

45. Ibid., 686.

46. Dávid Falvay, "St. Elizabeth of Hungary in Italian Vernacular Literature: *Vitae, Miracles, Revelations*, and the *Meditations on the Life of Crist*," in Ottó Gecser, et al., *Promoting the Saints: Cults and their Contexts from Late Antiquity until the Early Modern Period*, preface by Jacques Le Goff (Budapest: Central European University Press, 2011), 137–50. The *Golden Legend* did much to contribute to the popularity of the cult of Saint Elizabeth, not only in Hungary but throughout Christendom.

47. *The Golden Legend*, trans. Ryan, 689.

48. Ibid., 690. For the following, see ibid., 691, 696.

49. Ibid., 698.

50. Ibid., 724. For what follows, see ibid., 725, 727.

51. Jacobus de Voragine must be alluding here not to the emperor Maximinus I (235–238), but to the Caesar Maximinus II who governed Egypt and Syria from 305 to 313 and persecuted Christians with particular zeal.

52. See above for a more detailed discussion of All Saints within the framework of the definition of saints and their function in Christianity in general and within the *Golden Legend* in particular. I return here, briefly, to the chronological place that All Saints occupies within the *Golden Legend* and its role within the perspective of its close connection with the feast day that follows it, the Commemoration of All Souls.

53. *The Golden Legend*, trans. Ryan, 659.

54. Ibid.

55. Ibid., 665.

56. See Jacques Le Goff, *La Naisssance du Purgatoire* (Paris: Gallimard, 1981), in English translation by Arthur Goldhammer as *The Birth of Purgatory* (Chicago: University of Chicao Press, 1981); Jacques le Goff, *Un autre Moyen Âge*, Quarto (Paris: Gallimard, 1999).

57. *The Golden Legend*, trans. Ryan, 667.

58. Ibid., 674–75.

59. See the seven-page article by Claire Sotinel, "Pelagio I," in the large and extremely erudite *Enciclopedia Italiana dei papi*, published in 2000 by the Istituto Treccani, 3 vols. (Rome: Istituto del Enciclopedia italiana, 2000), 1: 529–36, which gives an abundant list of sources and bibliography.

60. Iacopo da Varagine, *Cronica della Città di Genova dalle Origini al 1297*, introduction and translation by Stefania Bertini Guidetti (Genoa: Edizioni culturali internazionali, 1995).

61. *The Golden Legend*, trans. Ryan, 754.

62. Ibid., 765.

63. Ibid., 770.

64. Stefano Mula, "L'histoire des Lombards: Son rôle et son importance dans la *Legenda aurea*," in Barbara Fleith and Franco Morenzoni, *De la sainteté à l'hagiographie: Genèse et usage de la* Légende dorée (Geneva: Droz, 2001), 75–95.

65. "The Dedication of a Church" is chapter 182 in *The Golden Legend*, trans. Ryan. Jean-Claude Schmitt, whom I thank, communicates to me that a chapter on the feast day of the Dedication of a Church also closes the *Rationales divinorum officiorum* of the liturgist Guillaume Durand of Mende, "both because that feast is *variable* from one church to another even while it is inscribed within a fixed, universal sanctorale, and because the *place*—the church, the altar—consecrated on that day welcomes all the saints."

66. Jacques de Voragine, *La Légende dorée*, ed. Boureau et al., 1487.

67. I recommend the reading of an interesting article by Dominique Donadieu-Rigaut, "La *Légende dorée* et ses images," in ibid., lvii–cxi; and Chloé Maillet, "La Parenté hagiographique d'après Jacques de Voragine et les manuscrits enluminés de la *Légende dorée* (1260–1490)," thèse soutenue a l'École de hautes études en sciences sociales, 6 September 2010, 3 vols. typewritten. I thank the author of this thesis and her thesis director, Jean-Claude Schmitt, for telling me of this study, which is highly interesting but does not apply to the topic of the present book.

68. *The Golden Legend*, trans. Ryan, 772.

69. The text I am referring to was first published in 1978 and has been republished as "Le merveilleux dans l'Occident médiéval," in Le Goff, *Un autre Moyen Âge*, 455–91.

70. *The Golden Legend*, trans. Ryan, 774.

71. Ibid., 781.

# Bibliography

## 1. Jacobus de Voragine and the *Golden Legend*

Barth, Ferdinand. "Legenden als Lehrdichtung: Beobachtungen zu den Märtyrerlegenden in der *Legenda aurea*." In *Europäische Lehrdichtung, Festschrift für Walter Naumann zum 70. Geburtstag* (Darmstadt: Wissenschaftliche Buchgesellschaft, 1981), 61–73.

Bataillon, Louis-Jacques. "Iacopo da Varazze e Tommaso d'Aquino." *Sapienza* 32 (1979), 22–29.

Bertini Guidetti, Stefania. "Enquête sur les techniques de compilation de Jacques de Varagine." *Cahiers d'histoire* 16 (1996): 5–24.

———. "Iacopo da Varagine e le 'Ystorie antique': Quando il mito diventa 'exemplum' nella storia." In *Posthomerica* I: *Tradizioni omeriche dall'Antichità al Rinascimento.* Edited by Franco Montanari and Stefano Pittaluga. Genoa: Dipartimento di archeologia, filologia classica e loro tradizioni, 1997, 139–57.

———. "Contrastare la crisi della chiesa cattedrale: Iacopo da Varagine e la construzione di un'ideologia propagandistica." In *Le Vie del Mediterraneo: Uomini, idee, ogetti (secoli 11–16).* Edited by Gabriella Airaldi. Genoa: ECIG, 1997, 155–82.

Boureau, Alain. *La Légende dorée: Le système narratif de Jacques de Voragine († 1298).* Preface by Jacques Le Goff. Paris: Cerf, 1984, 2007.

Cenerelli Campana, Carlo. "La tradizione venezia della 'Translatio sancti Nicolai' nel primo volgarizzamento italiano a stampa della *Legenda aurea* di Jacopo da Voragine." *Miscellanea Marciana* 7–9 (1992–94): 103–15.

Chierici, Joseph. "Il miracolo in Jacopo da Voragine, Gonzala de Berceo e Dante." *L'Alighieri* 19 (1978): 18–27.

Colledge, Edmund. "James of Voragine's 'Legendas Augustini' and His Sources." *Augustiniana* 35 (1985): 281–314.

Di Pietro Lombardi, Paola, Milena Ricci, and Anna Rosa Venturi Barbolini. *Legenda aurea: Iconografia religiosa nelle miniature della Biblioteca Estense universitaria.* Modena: Il Bulino, 2001.

Dunn-Lardeau, Brenda, and Dominique Coq, "Fifteenth and Sixteenth-Century Editions of the *Légende dorée.*" *Bibliothèque d'humanisme et Renaissance* 47 (1985): 87–101.

Fleith, Barbara. "Hagiographisches Interesse im 15. Jahrhundert: Erörtert an einem Jahrhundert Rezeptionsgeschichte der Legenda aurea." *Fifteenth-Century Studies* 9 (1984): 85–98.

———. "Die *Legenda aurea* und ihre dominikanischen Bruderlegendare: Aspekte der Quellenverhältnisse apokryphen Gedankenguts." *Apocrypha* 7 (1996): 167–91.

———. "The Patristic Sources of the *Legenda aurea*: A Research Report." In *The Reception of the Church Fathers in the West: From the Carolingians to the Maurists.* Edited by Irena Backus, 2 vols. Leiden and New York: Brill, 1997, 1: 231–87.

———, et al. *La Légende dorée de Jacques de Voragine: Le livre qui fascinait le Moyen Âge.* Geneva: Bibliothèque publique et universitaire de Genève, 1998.

———, and Franco Morenzoni. *De la sainteté à l'hagiographie: Genèse et usage de la Légende dorée.* Geneva: Droz, 2001.

Gaiffier, Baudouin de. "*Légende dorée* ou légende de plomb?" *Analecta Bollandiana* 83 (1965): 350–54.

———. "L'Historia apocrypha dans la Légende dorée." *Analecta Bollandiana* 91 (1973): 265–72.

Gounelle, Rémi. "Sens et usage d' 'apocryphus' dans la *Légende dorée.*" *Apocrypha* 5 (1994): 189–210.

Hamer, Richard, ed. *Three Lives from the Gilte Legende.* Heidelberg: Winter, 1978.

Huot-Girard, Giselle. "La justice immanente dans la Légende dorée." In *Épopées, légendes et miracles. Cahiers d'études médiévales.* Edited by G. H. Allard and J. Ménard, (Montreal: Bellarmine; Paris: Vrin, 1974), 135–47.

Knape, Joachim, and Karl Strobel. *Zur Deutung von Geschichte in Antike und Mittelalter: Plinius d.J. "Panegyricus," "Historia apocrypha" der "Legenda aurea."* Bamberg: Bayerische Verlagsanstalt, 1985.

Kunze, Konrad. "Jacobus a (de) Voragine (Varagine)." In *Die deutsche Literatur des Mittelalters: Verfasserlexikon.* 14 vols. Berlin and New York: De Gruyter, 1978–2007, vol. 4 (1983), cols. 448–66.

*Legenda aurea, Légende dorée (XIIIe–XVe s.),* Actes du colloque international de Perpignan. Edited by Brenda Dunn-Lardeau. *Le Moyen Âge français* 32 (1993).

Maggioni, Giovanni Paolo. "Dalla prima a la seconda redazione della *Legenda aurea*: Particularità e anomalie nella tradizione manoscritta delle compilazioni medievali." *Filologia medievale* 2 (1995): 259–77.

Martucci, Vittorio. "Manoscritti e stampe antiche della *Legenda aurea* di Jacopo da Varagine volgarizzata." *Filologia e critica* 5 (1980): 30–50.

Mombrini, Augusta. "La *Legenda aurea* di Jacopo da Varazze." *Memorie domenicane* 86 (1969): 19–42.

Nagy, Maria von, and Christoph von Nagy. *Die* Legenda aurea *und ihr Verfasser Jacobus de Voragine.* Bern: Franke, 1971.

Pagano, Antonio. "Etimologie medievali di Jacopo da Voragine." *Memorie domenicane* 53 (1936): 81–91.

———. "*L'Oratoria* di Jacopo da Voragine." *Memorie domenicane* 59 (1942): 77–99, 108, 112, 137–41.

Pouchelle, Marie-Christine, "Représentations du corps dans la *Légende dorée*." *Ethnologie française* 16 (1976): 293–308.

Reames, Sherry L. "St. Martin of Tours in the *Legenda aurea* and Before." *Viator* 12 (1981): 131–64.

Rhein, Reglinde. *Die* Legenda aurea *des Jacobus de Voragine: Die Entfaltung von Heiligkeit in "Historia" und "Doctrina".* Cologne: Böhlau, 1995.

Schnell, Rüdiger. "Konstanz und Metamorphosen eines Textes: Eine Überlieferungs- und geschlechtergeschichtliche Studie zur volksprachlichen Rezeption von Jacobus de Voragine." *Frümittelalterliche Studien* 33 (1999): 319–95.

Surdel, Alain, "Les quatre éléments dans les légendes hagiographiques du XIIIe siècle (*Legenda aurea, Abbreviato in gestis sanctorum*)." In *Les Quatre Éléments dans la culture médiévale.* Edited by Danielle Buschinger and André Crepin. Göppingen: Kümmerle Verlag, 1983, 49–62.

Vidmanovà, Anežka. "À propos de la diffusion de la *Légende dorée* dans les pays tchèques." In *L'Art au XIIIe siècle dans les pays tchèques.* Prague, 1983, 599–619.

Walter, Christian. *Prozess und Wahrheitsfindung in der* Legenda aurea. Kiel: Christian-Albrechts-Universität, 1977.

Williams-Krapp, Werner. "Die deutschen Übersetzungen der *Legenda aurea* des Jacobus de Voragine." *Beiträge zur Geschichte der deutschen Sprache und Literatur* 101 (1979): 252–76.

Winroth, Anders. "Thomas interpretatur abyssus vel geminus: The Etymologies in the *Golden Legend* of Jacobus de Varagine." In *Symbolae Septentrionales: Latin Studies Presented to Jan Öberg.* Stockholm: Sällskapet Runica et Mediaevalia, 1995, 113–35.

Witlin, C. J. "Les explicacions dels hagionims en la *Legenda aurea* i la tradicio medieval d'etimologies no-derivacionals." *Analecta sacra Tarraconensia* 48 (1975): 75–84.

## 2. Genoa in the Time of Jacobus de Voragine

Airaldi, Gabriella. *Jacopo da Varagine, tra santi e mercanti.* Milan: Camunia, 1988.

———. *Genova e la Liguria nel Medioevo.* Turin: UTET, 1986; Genoa: Frilli, 2007.

Balard, Michel. *La Romanie génoise: XIIe–début du XVe siècle*. 2 vols. Rome: École française de Rome, 1978.

Boureau, Alain. "Le Prêcheur et les marchands: Ordre divin et désordres du siècle dans la 'Chronique de Gênes' de Jacques de Voragine." *Médiévales* 4 (1983): 102–22.

Crouzet-Pavan, Élizabeth. *Enfers et Paradis: L'Italie de Dante et de Giotto*. Paris: Albin Michel, 2001, 2004.

Epstein, Steven A. *Genoa and the Genoese, 958–1528*. Chapel Hill and London: University of North Carolina Press, 1996.

Heers, Jacques. "Urbanisme et structure sociale à Gênes au Moyen Âge." In *Studi in onore di Amintore Fanfani*. 6 vols. Milan: Giuffrè, 1962, 1: 371–412.

Jones, P. J. *The Italian City-State: From Commune to Signoria*. Oxford and New York: Clarendon Press, 1977.

Lopez, Roberto S. *Storia delle colonie genovesi nel Mediterraneo*. (1938). 2nd ed. Genoa, 1996.

Maire Vigueur, Jean-Claude. *Cavaliers et citoyens: Guerres, conflits et société dans l'Italie communale, XIIe–XIIIe siècle*. Paris: École des hautes études en sciences sociales, 2003, 316–18.

"Les ordres mendiants et la ville en Italie centrale (v. 1220–v. 1350)." *Mémoires de l'École française de Rome* 89, no. 2 (1977): 577–773.

Petti Balbi, Giovanna. *Una città e il suo mare: Genova nel Medioevo*. Bologna: CLUEB, 1991.

Pistarino, Geo. *La Capitale del Mediterraneo: Genova nel Medioevo*. Bordighera: Istituto internazionale di studi liguri, 1993.

## 3. The "Beautiful" Thirteenth Century

Genicot, Léopold. *Le XIIIe siècle européen*. Paris, 1968. 2nd ed., revised. Paris: Presses Universitaires de France, 1984.

Le Goff, Jacques. *L'Apogée de la chrétienté v. 1180–v. 1330*. Paris: Bordas, 1982.

———. "Apostolat mendiant et faits urbains dans la France médiévale." *Annales E.S.C.* (1968): 335–48.

———. "Du ciel sur la terre: La mutation des valeurs du XIIe au XVIIIe siècle dans l'Occident chrétien." In Le Goff, *Héros du Moyen Âge, le saint et le roi*. Paris: Gallimard, 2004, 1263–87.

*Il Paradiso e la terra: Iacopo da Varazze e il suo tempo*. Atti del Convegno internazionale, Varazze, 1998. Edited by Stefania Bertini Guidetti. Tavarnuzze: SISMEL/ Edizioni del Galluzzo, 2001.

## 4. The Latin Legendaries

Boureau, Alain. "Saint Bernard dans les légendiers dominicains." In *Vies et légendes de saint Bernard de Clairvaux: Création, diffusion, réception (XIIe–XXe siècles)*. Edited by Patrick Arabeyre, Jacques Berlioz, and Phillippe Poirrier. Cîtaux: Présence cistercienne, 1993, 84–90.

———. "Vincent de Beauvais et les légendiers dominicains." In *Lector et compilator: Vincent de Beauvais, frère prêcheur: Un intellectuel et son milieu au XIIIe siècle.* Edited by Serge Lusignan and Monique Paulmier-Foucart. Grâne: Créaphis, 1997, 113–26.

———. "Barthélemy de Trente et l'invention de la *Legenda nova.*" In Sofia Boesch Gajano, ed., *Raccolte di Vite di Santi dal XII al XVIII secolo: Strutture, messaggi, fruizioni.* Fasano di Brindisi: Schena, 1990, 23–39.

Dolbeau, François. "Les Prologues de légendiers latins." In *Les Prologues médiévaux.* Actes du colloque international, Rome 1998. Edited by Jacqueline Hamesse. Turnhout: Brepols, 2000, 345–94.

Dondaine, Antoine. "Le dominicain français Jean de Mailly et la *Légende dorée.*" *Archives d'histoire dominicaine.* Paris: Cerf, 1946, 1: 53–102.

Maggioni, Giovanni Paolo. "La trasmissione dei legendari abbreviati del XIII secolo." *Filologia mediolatina* 9 (2002): 87–107.

Philippart, Guy. *Les Légendiers latins et autres manuscrits hagiographiques.* Turnhout: Brepols, 1977.

# 5. The Dominicans in the Thirteenth Century

Hinnebusch, William A. *The History of the Dominican Order.* 2 vols. New York: Alba House, 1966–1973.

Vicaire, Marie-Humbert. *Dominique et ses prêcheurs.* Fribourg: Éditions Universitaires; Paris: Cerf, 1977.

# 6. Liturgy and Christian Time in the Middle Ages

Bonniwel, William R., O.P. *A History of the Dominican Liturgy 1215–1945.* New York: Wagner, 1945.

Dalmais, Irénée Henri, Pierre Jounel, and Aimé Georges Martimort. *La Liturgie et le Temps.* Paris: Desclée, 1983. In English translation as *The Liturgy and Time.* London: G. Chaptan; Collegeville, MN: Liturgical Press, 1986.

*L'Église en prière: Introduction à la liturgie.* Edited by Aimé Georges Martimort. Paris: Desclée, 1961; 3rd ed., revised and corrected, Paris: Desclée, 1965.

Elich, Tom. "Using Liturgical Texts in the Middle Ages." In *Fountain of Life.* Edited by Gerard Austin. Washington, DC: Pastoral Press, 1991, 69–83.

Gy, Pierre-Marie. "Liturgistes." In *Dictionnaire encyclopédique du Moyen Âge.* Edited by André Vauchez. 2 vols. Paris: Cerf, 1997, 2: 899–900.

Jungmann, Joseph A. *Missarum Solemnia: Explication génétique de la messe romaine.* Paris: Persée, 1951, 1955. In English translation as *The Mass of the Roman Rite: Its Origins and Development (Missarum Solemnia).* Translated by Francis A. Brunner. 2 vols. New York: Benziger, 1951–1955.

# 7. Christian Time in the Middle Ages

Bidot, Eric. *Saint Augustin: Le Temps de Dieu*. Paris: Points, 2008.

———. "Tempo y memoria en la edad media." Special issue of *Temas medievales* 2 (Buenos Aires, 1992).

Duval, Frédéric. "Hagiographie: Jacopo da Vorazze (Jacques de Voragine), *Legenda aurea* ou *Légende dorée*." In Frédéric Duval. *Lectures françaises de la fin du Moyen Âge: Petite anthologie commentée de succès littéraires*. Geneva: Droz, 2007, 113–23.

Flasch, Kurt. *Was ist Zeit? Augustinus von Hippo, das XI. Buch der Confessiones*. Frankfurt: Klostermann, 1993.

Le Goff, Jacques. *Un autre Moyen Âge*. Paris: Gallimard, 1999. In English translation as *Time, Work and Culture in the Middle Ages*. Translated by Arthur Goldhammer. Chicago: University of Chicago Press, 1980.

Luneau, Auguste. *L'Histoire du salut chez les pères de l'Église, la doctrine des âges du monde*. Paris: Beauchesne, 1964.

Ribémont, Bernard, ed. *Le Temps, sa mesure et sa perception au Moyen Âge*. Actes du Colloque, Orléans, 1991. Caen: Paradigme, 1992.

*Sentimento del tiempo e periodizzazione della storia del Medioevo*. Atti del XXXVI Convegno storico internazionale Todi, 10–12 October 1999. Spoleto: Centro italiano di studi sull'alto medioevo, 2000.

Surdel, Alain. "Temps humain et temps divin dans la *Legenda aurea* (XIIIe siècle) et dans les mystères dramatiques (XVe siècle)." In *Le Temps et la Durée dans la littérature au Moyen Âge et à la Renaissance*. Colloque de Reims, 1984. Paris: Nizet, 1986, 85–102.

*Le Temps chrétien de la fin de l'Antiquité au Moyen Âge (IIIe–XIIIe siècle)*. Edited by Jean-Marie Leroux. CNRS colloquy. Paris, Éditions du Centre national de la recherche scientifique, 1984.

# 8. Saints and Sanctity under Christianity

Boesch-Gajano, Sofia. *La Santità*. Rome and Bari: Laterza, 1999.

———. *Agiografia altomedioevale*. Bologna: Il Mulino, 1976.

Brown, Peter. *The Cult of the Saints: Its Rise and Function in Latin Christianity*. Chicago: University of Chicago Press, 1981. In French translation as *Le Culte des saints, son essor et sa fonction dans la chrétienté latine*. Translated by Robert Lamont. Paris: Cerf, 1984; 2011.

Delcorno, Carlo. "Il raconto agiografico nella predicazione dei secoli XIII-XIV." In *Agiografia dell'Occidente cristiano, secoli XIII–XIV*. Atti dei Convegni dei Lincei XLVIII. Rome, 1980, 79–114.

*Les Fonctions des saints dans le monde occidental (IIIe–XIIIe siècle)*. Actes du Colloque, Rome, 1988. Rome: École française de Rome, 1991.

Gecser, Ottó, et al., *Promoting the Saints: Cults and Their Contexts from Late Antiquity until the Early Modern Period: Essays in Honor of Gábor Klaniczay for his 60th Birthday*. Budapest and New York: Central European University Press, 2011.

Iogna-Prat, Dominique, and Gilles Veinstein, eds. *Histoires des hommes de Dieu dans l'islam et le christianisme*. Paris: Flammarion, 2003.

Kleinberg, Aviad. *Histoire des saints: Leur rôle dans la formation de l'Occident*. Paris: Gallimard, 2005. In English translation as *Flesh Made Word: Saints' Stories and the Western Imagination*. Translated by Jane Marie Todd. Cambridge, MA: Belknap Press of Harvard University Press, 2008.

Leonardi, Claudio. *Agiografie medievali*. Edited by Antonella Degl'Innocenti and Francesco Santi. Florence: SISMEL/ Edizioni del Galluzzo, 2011.

Maggioni, Giovanni Paolo. "Storie malvagie e vite di santi: Storie apocrife, cattivi e demoni dei leggendari condensati del XIII secolo." In *Tra edificazione e piacere della lettura: Le vite dei santi in età medievale*. Atti del Convegno, 1996. Edited by Antonella degli'Innocenti and Fulvio Ferrari. Trent: Dipartimento di scienze filologiche e storiche, 1997, 131-43.

——. "Parole taciute, parole ritrovate: I racconti agiografici di Giovanni da Mailly, Bartolomeo da Trento e Iacopo da Voragine." *Hagiographica* 10 (2003): 183–200.

Vauchez, André. *La Sainteté en Occident aux derniers siècles du Moyen Âge d'après les procès de canonisation et les documents hagiographiques*. Rome: École française de Rome, 1981, 1982.

——. *Saints, prophètes et visionnaires, le pouvoir surnaturel au Moyen Âge*. Paris: Albin Michel, 1999.

# 9. Various Studies on Time

Attali, Jacques. *Histoires du temps*. Paris: Fayard, 1992.

Barreau, Hervé. *Le Temps*. Paris: Presses Universitaires de France, 1996.

Bloch, Marc. *Apologie pour l'histoire ou métier d'historien*. (1949) New edition, Paris: A. Colin, 1993, esp. pp. 48–66.

Bonnaud, Robert. *Victoires sur le temps: Essais comparatistes: Polybe le Grec et Sima Qian le Chinois*. Condeixa a Nova: Ligne d'ombre, 2007.

Braudel, Fernand. *Écrits sur l'histoire*. Paris: Flammarion, 1969, esp. pp. 9–133. In English translation as *On History*. Translated by Sarah Matthews. Chicago: University of Chicago Press, 1980.

Cerquiglini, Jacqueline. "Écrire le temps: Le lyrisme de la durée aux XIVe et XVe siècles." In *Le Temps et la Durée dans la littérature au Moyen Âge et à la Renaissance*, Actes du Colloque. Edited by Yvonne Bellenger. Paris: Nizet, 1986, 103–14.

Certeau, Michel de. *L'Écriture de l'histoire*. Paris: Gallimard, 1975. In English translation as *The Writing of History*. Translated by Tom Conley. New York: Columbia University Press, 1988.

Chesneaux, Jean. *Habiter le temps: Passé, présent, futur: Esquisse d'un dialogue politique*. Paris: Bayard, 1996.

Cullmann, Oscar. *Christ and Time: The Primitive Christian Conception of Time and History*. Translated from the German by Floyd V. Filson. Philadelphia: Westminster Press, 1950, 1964. In French translation as *Christ et le temps: Temps et histoire dans le christianisme primitif*. Neuchâtel and Paris: Delachaud & Nestlé, 1947.

Duby, Georges. *L'Histoire continue*. Paris: O. Jacob, 1991.

Elias, Norbert. *Time: An Essay*. Translated in part from the German by Edmund Jephcott. Oxford UK and Cambridge MA: Blackwell, 1992. In French translation as *Du Temps*. Translated by Michèle Hulin. Paris: Fayard, 1993.

Foucault, Michel. *L'Archéologie du savoir*. Paris: Gallimard, 1969. In English translation as *The Archaeology of Knowledge and the Discourse on Language*. Translated by A. M. Sheridan Smith. New York: Pantheon Books; Harper & Rowe, 1972.

Gautier-Dalché, Patrick. "Le temps et l'espace." In *Le Moyen Âge en lumière: Manuscrits enluminés des bibliothèques de France*. Edited by Jacques Dalarun. Paris: Fayard, 2002, 35–63.

Halbwachs, Maurice. *La Mémoire collective*. (1968) New edition, Paris: Presses Universitaires de France, 1997. In English translation as *On Collective Memory*. Translated by Lewis A. Coser. Chicago: University of Chicago Press, 1992, 2001.

Hartog, François. "Temps et histoire." *Annales HSS* 6 (November-December 1995): 1219–36.

Koselleck, Reinhart. *Le Futur passé: Contribution à la sémantique des temps historiques*. Paris: École des hautes études in sciences sociales, 1990. In English translation as *Futures Past: On the Semantics of Historical Time*. Translated by Keith Tribe. Cambridge, MA: MIT Press, 1985; New York: Columbia University Press, 2004.

Le Goff, Jacques. *Histoire et mémoire*. Paris: Gallimard, 1988. In English translation as *History and Memory*. Translated by Steven Rendall and Elizabeth Claman. New York: Columbia University Press, 1992.

———. *Pour un autre Moyen Âge: Temps, travail et culture en Occident: 18 essais*. Paris: Gallimard, 1977. In English translation as *Time, Work and Culture in the Middle Ages*. Translated by Arthur Goldhammer. Chicago: University of Chicago Press, 1980.

Noiriel, Gérard, ed. *Périodes: La construction du temps historique*, Actes du Colloque d'Histoire au Présent. Paris: École des hautes études en sciences sociales, 1991.

Paravicini Bagliani, Agostino, ed. *La Mémoire du temps au Moyen Âge*. Florence: SISMEL/ Edizioni del Galluzzo, 2005.

Pomian, Krzysztof. *L'Ordre du temps*. Paris: Gallimard, 1984.

Ricoeur, Paul. *Temps et récit*. 3 vols. Paris: Seuil, 1983–1985. In English translation as *Time and Narrative*. Translated by Kathleen McLaughlin and David Pellauer. 3 vols. Chicago: University of Chicago Press, 1984–1988.

Rousso, Henry. *La Hantise du passé*. Paris: Textuel, 1998. In English translation as *The Haunting Past: History, Memory, and Justice in Contemporary France*. Translated by Ralph Schoolcraft. Philadelphia: University of Pennsylvania Press, 2002.

Schmitt, Jean-Claude. "Le temps impensé de l'histoire ou double objet de l'historien?" *Cahiers de civilisation médiévale* 48 (2005): 31–52.

Thomas, Yan. "La vérité, le temps., le juge et l'historien." *Le Débat* 102 (November-December 1998): 17–36.

Weinrich, Harald. *Le Temps: Le récit et le commentaire*. Paris: Seuil, 1972. In English translation from the German as *On Borrowed Time: The Art and Economy of Living with Deadlines*. Chicago: University of Chicago Press, 2008.

# 10. Time and History

Ariès, Phillipe. *Le Temps de l'histoire*. Paris: Seuil, 1986.

Beaujouan, Guy. "Le temps historique." In *L'Histoire et ses méthodes*. Edited by Charles Samaran. Bibliothèque de la Pléiade. Paris: Gallimard, 1961, 52–67.

Braudel, Fernand. "Histoire et longue durée: La longue durée." *Annales E.S.C.* (1958): 725–53.

Cardini, Franco. *Il Cerchio sacro dell'anno: Il Libro delle Feste*. Rimini: Il Cerchio, 1995, 2004.

Fraisse, Paul. *Psychologie du temps*. (1964). 2nd ed., Paris: Presses Universitaires de France, 1967, 1970. In English translation as *The Psychology of Time*. Westport, CT: Greenwood Press, 1975.

Gurvitch, Georges. *La Multiplicité des temps sociaux*. Paris: Centre de documentation universitaire, 1958.

Hartog, François. "Ordre des temps: Chronographie, chronologie, histoire." In *Théologies et vérité du défi de l'histoire*. Recherches de science religieuse, 1910–2010. Leuven: Peeters, 2010, 279–89.

———. *Régimes d'historicité: Présentisme et expériences du temps*. Paris: Seuil, 2003.

Hulin, Michel. *La Face cachée du temps*. Paris: Fayard, 1985.

Le Goff, Jacques. "Temps." In *Dictionnaire raisonné de l'Occident médiéval*. Edited by Jacques Le Goff and Jean-Claude Schmitt. Paris: Fayard, 1999, 1, 113–22.

Milo, Daniel S. *Trahir le temps (Histoire)*. Paris: Les Belles Lettres, 1991.

Schmitt, Jean-Claude. "L'imaginaire du temps dans l'histoire chrétienne." *PRIS-MA* 25, nos. 1 and 2 (2009): 135–59.

# Index

Abel, 79
Abelard, 194n23
Abraham, 67, 70, 79, 178
Adam, 53, 77, 108; and original sin, 67, 84, 91, 100, 108; ransomed, 103; and time, 19, 51, 70, 84, 87, 100
Advent, 18, 35–50, 51, 181
Aegeus (proconsul of Achaia), 37, 38
Agatha, Saint, 45, 85
Agni de Lentino, Thomas, O.P., 119
Albert the Great, O.P., 4
Alexander (emperor), 50
Alexandria, 164
All Saints Day, 29, 31, 121, 165–67
All Souls Day, 29, 99, 121, 167–69
alms, almsgiving, 46, 55, 73, 81–82, 83
altar, 177–78
Amand, Saint, 85
Ambrose, Saint, 11–12, 28, 113–15; and Augustine, 149, 150; cited in *Golden Legend*, 77, 105, 110, 113; *De Virginibus*, 102; as source for *Golden Legend*, 34, 45, 154
Anastasia, Saint, 55–56
Anastasius (librarian of the apostolic see), 135
Andrew, Saint (apostle), 33, 34, 36–39, 43

Andrew II (king of Hungary), 161
angels, 53, 106, 137, 153, 160, 163; archangels, 152; and demons, 106, 154, 160, 163; guardian, 35, 154; and Mary, 124, 127; virgins as, 28–29
Anna, Saint, 93
Annunciation, 85
Anthony, Saint, 73–76
Antichrist, the, 34, 154
Antiochus, 180
apocrypha, 126; gospels, 9, 10, 23, 48, 49
apostles, 106, 107, 127; and Jesus, 57, 102, 104; as saints, 23, 33, 65
apparitions, 147, 154, 162, 178
Arcadius (emperor), 160
Aristotle, 148
Arnold de Liège, 30
Ascension Day, 86, 103, 106, 107, 121
Ash Wednesday, 21, 93
Augustine, Saint, 38, 156; cited in *Golden Legend*, 91, 101, 115, 116, 128; *The City of God*, 150; *Confessions*, 149; as learned, 145, 150; relics of, 150, 151–52; as source for *Golden Legend*, 10–11, 48, 59, 70, 73, 117, 148–52, 154; works of, 150

Augustus (Roman emperor), 148
Autpert, Ambroise, 91

Babylonian captivity, 87
Balzac, Honoré de, 46
baptism, 67, 114
Barlaam, Saint, 121
Bartholomaeus Anglicus, Franciscan, xiii
Bartholomew of Trent, O.P., xii, 6, 12, 40, 81, 97
Bede, the Venerable, Saint, 71, 92, 101, 123, 172
Beguines, 162
Beleth, John (Johannis), 12, 15–16, 27
Benedict, Saint, 85, 92, 97; relics of, 86, 172
Benedictine Order, 92
Bernard of Clairvaux, Saint, 145–48, 180; canonization of, 145; cited in the *Golden Legend*, 53; as source for *Golden Legend*, 13, 25, 69, 73, 107
Bible, 9, 155, 178; Old Testament, 123
birthdates, 125, 139, 146
Blaise, Saint, 85
Bollandists, 117
Bonaventure, Saint, 144
Boniface IV (pope), 27, 166
Boniface VIII (pope), 3
Boniface IX (pope), 137
Boureau, Alain, xi, 8, 11, 26, 68, 113, 116, 139, 152, 158, 176–77, 181
Brown, Peter, 22, 24
Brunel-Lobrichon, Geneviève, 187n8

Caesarius, Saint (bishop of Arles), 70
Caesarius of Heisterbach, 30
Caesar Maximinus II, 195n51
calendar, 77, 131; Christian, 16, 17, 25; Jewish, 16, 77; Roman, 16, 165
Callistus (pope), 89
Candlemas, 93
Carpophorus, Saint, 139
Cassiodorus, 127, 153
Catherine, Saint, 164–65
Charlemagne (emperor), 136, 169, 172
Charles V (king of France), x

Chenu, Father Marie-Dominic, 7, 54
childhood, children, 73, 114, 125, 149; Saint Nicholas as protector of, 39, 43, 44
Chosroës (king of the Persians), 129
Christ. *See* Jesus Christ
Christmas, 18, 19, 20, 68. *See also* Jesus Christ: the Nativity of
Christopher, Saint, 143–44
church, churches, 177; consecration of, 129, 179; construction of, 77; dedication of, 176–80; profanation of, 180
Cicero, 148–19
Cistercian Order, 145, 146, 147, 173
Clare, Saint, 161
Claudius (Roman emperor), 142
clothing, 82–83, 147, 162
Clovis (king of France), 37, 80–81
Cluniac Order, 168, 173
Constantia, Saint, 191n28
Constantine (the Great; Roman emperor), 42, 47, 67, 76, 158; conversion of, 66, 74, 109, 110, 128, 154; Donation of, 65–66
Constantine (father of emperor), 110
Constantine of Orvieto, 144
conversion, 149, 156, 172
Cosmas, Saint, 31
Council of Lyon, 174
Council of Trent, 16
cross: of Saint Andrew, 38; sign of the, 110–11
Cross, Holy/True, 38, 128–29; exaltation of the, 128–30; finding of the, 108–11, 128
crusades, 44, 53, 117, 148
Cyprian, 150
Cyriacus (pope), 137

Dacian (Roman prefect), 117
Dagobert (king of the Franks), 137, 172
Damasus (pope), 12
Damian, Saint, 31
Dante Alighieri, 99
David (king), 70, 122, 140
dead, 168; resurrection of the, 133

death, preparation for, 150
Decius (Roman emperor), 74, 133
Denis, Saint. *See* Dionysius (Denis), Saint
desert, 74, 97
devil, 35, 42, 54, 60, 68, 69, 91, 102, 111, 112, 125. *See also* Lucifer; Satan
devils, demons, 106, 111, 113, 128, 130, 153, 154, 160
Diana (goddess), 42
Dietrich, 164
Diocletian (Roman emperor), 25, 56, 117, 134, 139
Dionysius (Denis), Saint, 135–37
Dionysius the Areopagite, 135
Dolbeau, François, 14
Dominic, Saint, 15, 25, 144–45, 156
Dominican Order (Order of Preachers), xii, 5–6, 80, 108, 119, 124, 173; prayer and work and, 144–45, 147, 155, 182
Domitian (Roman emperor), 136
Donation of Constantine, 65–66
Donatus, 154
dragon: of Saint George, 116, 117; of Saint Michael, 153
dreams, 74, 146. *See also* apparitions; visions
Durand, Guillaume (bishop of Mende), 16, 27–28, 196n65

Easter, 19, 20, 89, 103; Easter Day, 84, 85, 92, 100; as a movable feast, 16, 78
Ebroïn (mayor of the palace), 125
Ecclesiastes, 17
eclipses, 136
ecstasy, 162
Edmond (king of England), 61
Eleutherius, Saint, 136
Elizabeth, Saint, 123, 140
Elizabeth of Hungary, Saint, 25, 156, 161–64, 174
Elizabeth of Schönau, 137
Ember Days, 21
Epiphanius, 127
Epiphany, 19, 68, 71–73
Étienne de Bourbon (Stephanus de Borbone), 30

etymology, xi, 122–13; criticism of, 35–36. *See also saints by name*
Eucher (bishop of Valais), 134
Eusebius of Caesarea, 92, 109, 127
Eve, 100, 108
exemplum, exempla, 27, 30, 125, 171; compilations of, 30

fasts, fasting, 86–87, 88, 89–90, 92
feasts, movable, 16, 77–78, 85, 100
Felicity, Saint, 132–33
Fleith, Barbara, 181
folklore, 31, 187n8
Franciscan Order, 147, 156, 17
Francis of Assisi, Saint, 25, 156–57, 159; and crèche, 193n11; and Dominic, 19, 144
Frederick II (Barbarossa; Holy Roman emperor), 73, 174

Gabriel (archangel), 140, 152
Gaiffier, Father Baudouin de, xi
Gallienus (Roman emperor), 74
Gauchet, Marcel, xiii
Genoa, 116, 118, 135, 141
geography, 29, 61, 141
George, Saint, 115–17
Gérard de Frachet, 144
Gervase of Tilbury, 179, 186n2
Gervasius, Saint, 31
God the Father, 107, 113, 143; and Abraham, 67, 178; and the Trinity, 71
*Golden Legend*, the: aim of, 14, 17; not a calendar, 11, 16; as compilation, xi; editions of, ix–x; as legendary, xi–xii, 18, 22; narrative in, 26; reputation of, ix, x; 153; saints in, 24, 31, 166; sources for, 9–13, 36; as *summa* on time, xii and passim
Good Friday, 90, 92
Gregory, Saint (Gregory I, the Great, pope), 85, 96–97, 153, 170; *Dialogues on Miracles*, 96, 97; as influence on Joachim de Voragine, 16, 142; and litany, 112; *Moralia*

Gregory, Saint (*continued*)
    *in Job*, 96; reform of, 181–82; and
      time, 92
Gregory IV (pope), 166
Gregory IX (pope), 124, 161, 174
Gregory of Tours, 117
Gui, Bernard, 6
Guillaume de Saint-Thierry (William,
    abbot of Saint Thierry), 145
Guillaume of Auxerre, 28
Gurevich, Aron J., 7
Gy, Father Pierre Marie, 15

Hadrian (Roman emperor), 153
heaven, heavens, 105, 106. *See also*
    Paradise
Helena, Saint, 108, 109–10, 128
Hell, 98, 99, 168
Henry II Plantagenet (king of England),
    64
Heraclius (Roman emperor), 129
heresy, heretics, 119, 133, 148, 149, 173
hermits, hermitism, 23, 74, 75
Herod Agrippa, 62
Herod Antipas, 62, 131, 139, 140
Herod the Great (Herod Ashkelon, king
    of Judea), 62
Hilary, Saint (bishop of Poitiers), 73, 158
Hilduin (abbot of Saint-Denis), 135
Holy Ghost, 20, 28. *See also* Holy Spirit
Holy Innocents, the, 54, 55, 59, 62–63
Holy Saturday, 90, 92
Holy Spirit, 54, 71, 80, 88, 106–8, 179
Holy Thursday, 93
Holy Week, 93
Honorius (Byzantine emperor), 131, 160
Honorius III (pope), 145
Houssiau, Monsignor Albert, 15
Hugh of Saint-Cher, O.P., 17
Hugh of Saint Victor, 173, 178, 192n10
Humbert of Romans, O.P., 15, 144
Huns, 137, 138

Iacopo da Carcano (*potestate* of Genoa), 3,
Ignatius, Saint, 85

images, 177–78
India, 22; and Saint Thomas, 47–48, 49,
    50, 61
Innocent, Saint, 134
Innocent IV (pope), 124, 174
Ireland, 98
Isaac, 80, 123
Isidore of Seville, xi, 12, 133
Islam, 22, 173–74. *See also* Muslims

Jacob, 80
Jacobus de Voragine: as archbishop of
    Genoa, 4, 35, 41; as an author, 4–5,
    27, 80, 117, 126, 129, 151, 165, 181;
    as a Dominican, 4, 5–6, 30, 35; as
    Genoese, 4, 147, 181; life and career
    of, 1–3; as a man of his time, 6–7;
    name of, 1; and nature, 159
Jacques de Vitry, 30
James, Saint, 62
Jean de Mailly, O.P., xii, 6, 12, 40, 44, 81,
    97, 134
Jeroboam, 180
Jerome, Saint, 154–57; Bible of, 155; cited
    in *Golden Legend*, 124, 127; and
    the lion, 12, 155; as source for the
    *Golden Legend*, 73, 142
Jesus Christ: apostles and, 33;
    appearances of, 102, 127; ascension
    of, 21, 103–6, 112; baptism of, 71;
    birth of, 52, 69, 139, 140; blood
    of, 69; circumcision of, 67, 68;
    crucifixion of, 47, 68–73, 110;
    fasting of, 88; foreskin of, 70;
    incarnation of, 26, 34, 52, 53, 100,
    103, 106, 128, 145, 180; in India,
    49; the Infant, 71, 72, 73, 93, 94,
    114, 122, 145; laughter and, 147,
    163; in Limbo, 103; miracles of, 71;
    names of, 69; the Nativity of, 20, 52,
    68, 100, 125, 140; passion of, 177;
    preaching of, 177; resurrection of,
    78, 89, 92, 100, 102, 103, 121, 132,
    146; and Saint Andrew, 36; and
    Saint Christopher, 144; and Saint
    Francis, 157; and Saint Stephen, 58;
    and Saint Thomas, 47, 49, 61; and

time, 34, 67, 84, 92, 126; and the
Trinity, 71; transfiguration of, 107
Jews, 57–58; conversion of the, 44; Jesus
as Jew among, 69; Judaic religion,
23, 173; and paganism, 54, 67
Job, 80, 90
John, Saint (apostle and evangelist), 55,
59–61, 107, 126; feast day of, 140
John, Saint (martyr), 31, 76
John Chrysostom, Saint, 50
John of Damascus, Saint, 28, 54, 126
John the Almsgiver, Saint, 73, 80, 81–83
John the Baptist, Saint, 62, 80, 123, 130,
131–32, 139–41; and baptism of
Jesus, 71; birth of, 20, 96, 125, 139,
140; body of, 141; decapitation of,
62, 131, 132, 140–41; feast of, 132,
139, 140; as precursor of Jesus, 96;
relics of, 5
John the Deacon, 40
Josaphat, Saint, 121
Joseph (son of Rachel), 123
Joseph, Saint, 190–91n4
Jubilee years, 8, 88
Judas Iscariot, 37, 90
Judas Maccabeus, 180
Judgment: Judgment Day, 152–53; Last,
174
Julian (Roman emperor), 158
Juliana, Saint, 85
Julian the Apostate (Roman emperor), 76
justice, 35, 42

kinship, 122–23
Kleinberg, Aviad, 26

Last Days, Last Times, 34, 152, 168
laughter, 147–48, 162–63
Law of God, 58, 88
Lazarus, 60
legendaries, 6, 45
Lent, 21, 84–85, 88–89, 92, 130
Leo I (Byzantine emperor), 112
Leo I, Saint (the Great, pope), 106
Lestocquoy, Monsignor J., xi

Liberius (pope), 154
Lion, Antoine, O.P., 192n8
Limbo, 103
Litany, Greater and Lesser, 21, 111–13
Liutprand (king of the Lombards), 151
Lombards, Longobards, 170, 171–72,
173, 176
Longinus, Saint, 85
Louis IX, Saint (king of France), 81–82
Louis the Pious (emperor), 135, 136
Lucian, 131
Lucifer, 153
Lucy, Saint (virgin), 33, 35, 45–47

Maggioni, Giovanni Paolo, 26, 175, 181
Magi, the, 50, 62, 71, 72–73, 188
magic, 179
Major Litany. *See* Litany, Greater and
Lesser
Mammon, 60
Marcian (Roman emperor), 138, 141
Mark, Saint (evangelist), 111, 112,
117–18
Mars (god), 93
Martin, Saint (bishop of Tours), 82,
157–63; feasts of, 158; life of, 158;
and nature, 159
martyrs, 63, 132; as saints, 23, 24, 59,
65, 105, 139; Saint Stephen first of
the, 131
marvels, 53, 178–79, 180, 186n2
Mary, the Blessed Virgin, 60, 80, 92,
102; and the annunciation, 85,
140; appearance to Jesus of, 102–3;
assumption of, 121, 122, 126; birth
of, 122, 123, 124–25, 139; cult
of, 72, 93, 94, 128, 193n7, 194n9;
death (dormition) of, 127; eternity
of, 128; immaculate conception
of, 123, 128, 139; life of, 123–26,
127–28; as mother of Jesus/God,
123, 140; nativity of, 20, 121;
purification of, 85, 92–95, 122–26;
virginity of, 53
Mary Magdalen, Saint, 34
Matthew, Saint (apostle), 37, 85
Maurice, Saint, 133–34

Maxentius (Roman emperor), 47, 164, 165
Maximian (Roman emperor), 117, 134
Maximinus (Roman emperor), 165, 195n51
Melchiades (pope), 139
Methodius, Saint (bishop of Olympus), 52
Michael (Bizantine emperor), 135
Michael, Saint (archangel), 103, 108, 152–54
Minor Litany. *See* Litany, Greater and Lesser
miracles, 133; and marvels, 53, 178–79, 186n2; as definition of sainthood, 23, 157; posthumous, 43, 157; and time, 129, 125, 129, 164
monasticism, 92, 97
Morris, Colin, 7
Moses, 58, 80, 180; and time, 19, 70, 84
Moses Maimonides, 105
Muhammad, 173
Mula, Stefano, 174–76
Muño de Zamora, O.P., 3
Murray, Alexander, 7, 54
music, 11, 16–17, 87, 97, 172, 178
Muslims, 22, 43, 173

Nabuzardan, 180
nature, xii, 19, 35, 37, 140, 147, 159; catastrophes of, 172–73
Nero (Roman emperor), 79, 142
Nicholas (Irishman), 99
Nicholas, Saint, 33, 35, 39–44, 173
Nicholas IV (pope), 3
Nicodemus, Saint: Gospel of, 108
Noah, 70, 79
numbers, 18–19, 24, 27, 86, 169; auspicious/inauspicious, 130, 142; forty, 94, 103–5, 130, 142; four, 19, 88–89; seven, 132; symbolism in, 87–89, 134; thirty, 130; twenty, 142

Odilo, Saint (abbot of Cluny), 168
Order of Preachers. *See* Dominican Order (Order of Preachers)
orders, mendicant, 168

pagans, paganism, 76–77, 138, 149; celebrations and feasts of, 70, 71, 88, 89, 93, 112, 166; conversion and, 37, 42, 55, 67, 149
Palm Sunday, 21, 93
Pancratius, Saint, 100–103
Pantheon (Rome), 27, 166
Paradise, 31, 98, 99, 103, 179
Patrick, Saint, 85, 92, 97–99
Paul, Saint (apostle), 73, 76, 77–80, 142–43; conversion of, 142–43; and Denis, 135, 136; Epistles of, 69
Paul, Saint (martyr), 31, 76–77
Paul the Deacon, 171
Paul the Hermit, Saint, 73, 74–75, 76
peace (*Pax romana*), 52
Pelagius, Saint (pope as Pelagius I), 121, 170–71, 181
Pelagius II (pope), 115,
Pentecost, 103, 106, 107, 108; and time, 107, 121
Peter, Saint (apostle), 62, 102, 118, 141–42; body of, 112; chair of, 85; and Saint Paul, 78, 79
Peter Lombard, 13, 192n10
Peter of Verona (Peter Martyr), Saint, 63, 118–20; as Dominican, 5; as martyr, 23, 63; as recent saint, 7, 25, 156
Peter the Venerable (abbot of Cluny), 54, 173
Petrus Comestor, 12, 13, 53, 63
Philip Augustus (Philip II, king of France), 81
Phocas (Byzantine emperor), 81
Pius VII (pope), 2
Pius IX (pope), 191n4
Pontius Pilate, 91–92, 179
popular culture, 31
poverty, 40, 60–61, 82, 97, 147
prayer, prayers: for the dead, 168; intercessory, 29, 31; and work, 75–76, 124
preaching, preachers, 5, 57, 102, 107–8, 182
prophecy, 140, 155
prostitution, 46
Protasius, Saint, 31
Purgatory, 32, 98–99, 104, 167, 168–69

Quadragesima, 21, 85, 88, 92
Quinquagesesima, 21, 85, 88, 92

Rabanus Maurus, 29
Rachel, 123
Raphael (archangel), 152
reading, 182; silent, 15
reason, 53–54
religions, monotheistic, 173–74
Remy (Remigius), Saint, 11, 80
Richard the Lionhearted, 116
Robert of Molesmes (abbot of Citeaux), 173
rogations, 111, 112, 113
Rome, 112, 142, 150; ancient, pagan, 10, 31; Christian, 10; as the Church, 159; pilgrimages to, 88
Rudolph of Habsburg (Holy Roman emperor), 174
Rusticus, Saint, 136

Saint-Denis, Abbey of, 135, 172, 194n21
sainthood, saintliness, 22–23
Saint Peter's, basilica of, 31
saints: birth as feast day of, 139, 140; canonization of, 23, 157; categories of, 28, 29, 33; days of cult of, 24–25; death as feast day of, 57, 105, 18, 139, 140; definition of, 22–23; as intermediaries, 167; number of, 166; and odor of sanctity, 131; relics of, 24, 28, 49–50, 57, 70, 86, 108, 110, 134, 141, 160; and time, 155; translation of relics of, 57, 108, 150, 160–61, 173
Samson, 123
Samuel, 13
sanctorale, xiii, 22–24, 86, 122, 130, 132, 149, 152, 165, 166, 167
Saracens. See Islam; Muslims
Sarah, 123
Satan, 67, 111, 130, 179. See also devil; Lucifer
Schmitt, Jean-Claude, 132, 139
scrofula (the king's itch), 194n21

sea: fear of the, 41; shipwrecks at, 37
Second Vatican Council, 99, 169
Secundus, Saint, 100
senses, 89, 90
Septuagesima, 18, 19, 21, 85, 87, 89, 92
Serapion, Saint, 83
Seth (son of Adam), 108–9
Seven Brothers, 132
Seven Sleepers, 133
Severianus, Saint, 139
Severus, Saint, 139
Sexagesima, 21, 85, 87–88, 92
Sheba (queen of), 108
Sigibert of Gembloux, 171
Simeon, 93
sin, original, 108, 112, 108, 146
sins: acedia; 75; seasonal, 90
Siricius (pope), 89
Siro, Saint, 4
Solomon (king), 108, 109, 180
Sotinel, Claire, 170
space, 143; and saints' relics, 86; and time, 29, 79, 86, 134, 148, 150, 173, 177, 181
Star, the (of the Magi), 62, 71, 72
Stella, Francesco, 175
Stephen, Saint (king of Hungary), 172
Stephen, Saint (martyr), 55, 56–61; body of, 130–31; lapidation of, 77
Sulpicius Severus, 158
Sylvester, Saint (pope Sylvester I), 55, 65–68, 70, 109

temporale, xiii, 19–20, 86, 122, 152, 166, 167
Theban legion, 124
Thecla, Saint, 141
Theodosius I (Roman emperor), 12, 126, 133
Theophilus, 125–26
Theresa of Avila, Saint, 191n4
Thomas, Saint (apostle), 33, 35, 47–50, 61, 63, 102
Thomas Aquinas, Saint, 49, 94
Thomas of Canterbury, Saint (Thomas à Becket), 25, 55, 63–65
Thomas of Cantimpré, xii

time: ages of, 70; of alms, 46; of angels, 152; calendar, 170–71, 181; and canonical hours, 179; Christian, 26, 27; cyclical, xiii, 78, 179; of deviation, 18, 19, 84–99, 100, 171, 180; end of, 154; eschatological, xiii, 20, 34, 68, 78, 79, 86, 87, 121, 129, 152, 167, 174; of gestures, 180; historic, 18–19, 171; of humanity, 18, 87, 97, 101, 106, 125, 138, 152, 159, 160, 162, 163, 165, 167, 169, 170; linear, xiii, 78, 132, 152; liturgical, 113, 129, 152, 166, 174, 179; of martyrdom, 164; pagan, 27; periods of, 68–69, 124; of pilgrimage, 19, 20, 51–83, 84, 121–80; of reconciliation, 19, 20, 51–83, 84, 85, 100–120, 121, 146, 180; of renewal, 18, 19. 33–50, 170; sacralization of, 17 and passim
Trajan (Roman emperor), 61
Trexler, Richard, 50
Trinity, 67, 71, 107

Uguccio of Pisa, 13
Urbain, Saint (pope), 121
Ursula, Saint, 137–38

Vaast, Saint, 85
Valentine, Saint, 85
Valla, Lorenzo, 66
Vandals, 150

Venice, 118
Vicaire, Father Marie-Humbert, 119
Victorinus, Saint, 139
victory, 153–54
vigil, 125
Vignay, Jean du, x
Vincent of Beauvais, xii, 171, 175, 176
Virès, Juan-Luis, xi
virgin, virgins, 55, 123–24; Mary as, 53; prostitutes as, 46; saints as, 28–29, 45, 161
virtue, virtues, 49, 49; humility as, 79, 96; saints exemplify, 158
visions, 64–65, 146, 178. See also apparitions; dreams

Weber, Max, xiii
William of Auxerre (bishop of Paris), 27
women: body of, 28; and childbearing; 94; inequality of, with men, 94; and knowledge, 164; place/importance of, 102; presence of, in Golden Legend, 29; spirituality in, 161–62; sterility in, 123
Word, 67
work, 75–76, 124, 155

year, first day of the, 16, 5, 77

Zachariah, 140